Big Ideas

To Ponder and To Use

Joseph Strayhorn, Jr.

Psychological Skills Press

1

ISBN :   978-1-931773-28-7

Wexford, PA, Psychological Skills Press

Author's email: jstray@gmail.com

Table of Contents

11

Introduction: the idea of big ideas itself

When people speak of "the life of the mind," they are talking about having fun thinking about ideas. One of the goals of this book is to help some readers learn to have fun in this way. And another is to provide some fun for those who already have come to enjoy the life of the mind.

But the goal is not only fun, but better lives. In lots of ways, education helps us to live life better: to be happier, to help other people to be happier. What is it about education that does this? It's not memorizing the state capitals for the states in the USA. It's not memorizing dates on which things happened in history. But I think it's due to getting certain ideas in mind. These ideas tend to enlarge our ways of thinking about the world. They help us to be more insightful people. They seem to come around from time to time in the course of getting an education , at random intervals. What if we tried to compile them and put them into one book and and to try to understand and think about them, one after the other ? Would it work? If you're reading this book, and if you continue to do so, you will be an experimenter who can contribute an answer to that question. How much does reading the big ideas turn out to help you in your conduct of life? This is what you're about to find out, if you continue.

For whom is this book written? It's hard for me to narrow down the imagined audience to any specific group. If you read some of the ideas and want to keep going, this book is for you!

You'll notice right away that the ideas are in more or less random order. You can start and finish reading at any place. Often you may want to put the book down and think about an idea rather than speeding on to the next one.

With a few exceptions, I don't go into the history of the various ideas, who first thought it up, who deserves credit, why the idea occurred to them, and so forth. I'm just interested in giving a brief explanation of what the idea is.

A good number of these ideas have changed my life for the better. If you find any of them very helpful for you, or if you think of a really good one I've left out, you can tell me your thoughts by writing to joestrayhorn@gmail.com.

Self-education

Where does education take place? For most of us, the reflex answer to this is "at a school." But most people who have learned a lot will tell you that most of what they have learned, they have not learned in school. They have learned it through self-education. How do people teach themselves things? The simplest way is simply by reading. Almost anything that you want to know, there are books or articles or other written things that can teach you about it. Sometimes seeing videos is better than just reading, and teaching videos are very much available on the Internet. Lots of times rather than just reading and watching videos, there is a need for lots of practice. For example someone who wants to learn to dance or to play a musical instrument needs to practice their movements many times. And it helps to be able to discuss what you've learned with other people.

One time, some people were taking a biology course. At the end of the course, there would be a test given to people all over the nation who had taken that type of course. The teacher in these people's class didn't believe in evolution. So the teacher skipped the part of the course that had to do with evolution. Some students were irritated, because they knew that they were going into the test without having studied subject matter that was certain to be on the test. They said, "I know we're going to do worse on the test because we weren't taught an important part of the course." But an even more important part of their educations should have been this idea: "You can pick up a book (or open an electronic book) and read and study any subject you want, without waiting for a teacher to assign it!" In other words, you can use self-education. Sometimes school gets us into the habit of thinking that we can't learn something without having been compelled to do so. This is a very unfortunate attitude.

One time someone was set to take a very important course in the fall. It was to be a difficult one, but one that medical school admissions people emphasized in figuring out whom to let in to medical school. This person very much wanted to go to medical school. At the same time, the person didn't have plans for the summer, and was finding himself quite bored during the summer. What do you think the person could do to make summer less boring? The person could have used his free time during the summer to start learning the material in the difficult course that he would be taking in the fall. There was nothing stopping him from buying a book or checking a book out from the library or finding information on the Internet and starting to master it. In other words, he could use his time for self education.

I read about the people who discovered the structure of DNA. They would occasionally run into problems that required some specialized knowledge to solve, knowledge that they didn't have. So they would look up what they needed to know and teach it to themselves as quickly as possible. They used self education to help themselves reach their goal.

Self-education doesn't have to be a lonely venture. I've been running an organization where two people take turns reading aloud to each other. It's possible that you would enjoy doing that with someone, using this book.

People who are good at self-education have a tremendous advantage in being successful in life.

Psychoeducation (or, social and emotional learning)

When people think about education, they tend to think about science, math, writing, reading, history -- the usual required courses. What they don't think about so often are subjects like the following:

How do you make good decisions?
How do you solve conflicts with other people?
How do you make unpleasant emotions such as anger and fear and sadness less intense, so that they don't interfere with your making good decisions?
How do you have fun and interesting conversations with other people?
How do you take control of what you say to yourself, to make things come out best?
How do you change your habits for the better?
How do you figure out good goals for yourself, and work successfully toward those goals?
How do you get better at self-discipline?
How do you cultivate good relationships?
How do you best handle it when bad things happen?
What are ways of being kind to yourself and to other people?
How do you increase your chances of being happy and making other people happy?

When people think of ways of getting people mentally healthier, they tend to think of 2 major ways of making things better: medicines and psychotherapy. And many of them think of psychotherapy as "talk therapy" --

that the major way that things get better is by the talking that the patient does -- the patient has "someone to talk to." Or by talking to a very good listener, the patients come to insights about themselves that help them get better.

The idea of psychoeducation is that there are lots of things people have learned about how to get mentally healthier, and lots of good can be accomplished simply by learning these things and by practicing the skills involved. People have discovered ideas about these topics that are really helpful, and they have written them down. They've also discovered exercises that people can do to practice using the ideas. People can gain from reading these ideas and doing the exercises. In so doing, they gain wisdom and skills, just as they do when they read about math and do math problems. The big idea is that people can be taught, and can learn, how to be psychologically healthy, just as they can learn other skills.

What sorts of things have people learned? Here are some examples. To prevent depression, observe the things you say to yourself and try to make your self-talk helpful rather than getting down on yourself. Try to celebrate the good things that happen and the good things you do, in your self-talk. To prevent depression, get regular aerobic exercise. To prevent depression, keep a regular sleep rhythm and get enough bright light, especially in the fall and winter. To reduce anxiety, practice relaxing in ways that turn down the "flight or fight response." To reduce anxiety, practice exposing yourself to the situations you want to get less scared of, beginning with the least scary and working your way up, practicing the thoughts, feelings, and behaviors you'd like to do in these situations. To reduce anxiety, pay attention to your self-talk and try not to estimate things as more awful than they really are. To solve conflicts with other people, avoid yelling at them and insulting them. To solve conflicts, try to focus on the options for what plan to adopt, and the pros and cons of those plans. When building relationships with people, try to feel good about your acts of kindness toward them, your acts that make them happier. If you want a child to be good, show the child lots of models of good behavior. If you want a child to be good, give them lots more attention and excitement in response to their good behaviors than in response to their bad behaviors. If you want family members to be mentally healthy, cultivate a "positive emotional climate" where people are kind to each other and have fun with each other. And so forth – for a much longer list!

There probably can never be enough psychotherapists to give talk therapy to everyone who needs to improve their mental health. But it is much more possible for people to get access to books and videos that teach the important ideas of psychoeducation. There are just a few things left to do, though. Separating out the writings that are good, from those that give bad advice is one of them. Once we've collected the good teachings, getting more people to actually read pay attention to these ideas, and use them, is another. These are very much on the to do list for this planet!

Multiple causes (multifactorial determination)

Suppose someone says, "I can prove that cigarettes are not harmful to health. My Aunt Beulah smoked cigarettes every day for 60 years and lived to be 95 years old." The person who says this doesn't understand how

19

causation usually works. It's usually not true that something has one, and only one cause. Usually, there are several causes, each of which make it more likely that something will happen. So, for example regarding early death due to lung cancer or heart disease, smoking is one causal factor. The person's genes are another as are how much exercise they get, what their diet is like, how much overweight they are, how much stress they are under, and how much air pollution they breathe. Each of these might make early death due to cancer or heart disease more likely.

What causes violence in society? Is it the models of violence and the practice of violent acts that people have carried out in fantasy through movies, television, and video games? Is it hostility or violence in their families? Is it the large number of guns in society? Is it the large amount of bullying that goes on? Is it the absence of training in ethics and nonviolence? Is it certain types of mental health problems, and the lack of treatment for those? Is it problems with how policing and law enforcement are carried out? People often debate about whether the cause of violence is one of these or another. However, it is entirely possible that all of these could contribute to the level of violence in society. It is possible that each of them can make violence more likely or more frequent. Believing that the cause of violence has to be either one thing or another is an error in thinking -- it overlooks the "multiple causes" idea.

Controlled studies and counterfactuals

How do we measure how much a certain vaccine helps, or how much a certain medication for an illness helps, or how much a certain educational technique helps? We could just go ahead and give the thing that we hope helps and look at the difference in people's condition before we give it and after we give it. Do they get better over the time they received the treatment? Sometimes people think that getting better after some treatment prove that the treatment actually caused things to get better. But here's the big problem: how do we know that things wouldn't have gotten better anyway ? This is the big reason why experiments in science need comparison groups. We take one group of people and give them the treatment; we also study another group of people who don't get the treatment. The group that doesn't get the treatment is called a control group. Being able to compare people who got the treatment with other people who didn't get the treatment helps us to figure out what causes things to happen.

People constantly try to make conclusions about causes without having a comparison group. For example, we elect someone as president and the president is in office for a couple of years, during which time the economy of a country gets worse. Is that president the reason why the economy got worse? Not necessarily. We don't know what would have happened had somebody else been president. Maybe without this particular president, things would have been much worse! And also there are many other things that can cause the economy to get better or worse that the president doesn't have any control over. (Please see our discussion on multiple causes, or multifactorial causation.)

The word counterfactual is sometimes used to describe what we have a control group in order to try to get. The word counterfactual is the answer to the question, "What would have happened if we hadn't had done this?"

or, "What would have happened if this event had not taken place ?" It's usually impossible to get a totally accurate counterfactual. To get one with total accuracy we would need to be able to rewind time and go back and start over with something happening differently and then see how things turn out differently. But having control groups can give us at least a guess about the counterfactual.

Suppose you have invented a treatment for an illness that you feel really sure works much better than any other treatment. How would you feel about withholding the treatment from a group of people, expecting them to do much worse than the treated group, so that you can prove that your treatment works? How would you feel if your family member were in the no-treatment group, and that family member died because they were not selected to get the treatment? For this reason, if there are ways of predicting the counterfactual other than having a control group, they should be explored and used when possible.

Randomization to study causation

Suppose someone gets two groups of people, and does an educational technique with one group and not with the other group. Suppose they found that the first group learns a lot better and a lot more. Do they know for sure that the educational technique caused that learning to happen? What if the group that got the special technique were people who were very motivated to learn , and the group who was the comparison group had absolutely no interest in learning the subject matter at hand. In that case the real reason the first group did better probably was that they somehow were selected to want to learn more. Maybe it had nothing to do with the teaching technique we're studying. To try to make the groups as equal as possible, people came up with a good idea. Suppose there were 52 people who signed up for the study. The experimenters would shuffle a deck of cards, and draw a card for each person. The people with a red card would be in the first group, and those with a black card would be in the second group. (They could use a random number table, or a computer randomizing program, or coin flips, or other random methods.) If the two different groups are assigned by random methods , it's still possible that one group could be more interested in learning than another group. But, it's unlikely that the groups would be very different, and large differences get less and less likely the more people you have in your study.

There are lots of problems with randomization and with insisting that we have to have randomized studies before we can figure out what causes what. Some people (this author included) believe that there are ways, other than randomization, to become confident that something causes something else, and that many researchers value randomization too much. Nonetheless, randomization to form different groups in experiments has been an extremely important idea in science and medicine.

Placebos

While we're on the subject of designing studies: Suppose someone studies the effect of a certain drug on a certain illness. One randomly selected group gets the drug, and the other group is just told, "You've been assigned to the no-treatment group. We'll see how you've done in about a month." Isn't it likely that the people who get the drug feel hopeful and expect to get better? And that that the people in the no-treatment group feel disappointed and maybe scared? If the researcher finds that the treated group has done better, people would say, "Maybe they did better because they were so much more hopeful." There is a good bit of evidence that increasing people's sense of hope has positive effects, with or without some positive drug effect.

For this reason, people who test drugs use *placebos*. They tell people, for example, "You may get a pill with the drug in it, or you may get a pill that looks just the same, only without any active ingredient. This pill that is not expected to do anything is called a placebo. You will not be told which you have gotten, until the trial is over." This way, both groups of people have the same degree of hope and expectation. Notice that people were told ahead of time that they may get a placebo – they were not deceived.

The idea of placebo groups has been extended from studies about drugs to studies of surgical procedures, psychotherapy, and education. There the idea is more problematic. Can you imagine, for example, trying to come up with a procedure that makes people feel like they're being taught math, and hopeful about getting better in math, when there is nothing in the procedure that really helps them learn math? And if you could come up with that, would it be a good thing to have people spend their time on?

If the difference that placebos make in people's states of mind really can make them healthier, doesn't it make sense to try to improve the state of mind in other ways, as a way of improving health? This is exactly what has been done through techniques of relaxation, meditation, and psychotherapy, and with some success.

The vicious cycle of revenge and punishment

Let's imagine two people, named Person A and Person B. Let's say that person B does something unpleasant to Person A. Person A thinks , "I'll teach Person B a lesson! I'll teach Person B not to do that bad thing! I'll get him back and get revenge and punish him." So Person A does something to person B that's unpleasant and punishing -- perhaps he slaps him in the face. Now, Person B thinks exactly the same sort of thing that Person A thought a while ago: "I'll teach Person A a lesson! I'll teach him not to do that bad thing! I'll get him back and get revenge and punish him." So Person B hits Person A with his fist. Then B hits back with a stick, A hits back with a chain, B attacks back with a knife, A attacks back with a gun, and someone is badly hurt or killed. Each person is punishing the other one to try to make the other person act better or to get revenge. But their punishment just provokes the other person to punish them. So there's a vicious cycle where the more punishment goes on, the more wishes there are for more punishment. Very often this vicious cycle ends up with someone being hurt badly or killed.

There are various remedies to the vicious cycle of revenge and punishment. One of them is called the rule of law. When someone has something bad done to him, he doesn't take it upon himself to punish the person. He goes to the authorities and reports the bad behavior and the authorities have systems of punishment that they use, for example having a trial in court, making the person pay money, or locking the person up. This is by no means the only alternative to the vicious cycle of revenge and punishment, but it's a very important one.

Another remedy to the vicious cycle of revenge and punishment is to teach the skills of kindness and forgiveness very widely, and for people to come to value these much more than they do now.

People have invented weapons with which they can bring about horrible destruction. Using ways to prevent the vicious cycle of revenge and punishment is necessary if human civilization is to survive.

Resistant, compliant, and goal-directed

These three words describe the attitudes and behaviors people have toward putting out effort to accomplish something. The thing to be accomplished can be learning a school subject, getting household chores done, learning a skill, doing work for a job, taking care of one's health, or anything else that takes effort toward a goal.

Resistant means that the person tries to get out of doing the work or putting out the effort. He argues that he should be able to have a day off. He says the work is already done, when it isn't. He tries not to be around when the work is being assigned. He gets asked to do the work, but he just doesn't do it. Or maybe he just refuses to do it.

Compliant means that the person does the work when someone in authority asks him to. But he only does what he's asked, and no more.

Goal-directed means that the person actually wants to accomplish what the work accomplishes. He doesn't need to have someone making him do the work or even assigning it to him -- he figures out what sort of effort accomplishes the goal, and puts out that effort on his own.

Which of these three do you think each of the following are examples?

1. Someone gets some math homework. The person does it as quickly as possible, and stops as soon as it's done and starts playing video games.

2. Someone gets some math homework. The person wants to be able to solve the type of problem the homework is about. The person reads a math textbook chapter several times until he feels like he really understands. He does the sample problems in the chapter to see if he gets them right. He does the assigned problems, and checks them to make sure he did them right. There's one that gives him trouble, and he looks up some more to read about that. He does it again, and makes up a few that are like that and practices with those.

3. Someone gets some math homework. The person has figured out that the teacher doesn't check the homework, so the person doesn't do it at all.

What do you think? Do you think #1 is compliant, #2 is goal-directed, and #3 is resistant?

Not all goals are worthy of being goal-directed for. Sometimes people ask us to do things that are just unnecessary wastes of time -- in such a case it might be a good idea to be compliant or resistant. And sometimes people ask us to do things that are downright wrong or bad ideas. In those cases it can be wise to be resistant. But a very frequent reason people are not goal-directed is just that they would rather goof off than work. Or they've never really thought about whether they want to achieve a goal or not.

Freedom and order

If you ruled the world, what would you make people do? The idea of freedom is that the best idea is to let them do what they want, unless there's a good reason to make and enforce rules that tell them otherwise.

What are good reasons for government to restrict someone's freedom? The main reason is that a certain behavior causes harm to someone else. If someone wants to dump poisonous chemicals into a river, drive at 120 miles an hour, rob someone at gunpoint, dump trash wherever they want to, physically hurt other people whenever they feel like it, cheat a bunch of people out of their money, or any of bunches of other harmful actions, it's good for government to stop them. This is why laws exist and why police and judges and prisons exist. When people speak about "law and order," they are talking about having enough rules and enforcement of rules that you don't just have everyone doing whatever they feel like doing. If someday society succeeds in teaching all people to be kind to others, law enforcement won't be so necessary. But that day is not expected to come any time soon!

Let's imagine you are still a ruler. What about if someone from a news organization wants to write about what a bad ruler you are? What if people want to march around protesting something you've done? If people are free to do these things, we call it "freedom of the press," and "freedom of assembly." If you're the only ruler and you're totally in charge, wouldn't you be tempted to tell your critics that they had to shut up and go home? That's why it's good for government people to have to obey rules too, and not to be able to make people do whatever they want.

Governments aren't the only organizations that make rules that limit people's freedom. The government might allow people to eat all the junk food they want, but parents might make rules setting limits on this for their kids. The government might allow people to goof off with their phones all day long if they want, but a school might require that people put them away when they are in class. A person might insist that the person they are married to let them know where they are at every single minute of the day, and never be alone with anyone else but them. (This last example is what I would call being very "overcontrolling.") Sometimes the rules people make that limit other people's freedom are reasonable, and sometimes they are not. A general principle is, give people freedom to choose, unless there's a good reason not to.

Checks and balances

The phrase, "checks and balances" refers to the power of a government person being stopped, or "checked," and "balanced out" by the power of someone else, so that one person doesn't have all the power. In the U.S. system of government, the congress can pass bills, but the president can reject these, or veto them, thus limiting the power of congress. But then if enough members of congress still want the law to be passed, they can override the president's veto. Once the bill becomes law, the supreme court can review it and decide that the constitution of the country doesn't allow it. A major purpose of the way the rules for government are set up in the constitution is to keep one person from having too

29

much power over everyone else. When one person gets to make all the rules and tell everyone else what to do, very often that one person messes things up very badly. Checks and balances are meant to prevent this.

When people get power, very often they want to get more power. Plus, people tend to get more excited about one famous leader than they do about a whole bunch of people who argue with each other. So if people in a country don't watch out, the system of checks and balances can stop being used. When there are no checks and balances, and one person has power over the entire government, the system is called a dictatorship. People in democratic systems should be careful that their country doesn't drift into dictatorship.

One advantage of a dictatorship is that government can make decisions very quickly and efficiently. You skip the steps of having lots of people arguing with each other and voting and trying to persuade people of things -- one person just makes a decision and that's what people carry out. If the dictator were extremely wise, unselfish, and good, thinks might work out great. But wise, good, and unselfish people don't tend to become dictators, and even if they do, having huge amounts of power doesn't appear to be good for people's personalities, in most cases. Someone said, "Power tends to corrupt; absolute power corrupts absolutely." And even if you could have a wise, unselfish, and good dictator, who would take over when the dictator gets too old or dies? The person the dictator names to be his or her successor could turn out to be a very mean person. If you study the history of nations and governments, you will probably conclude that governments with checks and balances make better decisions than those with dictatorships.

Biology, learning, situations

Why do people do what they do? We can put the influences on people's behavior into 3 groups: biology, learning, and situations. By biology, we refer to the type of brain the person inherited, whether the person has lead poisoning that is interfering with brain function, what the person's level of thyroid hormone is, whether the person has taken certain drugs, whether the person has gotten hit in the head and how hard, and so forth. By learning, we refer to the habits the person has gotten into: whether they have learned to feel good about their achievements and acts of kindness, whether they have learned to stay cool when things go wrong, what they've learned about how to have conversations with other people, how they've learned to think when they have a decision, and many other learnings that have to do with how they deal with life. By situations, we're talking about the things in the environment that they are having to deal with. Are they dealing with violent acts going on in the neighborhood, schooling that is way too hard for them, people who bully them, a parent who abuses them, or someone who is a really good teacher, or a friend who is really nice, a group of friends who are not into drugs, or a job that they really enjoy doing, or someone they are married to who is a really smart and nice person. Thinking about each of these three types of influence helps us understand other people.

Sources of nonpunitive power

Why are people violent, mean, or cruel with each other? Someone wants someone else to stop taunting them, so they punch the other person in the nose. Someone wants more money, so they commit an armed robbery. Someone wants more territory for his country, so he invades the country next to him with an army. In each case, they wanted one or more people to do something. Violence was the way they chose to try to get the power to influence the other person or people.

But there are ways of getting power without threatening to punish the other or hurting the other. The better people are at influencing each other in nonpunitive ways, the less they need to punish and threaten.

What are some of those ways? Here are some. 1. Reciprocity. You do something positive for the other person, in exchange for their doing something good to you. The exchange can be a formal agreement or informal expectations that both people keep true to. 2. Money. You earn money, in some honest way, so that you can hire people to accomplish your goals. 3. Competence in valued skills. You get very skilled at something people value. 4. Work capacity. You develop the ability to keep working a long time, to get what you want. 5. Friendship. You develop friends who will help you. 6. Modeling. You show people how to do what you want them to do. For example, a parent shows a child lots of examples of kindness and cooperation. 7. Prestige and social status. Power comes from gaining the admiration of people. 8. Walk-away power. You feel comfortable walking away from and saying no to a deal someone proposes. 9. Assertion. You feel comfortable communicating what you want. 10. Verbal persuasion. You are good at persuading people why they should or shouldn't do something. 11. Leadership. You know how to organize and lead a group. 12. Leadership jobs. You know how to get into positions of leadership. 13. Decision-making skill. You know how to make smart decisions, and your reputation for this makes other people want to listen to you. 14. Ethics. You're trying to get people to do good things, not bad ones. 15. Tolerance of others' hostility to you. You can handle criticism. 16. Organization skills. You know how to plan carefully and carry out your plans. 17. The law. You have more power when what you're trying to do is legal and the law is on your side. 18. Clear goals. You have more power to accomplish what you want, if you know what you want.

Free will versus determinism

Here's what "determinism" means: Everything we do, think, and feel is ultimately caused by the genes we inherit plus everything that has ever happened to us -- our heredity and our environment. Even though we feel like we are deciding something, the reasons we decide what we do, according to this point of view, depend on our heredity and environment, and both of those are beyond our control. The "determinist" point of view says that when you put two chemicals together and they react, there's no willing or choosing involved -- the molecules just follow physical laws. Well, the determinist would say, each little firing of a neuron in our brain is the result of such a chemical reaction, and what we do, think, and feel is the result of those firings of neurons.

If you're a determinist, it should be easy to forgive people. When people make mistakes or do bad things, they're just doing what their heredity and environment made them choose to do. If you could know every little thing about every neuron in their brain and every signal that came to them from the outside world, it would be possible to predict perfectly what they would do (or at least the determinists think so).

The people who argue for free will think that even though heredity and environment influence us, we nevertheless retain some power to rise above those and make our own choices. The free will advocates would say to the determinists, "You can talk about predicting every little thing a person will do, but no one has ever come close to doing that yet, and probably never will. We can't even predict with great accuracy who will or will not be a good employee, or who will be violent or peaceful, or who will be good to be married to, much less every little behavior that someone does. Probably part of the reason you can't predict is that people are constantly making choices that aren't totally determined by anything we can know about the person." The people who believe in free will might say to the determinists, "If everything that happens is determined by what comes before it, just like a chemical reaction is, then you want me to believe that the whole course of human history, including every move in every chess game ever played, every time I jiggle my foot, which pair of socks I randomly pick out, was already destined to happen, from the moment the universe was first formed? Everything that has ever happened or will happen was all encoded somehow and predestined billions of years ago, when the universe began?"

It feels good to believe that there is something inside us that can actually choose what to do, regardless of what has happened to us and how our bodies were formed.

Can there be both free will and determinism? Can it be that our heredity and environment do influence what we do in very major ways, but we still have at least some freedom to make choices?

Thinking about free will versus determinism seems to stretch people's minds. Thinking about the determinism that exists tends to make us more compassionate toward others. Thinking about free will tends to make us take responsibility for our own choices.

The golden rule

Treat others as you would like to be treated. Do unto others as you would have them do unto you. As you wish that people would act toward you, act that way toward other people. Don't do to other people what you wouldn't want someone to do to you. All these are different ways that the "golden rule" has been stated. The golden rule is sometimes thought of as at the center of deciding what is right and wrong to do. If you don't want someone to be violent toward you and hurt you, don't be violent toward other people. If you don't want people to lie to you and try to cheat you, don't do that to others. If you like for people to offer to help, to be good listeners, to give criticism in a very gentle way, to teach you good things, do the same for other people.

One of the problems with interpreting the golden rule too literally is that people are very different, and how you would like to be treated doesn't necessarily equal how the other person would like to be treated. For example,

Person A would just love for someone to give him a shotgun and a bottle of whiskey for a present. So he gives such a present to Person B. But Person B happens not to drink alcohol at all, and to be very much against guns. A young man sees a young lady and thinks that he would love it if the young lady would come up and start flirting with him, so he acts that way to the lady. But the young lady feels her privacy invaded by males her age coming up and "hitting on her," and feels scared or angry rather than having fun.

Even if you know the way the person wants to be treated, sometimes that way is not good for them. For example, suppose the person wants to be given drugs of abuse. Treating them the way they want to be treated is not the most ethical thing to do.

So a revision to the golden rule might be: Try to imagine as accurately as possible how the other person would like to be treated if they were making the best choice for themselves, and treat them in that way. Use your own experience to help you figure this out, but don't assume that the other person is the same as you.

However, if people would just use the unrevised version of the golden rule, which pretty much eliminates violence and cruelty, that would be good enough for starters!

The categorical imperative

Here's another ethical rule that's very similar to the golden rule: Act in such a way that you can wish that everyone would use the same sort of reasoning when they choose how to act. In other words, to test whether an action is right or wrong, you think, "Would I like for everyone to use the same principle that I am using in choosing this action?" This was an ethical rule as stated by a man named Immanuel Kant, and it has been called "the categorical imperative." So for example, I wouldn't like for everyone in the world to use the principle, "If you're angry at anyone, you're justified in being violent toward that person." Therefore, it isn't right for me to be violent toward someone just because I'm very angry at the person.

One of the problems with using Kant's rule is picking what the principle is behind a certain action. For example, suppose I'm considering going for a hike in the local state park. Can I wish that everyone would also go, this very day, to their nearest state park and take a walk? No, because the parks would then be overrun with crowds of people. Can I wish that everyone would enjoy getting some exercise in a harmless and peaceful way, as a form of recreation? Yes, I can certainly wish for that. Can I wish that everyone would appreciate nature? Yes, for sure. The point is that what principle you think of as being behind of certain behavior influences whether you think it's right or wrong by Kant's criterion.

Suppose that a college takes people's races into account when deciding whom to admit to the college, so that there will be a diverse group of people attending the college. If we say that the principle is, "It's okay to discriminate on the basis of race when you are deciding which persons to select for something," the action doesn't sound like a good one. On the other hand, if we say that the principle is, "It's good for students to develop in a culture where people of different races are among their companions," the action sounds like a much better one. So whether a given behavior is right or wrong by Kant's criterion depends a lot on what you think is the principle behind the behavior. There are lots of people who have engaged in violence, believing that "I am acting on the principle that there should be justice and goodness, and bad people should be overthrown." One of the men who did horrible things for the Nazi regime actually tried to justify his actions by Kant's rule, saying that the principle was that every person should do their "duty."

Another problem with the categorical imperative is that the question, "What if everybody used the same principle?" is not very useful when you know for sure that everyone is not going to use that principle. For example, suppose I decide to save money and save the earth's resources by severely restricting my purchases. I have fun making do with as few possessions as possible. Someone might argue, "If everyone did that, (especially if everyone started doing it at the same time), the economy of the world would be thrown into a major depression and huge numbers of people would be put out of work." But that's not really relevant to whether my decision is ethical, because I know that my being frugal will not influence huge numbers of other people (maybe not even one person) to act that way. It's better for me to base my decisions on what really is likely to happen rather than something that I feel sure won't happen.

So there are problems with using the categorical imperative. But the world still would probably be a better place if more people thought about it, rather than simply following the rule of, "I'll do whatever I feel like."

Not using people, versus social exchange

"You don't care about me! You're just using me." When people say this, they are thinking that the second person is being selfish, trying to get out of them something they want, without any consideration of the first person's needs. Another idea of Kant's is that we should consider other people to be ends rather than means to ends. His statement draws a distinction between an "end," or a goal, and a "means to an end," or something that lets you get to that goal. He is saying, each person's welfare is a goal, and we shouldn't think of another person purely as something we use to get some other goal.

But this can get a little complicated. Let's say I hire someone to drive me someplace. I'm "just using" the other person to get somewhere. But the other person is "just using" me to get some money. We are both using each other, but we're both better off for it -- I get to where I want to go, and the other person gets some money. There's nothing wrong with this. Why not? Because both people entered into this deal voluntarily. They each knew what they were getting into. They both figured they'd be better off with the deal than without it. This sort of thing goes on all the time, and it's great that it does. It has been called "social exchange."

Even if we imagine a very happy marriage between two people, social exchange is going on. Each person is "using" the other person to get companionship, affection, and whatever else about being married makes them happy. When one of them says, "Would you like to take a walk together?" they are proposing to "use" the other person to make the walk more pleasant. But they are also hoping that the other person will be happier by taking the walk than by not. If they go walking and have a good time, there is a successful social exchange.

When is "using" another person to get your needs met unethical? It's more likely to be so when you use force with the other person rather than when the other person enters the deal willingly. When a dictator forces people to join the army (or else go to jail) and forces them to fight (or else get shot), the soldiers are being used as means to ends. It's also more likely to be unethical when there is deception or outright lying that causes the other person to enter the deal. If someone sells someone the right to go to a school, telling the person that the graduates get great jobs and the students all love their professors, when in fact almost none of the students end up graduating and the classes are worthless, the salesperson is a "con artist" who is dishonestly using the other people to get money from people without caring about whether the deal works out well for them.

So a way of altering Kant's rule about not using people is as follows: feel free to let other people help you achieve your goals, (in other words, to "use" them) as long as the way that you do it also helps them to achieve their goals!

Living things are made of cells

Suppose you take an ink smear or a smear of salt water and look at it under a microscope. Then you take a smear of some blood or a thin bit of skin or a slice of muscle tissue from a piece of meat, or a slide made from some algae, or from the leaf of a plant, and look at it under the microscope. You see something very different for the tissues that are taken from living things: they are made up of cells. The cell is a basic unit of living things. Cells are typically drawn as if they are round, but they can be various different shapes. But they have an inside and an outside, and something separating the inside from the outside. For plants the wall around the cell is usually much stiffer than in animals. When plants and animals grow, cells split in two to form more cells. Cells have a nucleus, where there are strands of DNA; the DNA provides a code that tells the cell how to make the enzymes that do whatever the cell is supposed to do. The DNA also goes into the new cells and tells them to act in the same way that their parents did – for example, it tells the liver cells, "You are supposed to act like a liver cell and not like a skin cell." The cells are using up energy and needing nourishment and oxygen, and giving off waste products. For any given organ of the body, for example the lungs, the brain, the liver, the intestine, the skin, there's a large body of information on how the cells of that particular organ work.

If all cells in an organ divide, there is twice as much tissue as there was before. Somehow or other the process needs to stop. It's amazing that our bodies "know" when to make tissues grow and when to make them stop growing. Sometimes the body makes mistakes in these decisions, and certain cells keep dividing without getting the signal to stop. When this happens, it's called cancer. Those of us who don't have cancer can be very thankful for the processes in the body that tell cells when to divide and make more of themselves, and when to stop.

Groups of cells that do the same thing are called tissues – for example there are muscle tissue, skin tissue, brain tissue, liver tissue, and so forth. The whole batch of tissue that forms something that does something is called an organ. For example, the liver, the brain, the lungs, are organs. Groups of organs that carry out a certain function are called systems. For example, the circulatory system includes the heart, all the blood vessels, the blood itself, and the organs that make the blood. The nervous system includes the brain, the spinal cord, and the nerves. All the systems go together to make an organism – for example, you or me! But the basic building blocks for all of this are cells.

Contracts and contract law

People's "using" other people in a forceful or deceptive way is bad, but people's "using" each other in social exchanges where each gets something they want more than what they are giving up are great. Those sorts of arrangements are key to all employment: the employer decides, I want your work more than the money I pay you, and the employee decides, I want the money more than I want to do something other than work. Both come out ahead. There is such an exchange whenever someone rents a place to stay or live: I want to be in the space more than I want the money, and the landlord wants the money more than she wants to be in the space.

When people agree on social exchanges, things come up that they could argue over. Someone agrees to buy a house, but then decides that they would rather not. Someone rents an apartment, but then there's a plumbing problem and there's a lot of damage to the apartment. Someone hires someone to work 30 hours a week, but the person is expected to do the same amount of work as those working 40 hours a week. Someone agrees to fix the roof on someone's house, but they keep putting off doing the work.

For this reason, another big idea grew up: that the people would write down what they were agreeing to. They would spell out in as much detail as possible what each person was giving and what they were getting. They would try to anticipate what problems might come up, and they would agree in advance about what would be done. Then, when something happened, they could go back to this written agreement and use it to have a peaceful decision of how to settle things. These written agreements are called contracts.

What happens if one person says, "I know I signed the agreement saying I would pay you this much by this date. But I changed my mind. I don't think it's worth that much. In fact, I don't feel like paying you at all." Do they go and get their weapons and fight it out with each other? To keep that from happening, governments take an interest in people's agreements with each other. Lawyers get involved in these agreements, and if there's a dispute, people can go to courts and let a judge, a magistrate, or a jury decide who should get or do what. The enforcement of people's agreements by courts is another big idea -- it is what we call contract law. If it works well, it lets people make social exchanges without fighting with each other.

The greatest happiness for the greatest number

The greatest happiness for the greatest number principle is another way of deciding what is right and wrong to do. A simple statement of this principle is that we should choose the action that will increase the total happiness of the world the most. We do kind actions because they make people happy and we avoid cruel actions because they make people unhappy. If there's something we can do that can make lots of people very happy, that action is preferable to something else that would make only one or two people very happy. So if I have a choice between finding a cure for cancer and giving someone a trip to an amusement park, finding the cure wins out! So the more happiness we create in the more people, the better our actions are, according to this ethical system.

This way of thinking about what's right and wrong has been called utilitarianism. Some early writers about this were Jeremy Bentham and John Stuart Mill. People sometimes use the word utility to mean how well-off someone is: how good their life is, how much their circumstances are preferable to some other circumstances, the quality of their life, and not just how they feel at any given moment. The ethical philosophy of utilitarianism is about trying to "maximize utility."

One of the questions for this sort of philosophy is, whose utility are we trying to maximize? Does everybody in the world get equal weight, or do I have more responsibility for the happiness of some people than other people? For example, perhaps I could increase the total happiness of the world the most by giving away almost all the money I own to help the poorest people in the world. But this would probably decrease my own happiness and those of my family members. It seems logical that I hold more loyalty to my own family members than I do to people I've never met. But I still want to help those people that I've never met to some degree. So instead of maximizing the total happiness of the world, counting everybody equally, maybe I should give much more weight to the happiness of some people than others. For example, my own happiness and those of my family members, my loyal friends, and the people I affect in my work all get multiplied by a larger number in this formula than some people far away. Those people that I owe more loyalty to and have more responsibility for, are more important for me to try to make happy. But the people far away, even if they are not a member of my "tribe," do enter into the formula! They don't get a zero weight! I want to try to do something for them too!

Some people have argued that trying to maximize happiness results in ethical decisions that just seem wrong, sometimes. For example, suppose someone is very old and has a brain illness that has destroyed the person's ability to think and remember. Unlike some people in this situation, suppose that the person seems to be very unhappy and very tormented by their illness. Suppose that someone calculates that the person and those who are caring for him would all be happier if someone were to euthanize, or kill, this person, the same way we do with dogs or cats who have gotten very old and sick. If we think that this would be wrong, does this mean that utilitarianism is giving us the wrong answer?

In reply to this question, some would say that the problem is not with utilitarianism but with the calculation of what happens to happiness. They would argue that even though the person might be happier and all the person's relatives might be happier, nonetheless society is worse off because the precedent against killing people has been weakened. The word "precedent" is something of a big idea in itself. When people do something, they set a precedent, or make it more customary, for other people to do the same thing, or similar things. In our example, the happiness of society might be lowered because the weakening of the precedent against killing leads other people to be killed for bad reasons. This more nuanced version of utilitarianism has sometimes been called "rule utilitarianism." It draws attention to the fact that when we try to predict the effects on happiness, we have to take into account not just the people directly affected by the action, but also what happens to the rules and the precedents of society.

In trying to "maximize utility," should we think just about people? Many people (myself included) think that it is an advance of utilitarian ethics to also take into account the happiness of animals. The greatest happiness for the greatest number includes not raising chickens in conditions where you don't let them even move around! It includes not dumping into water waste chemicals that kill or sicken the animals living it and around it. It includes trying to make sure that people don't mistreat dogs and cats and other pets. (But my own sympathies for animals stop when we start thinking about the happiness of ticks, mosquitos, and the types of worms that get into people's bodies!)

If people truly focused on the goal of trying to choose the actions that would maximize some version of the total happiness of this planet, and thought very carefully trying to predict what the consequences of their actions would be on such happiness, the world would surely be a much happier place!

As it is, many people are focused only on their own happiness, and they don't even do a very good job of maximizing that! One of the major reasons for this is the subject of the next big idea.

Delay of gratification or self-discipline

Many years ago, among certain groups there was a slogan that went to, "If it feels good, do it." Unfortunately, it became obvious that this motto for decision-making turned out to be a good way to become addicted to drugs, become very overweight, produce lots of unplanned pregnancies, or fail in school and in business. The problem is that what feels good in the short run often produces results that don't feel good in the long run. Many times in order to produce the best long-term results, we have to make choices that pass up short-term pleasure. Someone would in the short run enjoy playing a videogame more than they would enjoy studying for a biology test. But studying for the biology test produces the outcome that makes them happiest in the long run. If they study for the biology test and pass up the videogame, they are using a very important skill: the skill of self discipline, otherwise known as the skill of delay of gratification.

It can be lots of fun, in the moment, to drive a car really fast. But the long-term consequences of a car wreck make it very worthwhile to pass up this form of pleasure. It can be very pleasant, when one comes into some money, to spend it on whatever strikes their fancy at the moment. It takes self-discipline to save money, but the long-term consequences are very much more pleasant than spending without restraint.

My guess is that many people never think about the fact that we often have to give up short-term pleasure to maximize our long term happiness, or to achieve some other goal that we care about greatly. Simply thinking about the meaning of the word self-discipline could be a life-changing idea for many people.

You'll notice that I said we *often* have to give up short-term pleasure to maximize long-term happiness. Often, but not always! There is a place in life for having fun and having short term pleasure, especially if it's of the sort that doesn't have any bad consequences! So, we don't have to give up eating stuff that tastes good! We don't have to give up reading stories that don't teach us much of anything, but are just fun to read! We don't have to give up going to parties! (But I would vote for totally avoiding ever getting drunk at a party!)

Goals -- responding to a vision of a future outcome

Self-discipline means doing what achieves our important goals rather than just doing what seems to feel good at the moment. But it's hard to use self-discipline to achieve goals if we don't have any goals!

Goals are what we want to try to make happen. They are our visions and dreams for the future, that we want to make come true. Having a happy marriage, having a fulfilling job, having enough money, having good friends, being in good physical condition, being as healthy as possible, making good grades, going to a desirable school, becoming an expert in something in a way that people look up to, learning lots about the world, making the world a better place, preventing violence, preventing mental health problems, having good relationships with family members, making good decisions, living in a safe place ... all these are example of goals that people might adopt.

Having goals can make activities lots more fun. For example, if someone has a goal of getting very strong, working out with weights can be lots of fun, because with every repetition, one can think, "This is getting me a little closer to my goal!" On the other hand, if one has no interest in getting stronger or in better shape, the person might think, "What sense does this make? Just to pick something up and put it back down, that's silly!" If someone has a goal of trying to build a better and better relationship with a family member, it can be lots of fun to go for a walk together and chat. If the person doesn't have that goal, they might think, "I don't have anything I particularly want to tell them, and there's nothing I want to know from them either. So what's the point?" If someone has the goal of becoming an educated person and becoming very expert at something, when that person studies schoolwork, they can think, "I'm building the skills that will help me become an expert! I'm getting better and better at learning!" If they have no such goal, they might think, "This is not nearly as interesting as watching a television show. Why should I do this?"

Someone said, "If you know where you want to go, you're much more likely to get there!" People who have goals are much more likely to achieve things in life. Some people have found that those who actually write down their goals, and look frequently at what they've written, tend to accomplish those goals more readily. And those who not only set goals, but make very detailed plans about how to achieve them, and work very hard to follow those plans, are even more likely to succeed.

Another part of this big idea is that of "worthy" goals. If someone sets a goal of getting into a book of world records for balancing the largest number of oranges on top of each other, that's a goal, all right. But it might not be as "worthy" a goal as trying to improve as many people's vision as possible by learning to do eye surgery and doing it well. But piling up the oranges might be a much more "worthy" goal than trying to knock out as many people as possible in mixed martial arts. What makes a worthy goal? If we refer to our utilitarian ethics idea, a worthy goal is one that increases happiness or utility in oneself and others. And if we refer to our self-discipline idea, we are talking about long term happiness and not just short term pleasure.

So here's the summary of this big idea: we choose worthy goals, we write them down, we make detailed plans for how to achieve them, we work hard to carry out those plans, and: last but not least, we feel good about every little bit of progress we make! We even feel good about the work we do, even if it doesn't seem to produce any progress, because sometimes on the way to goals we need to try out some things that don't work!

Meaning and purpose are self-assigned

For centuries, people have been asking, "What is the meaning of life?" which is usually synonymous with, "What is the purpose of life?" "What's the point of it all?" "What's it about?" "What am I supposed to do, and why should I do it?"

Sometimes people have the feeling that they're waiting for someone to tell them the answer to the question of what the purpose of life should be, or they're waiting to

50

discover it somewhere. Or sometimes they get the depressing idea that there is no meaning or purpose.

The big idea of this section is that people can create and decide upon their own purposes in life. The answer to this seemingly very profound and mystical question is pretty much synonymous with the question we mentioned earlier: "What goals would you like to achieve?"

People are good at caring about achieving the object of a game, once they decide what the object is. If the object is to get rid of all your cards, or capture all the opponent's pieces, get four tokens in a line, get the ball through a hoop, get the ball over a line, and so forth, people can convince themselves that achieving such goals to win games are extremely important and worthy of great emotion. Does it really make any difference how many times a ball goes through one hoop and how few times it goes through the other? There's really "no point" to it. But people have lots of fun with basketball by just deciding that it does make a difference to them, and they are going to work hard toward achieving a lot in the game -- or even, that they are going to root for members of the tribe they have adopted, to try to help them achieve in the game.

The essence of this big idea is that we get to do the same thing with life. We can decide that the object of the game is to enjoy life ourselves and help others to have happy lives also. We can decide that when unavoidable suffering comes, the object of the game is to bear it with fortitude. We don't need anyone's permission to choose these objects for the game (which I happen to think are good choices).

On the other hand, we can make all sorts of other choices. We can decide that life is a competition, and the object of the game is to win, to defeat our competitors. We can decide that the more people we can dominate, the better we're doing in the game. Lots of people decide that "the person who has the most money and possessions at the end of the game wins," i.e. that the object is the same as in the game called "Monopoly." Some people decide that the person who looks the most attractive wins -- (if you choose this as the object of the game, old age tends to be a bummer!) Some decide that the person who most easily gets the most romantic partners wins (likewise for this one in old age!) Some decide that the object of the game is to become as famous as possible. Unfortunately, perhaps as many people are famous for doing bad things as for doing good things.

Phrasing the question, "What is the meaning of life" or "What is the purpose of life" is perhaps not a good idea. We need plurals rather than singulars, because life can have lots of purposes or goals. Someone can want both to defeat some threatening adversaries and cooperate with some loved ones and make them happy. Someone can want to create happiness in self and others through a certain career, and can have 15 other goals that make that career possible, including school success, and have 10 other goals that foster school success, and so forth. It's also very possible that the "purposes of life" can change over time. What gives us a sense of meaning and purpose at age 15 doesn't have to keep doing so at age 75, and vice versa!

But the point of this big idea is that we have the freedom to choose what goals and directions we want for our lives.

The race between destruction and nonviolence

For as long as human beings have existed, people have been able to get an advantage over other people when they, or the side that they're on, has better weapons -- more effective ways of killing and hurting their enemies. Very long ago some people discovered how to make swords out of metal. A few centuries ago, they discovered gunpowder. In the late 1800's, Alfred Nobel invented dynamite. He wrote something like this: "My dynamite will sooner lead to peace than a thousand world conventions. As soon as men will find that in one instant, whole armies can be utterly destroyed, they surely will abide by golden peace." Well, it didn't exactly turn out that way, did it? In the 1940's nuclear weapons came into the world and were used to produce horrible destruction. Today's nuclear weapons are many times more powerful than those of the mid twentieth century. The total weaponry of the world is enough to destroy human civilization as we know it, and perhaps all human life. But "golden peace" is a dream rather than a reality. War is raging in some parts of the world. In the USA, huge amounts of money go to weapons and armed forces. The threat of nuclear war is being brought up often by world leaders.

The technology of nonviolence has to do less with the invention of machines, and more with the discovery of ways that people can act toward each other in peaceful ways, and the development of customs, procedures, and attitudes among people in favor of nonviolence. An example of this is the "rule of law," in which, for example, people take their disagreements to court and agree to abide by whatever the court decides, rather than physically fighting with each other. For a long time people have had the idea of a world court, where nations would take their disputes and get decisions, instead of having wars with each other. But people in countries are very reluctant to give up any of their "sovereignty," meaning their ability to make their own decisions without being controlled by anyone outside the country. Another part of the "technology of nonviolence" is helping people simply to appreciate and revere nonviolence rather than to celebrate and idolize the best fighters. Still another part of peace technology is the study of how people speak to each other in ways that get problems solved -- for example, by giving evidence for the predicted consequences of a given option, rather than insulting the other person. Another part might be agreements on how the decision to wage war is reached, for example requiring that no one person could make the decision by themselves. Requiring that committees with adequate representation by women consent to warfare before launching the guns and tanks and bombs is not too far-fetched an idea, since women (as a group, even though some individuals have been exceptions) have in all places and times been less inclined to violence than men have been.

We can view the Planet Earth as in a race: will violence destroy civilization first, or will advances in nonviolence keep us from self-destructing? This is perhaps the most important question for humanity.

Probability

The word *probability* has to do with the likelihood, or the chance, that something will happen, or even that something has happened. If we're absolutely sure something will happen, we say that the probability is 1, or 100%. If we're absolutely sure it won't happen, we say that the probability is 0, or 0%. What is the probability that when we flip a coin, the coin will come up heads? We say that it is 50%, or ½, or .5. If we pick one card from a deck of 52 cards, what's the probability that it will be the ace of spades? (There's one and only one of those in the deck.) The probability is 1/52. What's the probability that it will NOT be the ace of spades? 51/52. We can sometimes use the chances of drawing cards or getting numbers in a die roll or flipping coins as comparisons that help us decide how likely we think some other more important things are.

The big idea of probability implies that we don't go through life just knowing some things to be true and others not to be true. There are different degrees of certainty that are possible. What if you're on a jury, and you are deciding whether to convict someone of a crime. Suppose that after hearing all the evidence, you think the chance that this person committed the crime is about 25% -- the chance of flipping two coins and having 2 heads come up. This happens about 1 out of 4 coin flips. So your estimate of the chance that the defendant did the crime is a lot higher than the chance that some random person in the same city did it, which is pretty close to zero. Is this a high enough chance for you to vote to convict the person? No – you are supposed to think that the person did it "beyond a reasonable doubt," and that isn't the case when you think there's a 25% chance that he did it (and a 75% chance that he didn't!) On the other hand, if you think that there's a 99.5% chance that he did it, you would probably vote to convict, even though you think that it's remotely possible that he's innocent.

Sets, subsets, supersets, unions, intersections

A group of things or ideas or numbers or words or people or anything else is a set. We can define what's in and out of a certain set by listing the members or by giving a rule. An example of a list is to say, a certain set of cities consists of New York, Chicago, and Los Angeles. An example of a rule is to refer to the set of the three most populous cities in the USA.

If every member of a certain set is also in another set, we say that the first is a subset of the second. For example, the set of Beagles is a subset of the set of dogs. If a first set contains every member of a second set, we say it's a superset of the second. The set of dogs is a superset of the set of Beagles.

The union of two sets is everything that is in either one of them. For example, the union of {a,b,c} and {c,d,e} is {a,b,c,d,e}.

The intersection of two sets is every element that is in both of them. For example, the intersection of {a,b,c} and {c,d,e} is {c}.

These ideas have all sorts of applications. They are widely used in the study of probability. What's the probability of drawing a red face card from a standard deck of cards? There are 6 members in the set of red face cards: {jack of hearts, jack of diamonds, queen of hearts, queen of diamonds, king of hearts, king of diamonds}. There are 52 members in the set of cards in the deck. The probability of drawing a red face card is 6/52, or about 11.5%.

How would you explain to someone that the probability of having a stroke has to be greater than the probability of having a stroke leading to weakness on one side of the body? You'd probably be clearest if you said that the set of people with stroke and one-sided weakness is a subset of the set of people with stroke. You can't have a subset that has more members than the original set.

Suppose you want to look up articles on therapy, treatment, or intervention for aggression, violence, or anger? You would ask your software to
1. Create the union of the sets of articles on therapy, treatment, or intervention.
2. Create the union of the sets of articles on aggression, violence, or anger.
3. Find the intersections of the two sets you created.

Probabilities of intersections and unions

Let's imagine that we have four cards with the following written on them:
A a B b
If we pick a card at random, what's the probability of picking the letter a (either A or a)? It's 2/4, or 1/2, or 50%, because there are 2 ways of picking that letter and 4 ways of picking something. What's the probability of picking a capital letter? That also is 1/2, because there are two capital letters, out of 4 ways of picking a card.
What's the probability of picking one that is BOTH a capital letter and the letter A?The answer to this is 1/4, because there's only one card that would have a success

with that -- the one with A on it. (A is the intersection of the set of capitals and the set of a's.)

What's the probability of picking a card that is EITHER a capital letter OR the letter A? The answer to that is 3/4, because there are 3 cards that meet this condition, and only one that doesn't. (A, a, and B are the union of the set of capitals and the set of a's.)

There are rules and formulas that explain how to combine individual probabilities, but in this section, the big idea is that we can talk about the probability of this condition AND that condition, and we can also talk about the probability of this condition OR that condition; the first of these can't be greater than the second.

There are many times in life when it's useful to think about the probabilities of intersections or unions. For example, suppose you're running a project where the project will succeed only if each of 5 people does their job right. Suppose there's a different project that will succeed at least to some degree if any of 5 people does their job right. All other things equal (the competence of the people, the difficulty of the tasks) which project has the better chance of success? The second!

Mutually exclusive and independent events

Suppose there are two events such that if either one of them happens, the other can't happen. If you flip a coin and get heads, you can't also get tails on the same flip -- heads and tails are mutually exclusive. If you roll a die, outcomes of one dot or two dots are mutually exclusive. If you get Doctor X to take out your appendix, you can't get Doctor Y to do it (the two doctors don't want to work together on the job). If you marry person A, you can't also marry person B, at least not at the same time, in most countries! When you get treated for cancer, you either survive for 5 years, or you don't -- you can't do both of them. All these are mutually exclusive events. On the other hand, many events are not mutually exclusive. If you're wanting to do better on a test, you can read very carefully what you're going to be tested over, and practice taking sample tests from a test prep book, and make up your own questions and answers -- none of these are mutually exclusive. If I'm wanting to be more healthy, I can get more exercise and improve my diet -- these aren't mutually exclusive, so I don't need to pick between them. It's often very useful to recognize when events are mutually exclusive and when they aren't.

Two events are independent if the occurrence of the first doesn't affect the chance of the second. For example, I flip a coin twice. The chance of getting heads on the second flip doesn't depend on what I got on the first flip. The two events are independent of each other. If I roll two dice, the outcome with the second is independent of the outcome with the first. The probability of warm weather in the spring is probably independent of whether a ground hog sees his shadow on a certain day. Whether one person in a school classroom gets cancer is pretty much independent of whether another student gets cancer. (The phrase "pretty much independent" is meant to communicate that sometimes one event increases the other a tiny bit, a small bit, a medium bit, or a large amount -- the effects of events on one another can vary.)

Now that we've talked about independent and mutually exclusive events, we can name a couple of rules about probability. When two events are mutually exclusive, the chance that one or the other of them will occur is the sum of their probabilities. For example, when we roll a die, the chance of rolling a 1 and the chance of rolling a 2 are each 1/6; the chance of rolling either a 1 or a 2 is 1/6 + 1/6, or 2/6, or 1/3. When two events are independent, the chance that both will occur is the product of their probabilities. For example, if you roll two dice, the chance that you will roll a 1 on both dice is 1/6 times 1/6, or 1/36.

Democracy

When there is a group of people, who gets to decide what they do? Who gets to make the rules? If one person gets the power to tell everyone else what to do, we can call that a dictatorship, or autocracy. The idea of democracy is that the people who are affected by the decisions of government should get to decide what the government does. If we let the people vote directly on the important decisions, that is the most democratic form of government. Should we build a certain road, should we make a certain drug illegal, should we send soldiers to a certain place to fight -- for each of these, we would have a vote.

The trouble with this "pure democratic form" of democracy is that it takes a lot of work for people to gather and ponder the information necessary to make good decisions on the thousands of choice points that governments deal with, and most people don't have the time and energy to inform themselves about these. So if we leave all the decisions up to the people, we will have decisions being made by people who don't know enough to make good ones.

Representative government

In representative government, the people elect people to make the government's decisions. This is meant to get around the problem with "pure" democracy that we talked about -- at least in theory the representatives have the time to do lots of research that helps them make better decisions than the average person, who is busy making their living some other way. If the representatives make good decisions, the people vote them back into office, and if they make decisions that make the people unhappy, the people vote in someone else.

For representative government to work well, the voters have to do some good thinking in order to figure out what causes what, and who is responsible for what. For example, suppose some people in the legislature want the president to be voted out. So they purposely make decisions that result in very bad economic conditions -- fewer jobs, more poverty, higher taxes for the people who can't afford them. They do this, predicting that the president will be blamed for the bad results, and if they are right, the ignorance of the voters has interfered greatly with the workings of government. Both democracy and representative government depend upon voters who can correctly figure things out.

For representative government to work well, something else should happen: the representatives should try to do what is really best for the country rather than just do what gets their poll numbers higher with the people that will elect them. If the representatives know that most of the voters in their district have some very racist or otherwise wrong beliefs, they can perhaps hang onto their power by spouting off the wrong beliefs that the voters have.

Barriers to war, versus "Rally around the flag"

Let's start with the "Rally Around the Flag" effect. When a leader decides to launch a war, even if the war is of the sort that most people later decide was stupid to start, the leader's popularity tends to go up. People tend to put their trust and hope in their leader, when they are in war against another country. Why is this? Perhaps evolution has something to do with it. Perhaps through the thousands of years that people banded into tribes that fought with other tribes, tribes tended to survive when people had a reflex to stick together and be loyal to each other. They probably also survived more often when they obeyed a leader rather than having everybody decide for themselves what should be done, and arguing among each other about how to do it. Having a "common enemy" perhaps for that reason tends to bind people together, and to their leader. This has been called the "Rally around the flag" effect. Unfortunately, it gives leaders a big incentive to start wars.

People who work for peace have focused many of their efforts on getting rid of weapons, particularly on getting rid of nuclear weapons. But it appears increasingly unlikely that this goal will be achieved, at least not in the lifetime of anyone reading this. Why? Because nuclear weapons are a guarantee that your country won't be conquered and overrun by another country, and people tend not to give up that guarantee once they have it.

What else can peace workers set as a goal, something that nations can agree on, that will make war less likely, other than getting rid of weapons? One possibility would be a treaty where nations agree that war can not be launched by one person, or even a small number of people. There has to be a special committee, made up of different types of people, who would have to agree that war was necessary, before the soldiers could be put into motion. Or maybe there would have to be a vote by all the people of the country. Or, as long as we are dreaming, perhaps even the people who vote for the war would be the only ones forced to fight in it and fund it!

There are hugely different ways that this could be carried out, and they would all present obstacles and problems. And the rally around the flag effect would tend to make committee members jump on board and support a persuasive leader. But even efforts toward some plan like this might make the world a better place. It might reduce the danger in our current world, where there are a good number of dictators who can single handedly plunge their countries into war whenever they want to.

Influence of vocabulary on thought

It's easier for us to think certain thoughts if we know the words that most easily express those thoughts. Some researchers observed that people who lived in very cold regions used lots of different words for different types of snow. Because the distinctions between for example wet and sticky snow and dry and powdery snow were important to them, they developed words with which to talk about these differences. People who lived in very warm regions would not need these words.

This idea explains why nearly every area of specialized knowledge develops its own words with which to think about what's important for that subject. Chess players talk about forks and pins; musicians think about keys and arpeggios; economists think about inflation, aggregate demand, and price elasticity; cell biologists think about mitochondria and vacuoles; and on and on.

If people have the words *self-discipline* and *fortitude* in their vocabularies, it's probably easier for them think, "This is a situation where it's time for me to use self-discipline," or "I don't like what happened, but at least I handled it with fortitude." If they know the meaning of the word option, it's probably easier for them to think, "This is an important choice point; what are my options?"

So we can sometimes help people to handle life better, partly just by teaching them the meaning of certain words.

Compound interest

If you lend money to a person, a company, or a government, you get paid for letting the other people use your money; that payment is *interest*. This is a good reason not to spend money, but to invest it by lending it out instead -- you get paid back more than you lent.

Suppose you put money into an account where the interest you get, automatically gets re-invested by lending it back out. Now the amount of money that is collecting interest for you grows and grows over time. The interest payments get bigger and bigger. This is a situation where you are benefiting from compound interest.

Let's say you lend $1000, and the annual interest rate is 5%. Without compounding (for example if you took the interest and spent it), you would earn $50 a year in interest. In 50 years, you would have earned $2,500. That's not bad!

But let's say you let all the interest stay in the account and let it earn interest itself. So after a year, you would have $1050 in the account. 5% of that is $52.50. So after two years, you would have $1050+$52.50=$1102.50 in the account. If we kept that up, how much would you have after 50 years? The answer is $11,467.40!

The way money grows if you don't spend it, and you also don't spend the money you make from investing it, has been called "the magic of compound interest."

Activation energy, and its analogy to human activities

When you put two chemicals together, do they react with each other to make a new chemical? Sometimes they start reacting as soon as you put them together. But sometimes, even though their reaction would generate enough energy to keep the reaction going once it gets started, you need to put some energy in at the beginning, to start the reaction off. This is called the activation energy.

A very common example is a wood fire. When wood burns, it gives off lots of energy in the form of heat. This can make other wood start reacting with the oxygen in the air. But unless something starts the reaction going, wood and air can sit around together for a long time without any fire starting. The reaction generates energy once it gets going, but it needs to absorb some "activation energy" first, to get it going.

It's sometimes useful to use the idea of activation energy as an analogy to things that go on in life that are not really chemical reactions. We can think about the "activation energy" we need to get started in some activities that generate their own energy once they get started. For example:

It is fun and energizing to socialize with a group of people, but first someone needs to generate the energy to overcome shyness and get started talking with others.

It feels energizing to exercise, but first one must generate the energy to get started.

A business makes money, but first it takes money to start it up.

Using specialized skills can have a big payoff, but first one has to generate the energy to gain those skills.

Levers and other non-motorized machines

Have you ever seen someone pry a nail out of a board using the two prongs on the non-banging end of a hammer head? Or use a screwdriver to pry open a can of paint? Or use a screwdriver to put a screw into a piece of wood? I'm sure you're familiar with using a knife or scissors or ax to cut something. And almost everywhere we see cars, trucks, bikes, skates, skateboards, and other things that travel on wheels. All the tools that I've mentioned use principles of physics that make us able to do things without having to be so strong as to do it without the tools. Imagine how strong your fingers would have to be to just push a nail or screw into a piece of wood, all by themselves.

Many of the devices I've mentioned make it so that you don't have to push as hard, in return for pushing over a larger distance. For example, when you use a screwdriver to pry open a paint can, you move the handle of the screwdriver several inches, but the end that is connected with the lid only moves a fraction of an inch. This arrangement puts much more force on the lid than you could apply if you just used your fingers to pull on it. When you cut with a knife, you push with a certain force on the knife handle -- the force is spread out over the surface of the handle. But if the knife is sharp, the area of the cutting part is very small, so you are concentrating a large amount of force onto a very small area, and that part of what you're cutting comes apart. The same principle applies to using an ax. Imagine trying to break a big fallen tree in two without an ax. With an ax, it's a lot of work, but it can be done.

The wheel was a huge discovery for human beings, somewhere a very long time ago. Part of the way that wheels work is by reducing the friction that resists things from being moved from one place to another. Imagine grocery carts that didn't have wheels on the bottom, but just legs like a table. You would have to push a lot harder to get a cart to move! If you compare a grocery cart with a grocery basket that you carry, the cart also lets you not have to work to hold the basket off the floor.

Another example of device that lets you do things without being so strong is the "inclined plane," otherwise known as a ramp. Suppose you have a grocery cart full of stuff, and you need to move it to a place that's a couple of meters high, that is at the top of a little cliff that goes straight up. You can just pick up the whole cart and lift it straight up, if you're super-strong and super-big. But you can be just an ordinary person and roll the cart up a ramp, particularly if the ramp is long enough that you don't have to go up a very steep incline. Again, you're applying less force over a larger distance.

When I walk up lots of steps to get to a high floor of the apartment I'm staying in, I'm using a version of the inclined plane. I make lots of little pushes that eventually get me very high, instead of one big push from jumping all the way up. I don't need to be Superman and able of "leap tall buildings in a single bound" to be able to get myself just as high up!

Fundamental forces

Most of the things we think of as "happening" are the result of things moving. Even when we sit with our eyes closed and think, our thoughts are the results of the motions of atoms in our brains. And why do things start or stop moving? Because something at some time pushed or pulled on it. Pushes and pulls are called forces.

As far as scientists know, there are only four types of forces in the whole universe. They are:

1. Gravity
2. Electromagnetic force
3. The strong nuclear force
4. The weak nuclear force.

People are familiar with gravity as the force that makes things fall to the earth. Some people don't realize that every two objects in the whole universe attract each other with gravitational force. If you put two balls on a table, why doesn't gravity pull them together? Because the force of gravity is not strong enough to overcome the friction forces that hold them in place. The force of gravity gets bigger the heavier the two objects are, and it gets less the greater the distance between them is. (If you want to be exact, the force gets less in proportion to the square of the distance, or the distance multiplied by itself.) If you're on the moon, gravity pulls you down with much less force than if you're on the earth, because the moon isn't nearly as massive as the earth. Gravity is what holds the moon in its orbit around the earth, and what holds the earth in its orbit around the sun.

Electromagnetic force is that between charged particles. There are two different types of electrical charges that particles or objects can have; we call them positive and negative. A positive and a negative charge attract each other, and two positive or two negative charges repel each other. The force with which they pull each other together or push each other apart increases with the amount of charge (how strongly negative or positive they are) and decreases with the square of the distance apart that they are. Sounds a lot like what we said about gravity, doesn't it? Most people don't know that most of the forces that we exert, for example when we push on something and it moves, or when we hit a ball with a bat, are electromagnetic forces. When a bat and ball get really, really close to each other, the negative charges revolving around the atoms of the bat start to repel the negative charges revolving around the atoms in the ball. And that electromagnetic force is what sends the ball moving fast away from the bat!

In another section, there's another big idea about the structure of atoms. In the nucleus of most atoms there are a bunch of protons (which are positively charged) and neutrons (which are neutrally charged -- neither positive nor negative). The positive charges of the protons should repel each other, right, according to what we just discussed in the last paragraph? How do you have protons and neutrons stuck in a tight little ball, with the negatively charged electrons orbiting around them? Why don't the protons repel each other and fly off from each other, making most elements impossible? The answer is the "strong nuclear force." It somehow exerts a force that allows those protons to huddle together.

I'm not going to try to explain the weak nuclear force.

But here is a big question. The strength of these forces are in a certain ratio to each other. If these ratios were much different from what they are, we wouldn't exist. Elements, chemical reactions, and much of what goes on in the universe wouldn't go on. To give you an example of this, suppose there were no such thing as a repelling force, only attracting forces. All the particles in the whole universe would be pulled toward each other into a tight ball that would just sit there and do nothing. Or suppose every particle in the universe repelled every other particle, and there were no forces of attraction. All the particles would just spread out over the universe, each of them getting as far away from the others as possible. How did it happen that the ratios of the fundamental forces just happened to be such that we got to exist? One possible answer (assuming you like getting to be alive) is, "We just got lucky." Another possible answer is, "Whoever or whatever caused the universe to exist in the first place preferred it to be interesting and not boring." If you find an answer, that can really be proved, please let me know!

Two big goals: lasting happiness for self and others

What's the object of the game of life? What's the point? We can pick how we want to answer this question. What's a good answer to choose? Many wise people have focused on two big goals:

Lasting Happiness of self

and

Lasting Happiness of the other people we affect.

In other words, we want to be kind to ourselves and kind to others.

People have expressed these goals in various ways. "Love thy neighbor as thyself" is a famous way of putting this in religious writings. Another wise person (named Hillel) wrote, "If I am not for myself, who is for me? And if I am only for myself, what am I?"

The word *lasting* is meant to communicate that short-term, momentary pleasure is not what we are talking about primarily with these goals. Eating candy or taking a certain drug might be pleasurable in the short term, but often these short term pleasures are not what make us happiest over time. Having good relationships, developing a meaningful career, cultivating fun hobbies to do with other people, enjoying learning, and others tend to produce happiness that sticks around longer.

Why should we work toward our own happiness? If we define a "happier" condition as one we prefer to a different one, to say that "we prefer to be happy" is true by definition -- "we prefer to be in circumstances that we prefer."

Why should people be unselfish? Why should they care about their effects on other people's happiness? I would argue that even if one really only wanted to maximize their own happiness, working toward making other people happy would be the best way to do it. Why is that? Because people are social animals, and we get most of our happiness from good relations with other people.

And if we want to have good relations, we need to be kind to others. Another argument is that the game of life has to have some sort of objective. We need to be trying for something, or else it isn't fun -- just as a game isn't fun unless there's something we are trying to do. Trying to improve the human condition, trying to make things better for other people, both living and yet to be born (as well as our nonhuman animal relatives) is an object for the game that seems to resonate with our inborn wishes to help out members of our tribe. It's good if we can consider all of humanity, plus a good fraction of the animal kingdom, as members of our tribe whom we want to help out. (Sorry, ticks and mosquitos, as I said earlier, you don't make it into my tribe.)

Not everyone agrees that the best goals are lasting happiness for oneself and others. For some people, winning, being dominant, defeating one's competitors and enemies, is the primary goal of life. For others, being rich, being famous, being attractive, or being powerful are the major goals that dominate life. And for many other people, the question, "What are the central goals you are striving for?" results in an answer of, "I don't know," or "I don't have any goals."

It's important to realize that sometimes a great deal of patience is needed before happiness-related goals are achieved. In other words, if we are not happy at this moment, or this year, or this decade, that doesn't mean the game is lost! I think of the story of Nelson Mandela, who was imprisoned for 27 years. But after all those years of imprisonment, he helped South Africa overcome a system based on racial discrimination (called apartheid) and became the first black president of South Africa.

Sometimes many years of unhappiness are worthwhile to bear, for the sake of the final result. So the important addendum to the goals of happiness of self and others is: if neither of these is working out well, use fortitude, hang in there, and think about the long term rather than just this moment.

Does being a good make you happy? It depends on the environment.

In this book, you get from me the message that trying to make other people happy is a great way to become happy yourself. But someone might say to me, "You are just lucky. You live in an environment where you can help people, and get paid enough to be comfortable in return. You can help people, and those people are often grateful. The ways you have been trained to be kind to people are valued by society, and you get respect from people for that reason."

The person might continue, "But what if you lived in a world where anyone who spent time helping someone else was thought to be a sucker? What if giving anyone anything just resulted in people's trying to forcibly get everything else that you had? What if you had to lie and steal to keep from dying? What if the environment you lived in had every person fighting against everyone else, and if you refused to use violence, you just came to a quick death?"

I would have to agree with that person -- indeed I am lucky to live in an environment where doing good things for other people tends to bring rewards for oneself. And I would probably go so far as to say that a major aspect of the definition of a "good environment to live in" is the conditions where being kind to others tends to bring about good results for oneself.

How does a society bring about these conditions? The conditions for reward of goodness partly come as a result of what people choose to spend their money on. For example, in a society where many people will spend money to watch people fight with one another, but few people want to spend money to attract good teachers to work at school, you get more fighters and fewer good teachers. The conditions also depend on what behaviors people praise and admire. If someone risks his life to try to save the life of a stranger's child, do people say, "That person is a hero," or "That person is stupid"? If a young man is kind and loving, will the young woman he is attracted to be more attracted to him for that reason, or will she prefer a "bad boy"? In other words, the more people value good behaviors, the more it will be true that kind people tend to be happier.

The phrase "dog eat dog world" has been applied to the situation where everyone can be for themselves only by being against everyone else. The novel, *The Hunger Games*, tells a story where adolescents are forced into a situation where they have to all fight against one another and see who is left at the end. Trying to make human societies less "dog eat dog" and less like *The Hunger Games* is an extremely admirable goal in itself.

Inductive reasoning -- scientific method versus truth from authority

How do we know what we know? With the scientific method, we come to conclusions by making observations: by seeing or hearing things (and occasionally

74

by tasting, smelling, or touching them) and keeping track of what we've observed. We try to set things up so that we can conclude the most from our observations -- for example, if we want to know whether a certain teaching method helps people behave better, we don't usually at the same time start a drug that is also meant to help them behave better, because then we can't tell what caused the results. The methods that people use to set up experiments to figure out what causes what are the subject of many books. But the point we're talking about now is that we get knowledge from our senses. We observe something happening over and over, and we conclude that it will happen that way in the future.

The notion that observing is believing has its competitors. One of the major ones is, "What you should believe is what the people in power and authority tell you to believe." Galileo, who made some of the biggest discoveries in astronomy and physics, was threatened by the leaders of the church at the time, (in the 1600s) to try to get him to renounce and withhold his scientific findings. The rule that "We make our conclusions so as to be most consistent with our observations" ran into conflict with a different rule: "We make the conclusions that help the people in power stay in power."

Another competitor to the notion that observing is believing is that people can just generate knowledge independent of any observations. Someone sees a vision or has a dream or is visited by a spirit who tells that person something -- this has sometimes competed strongly with the scientific method.

The scientific method only works well if people report their observations honestly and accurately. But there's a way of checking up on people: it's called replication. When someone reports some observations and a scientific conclusion, other people can use the same methods and make their own observations and see if these lead to the same conclusion.

The vast majority of things that we know do not come from our own direct observations. Rather they come from someone else's, perhaps checked by various other people. The fact that scientific knowledge can grow and grow, with new investigations building on past ones, represents a major triumph of trust. We can trust people to try to report their observations as accurately as they can, partly because we know that replication allows people to check up on them. Part of the very important culture of science is the set of customs and habits that keep scientists from making up data and publishing what they want to be true rather than what is really true.

The news media, like the scientific community, perform the service of gathering and delivering information. At the time of this writing in the USA, there is a great deal of "polarization" -- division of people into right wing versus left wing, conservative versus liberal, red versus blue. News organizations appear to be much influenced by the need to say what their readers and viewers want to hear. As a result, the news reporting can be greatly slanted toward the philosophy of the viewers they are aiming to reach; this in turn influences the viewers to be more set in their views. The way out of this problem is yet to be accomplished.

Bringing people together, versus loneliness and social isolation

For a relatively small amount of money, one can buy the books which, if studied diligently, will let someone know as much as the average college graduate knows -- without ever going to college. One can exercise very strenuously and effectively without ever going to a gym. One can have religious experiences without ever setting foot inside a church. One can listen to the best version of music through recordings, without ever going to a concert. One can abuse alcohol without going to a bar! Plays, political demonstrations, getting and eating food, running a business -- as experience with COVID-19 demonstrated, it is possible for people to carry out lots of things without coming together with other people.

But that experience also demonstrated that staying apart from one another tends to make people less happy. People are social animals. They need each other to encourage -- or pressure -- one another to meet goals rather than just to goof off, to structure their days rather than to sleep all day and stay up all night. People who are "connected" with other people, who have good "social support," are healthier than those who aren't, both physically and mentally. Many of the most important institutions people have developed, including workplaces and schools, are needed perhaps as much to help people overcome their loneliness as they are to accomplish their more obvious goals. Loneliness and disconnection of people from one another is a very important problem for society to find better ways of solving.

Circadian rhythms, especially sleep rhythms, and four clock-resetters

Suppose someone regularly goes to sleep about 2:00 or 3:00 a.m. and sleeps till noon or later. Then the person needs to be somewhere at 8:00 a.m. some morning, which means the person will have to get up about 6:30 am. So in order to be well-rested, the person decides to go to bed at 9:30 p.m. the night before. What do you think is likely to happen? According to research and other observations, the person is very likely to feel wide awake for a long time and find it impossible to fall asleep until they are lots closer to the accustomed time. In addition, when the person hears an alarm clock at 6:30 am, they are likely to find it very unpleasant to wake up and get moving -- they will be strongly tempted to go back to sleep.

What is the reason for this? We all have a timekeeper in our brains. The time for getting sleepy and the time for waking up, as well as rhythms for various hormones and other body processes, get set in this timekeeper. It's not a simple and easy task to reset it. Scientists have figured out that the timekeeper is located in the hypothalamus of the brain, in a part called the suprachiasmatic nucleus.

Many teenagers and young adults tend to run into problems from having their clocks set too late. Lots of them have difficulty getting up and going to school for this reason. How can you get your clock set earlier, if you want to?

There are 4 major ways to set the clock earlier. The first is simply to get out of bed and start the day's activities earlier -- sometimes it's best to do it gradually, a little earlier each day. The second is to be in some bright light in the morning, again moving the bright light time gradually earlier. Bright light tells the body that it's daytime and the time for activity has begun. The third resetter is exercise. Exercise also tells the body, "You're really awake; the day has started." And the fourth is eating breakfast. Food intake also is a signal that wake-up time has arrived.

On the other hand, if late at night, someone eats, exercises, sees bright lights, and stays out of bed, this tends to set the clock later.

Getting your clock set where you're really ready to wake up and fall asleep at the times you want to does a lot more than just make it easier to fall asleep and wake up. It helps you get enough sleep; it helps you be sharper mentally and physically; it also appears to improve the mood and make you less likely to be depressed. It's much easier to have good sleep when you go to bed and get up about the same time each night and morning. Unfortunately, it's much easier to advise people to do this than it is for people to actually carry this out!

Approach and avoidance motivation

Why do people do what they do? One way we can divide up the pie in thinking about people's motives is that 1) they may be trying to make something good happen, and 2) they may be trying to make something bad not happen. We call these approach motivation and avoidance motivation.

Both of these types of motivation are very important for survival. Approach motivation makes us want to eat -- we want the pleasure that food gives us. Avoidance motivation tends to make us decide not to eat too much junk -- we want to avoid the displeasure that would come from having a heart attack or any of the other health problems that too much junk food can give us. Approach motivation makes us want to go and visit a friend; if we're driving to see the friend, avoidance motivation makes us not want to go too fast, so as to avoid a speeding ticket or a wreck. Some people do schoolwork because it's interesting and fun, or because they love getting good grades; these are driven by approach motivation. Other people don't feel particularly good when they get a good grade, but they feel very bad when they get a bad grade. They are driven by avoidance motivation.

Is it possible to have very strong approach motivation without having at least fairly strong avoidance motivation with it? For example, can a basketball player who is shooting a couple of foul shots anticipate great pleasure if they go in, without anticipating great displeasure if they go out? Or to get to a more important question: is it possible to have a very strong good feeling from making someone else feel good, without having a strong bad feeling from hurting someone else? It think the two usually go together. For this reason, in my opinion the people who say that shame and guilt are emotions that we want to get rid of altogether, are altogether wrong. Knowing that one would feel ashamed and guilty over doing hurtful things is part of what keeps us from doing those things. That avoidance motivation is part of what is meant by a "conscience."

Some behavior problems have been understood by thinking of too much approach and not enough avoidance: that is, too much sensitivity to good consequences and not enough sensitivity to the bad. For example, some people who appear addicted to gambling seem to get a really good feeling when they win money, and not a very bad feeling when they lose it.

Thus it's not possible or desirable to eliminate all avoidance motivation. Our desires not to get hurt, not to make other people mad at us, and to keep bad things from happening are very important. Still, part of the reason these concepts are important is that if you are running a business, teaching a school classroom, influencing others in your family, or influencing even one other person in a relationship, you tend to make people happier if you try to use approach motivation whenever possible. For example, if you're the boss of a business, you can wait for your employees to make mistakes or perform poorly, and criticize or threaten or fire them. When they do things right, you see no reason to do anything. If this is the way you run the business, you're relying on avoidance motivation, and your employees are likely not to be very happy. On the other hand, you can try to get your employees excited about the goals of the company, and celebrate and congratulate when people do things that foster these goals. You can try to measure people's performance and be sure to let them know when their performance is good. If this is the way you run the business, you are relying on approach motivation. The higher the fraction of approach motivation and the lower the fraction of avoidance motivation, the happier the employees are likely to be. The same idea applies to other types of relationships.

The emotional climate

The concept of "emotional climate" (also known as the "interpersonal environment") applies to any group of people. It applies to a relationship between two people; it can apply to a classroom, a school, a workplace, and very importantly, to a family. It has to do with the average way that people feel about one another. If people very often feel angry, scared, ashamed, upset, or other unpleasant feelings toward one another, there tends to be a "negative emotional climate." If they very often have fun with each other, feel happy, feel proud of one another, feel liking or loving, or feel other pleasant emotions toward one another, then there tends to be a "positive emotional climate."

How often do people criticize or insult one another? The rate of critical statements is very connected to the emotional climate. How often do they raise their voices in anger at one another? How often do they try to physically hurt one another? How much do they trust one another? How often do they help the other person? How often do they make a positive comment about the other person, or something the person has done?

People who live, go to school, and work in positive emotional climates tend to have better mental health than people who are in negative emotional climates. Positive emotional climates tend to result in happier and less violent people. Promoting positive emotional climates in all sorts of human groups, and even for the planet as a whole, should be one of humanity's foremost goals.

The big idea of emotional climates is very closely aligned to the idea of approach versus avoidance motivation, isn't it? In negative emotional climates, people tend to try to influence each other through avoidance motivation, whereas in positive emotional climates, there's a much higher fraction of approach motivation.

Investment, saving, donation, and consumption

If you earn some money, what do you do with it? There are four main choices (not counting silly ones like burning it, throwing it in the trash, or papering a wall with it).

The first is consumption. This means you buy some good or service with the money. You get some food, you pay a dentist, you get some electricity to heat your house, you pay a lawyer to defend you in court.

The second is donation. This means you give the money to someone else, or to some organization, because you want to do something kind, to make people happier.

The third is saving. This means you keep it, so you'll have it to spend some time later if you need it. You're not hoping to make much money off it -- your main priority is just not to lose it, so you'll have it later on. A bank account is typically where people keep the money they save.

The third is investment. With this, you usually take some risk of losing some or all of your money, in order to make more money. For example, someone buys a house, planning to rent it out to people. If they get a lot more money in rent than they have to spend in repairs, their investment has paid off. If the people who rent the house destroy it, the investment loses money. Another way to invest money is to make a loan to a person or a company; a loan to a company is called a bond. Another way is to buy a small fraction of a company, which is called buying stock, with hopes of benefiting from the profits the company makes.

Sometimes people invest money with hopes of gaining something other than money in return. For example, someone invests money to start a company that works for peace and nonviolence in the world. The person hopes not for a financial payoff, but for the knowledge that they are having some good effects.

Many people tend to use whatever money they get for consumption. For them there is a reflex: money comes in, money goes out to get something with it. But the more people can divert some of their income to savings and investment, the more "financially secure" they are. That means that they are ready for something unexpected that will cost them money. And the more they donate to really good causes, the more they improve the happiness of the world.

The ethics of consumption versus donation

I credit the story used to illustrate this idea to the philosopher, Peter Singer.

Suppose a train goes out of control, and starts barreling down the tracks with no one in the train. There is a fork in the track, and you can flip a switch and determine which of two paths the runaway train will take. On one of the paths are some young children. On another is your own nice car. Do you save the children, or do you let the train run over them so as to save your car?

Most people would say that the obvious ethical choice is to sacrifice the car to save the lives of the children.

If this is the case, then let's think about the fact that children are dying of starvation, violence, and disease in lots of places in the world, and that there are charitable agencies that can save more of them if they have more money. If we spend a lot of money on a really nice car, really fine restaurants, expensive clothes, expensive travel, and other luxuries, when we could have donated the money to save the children's lives, are we not making an ethical choice very similar to letting the train run over the children rather than sacrificing the car? The difference is that the children in real life may be far away and out of our sight and not in our "tribe." But they are human beings just like us. The conclusion is: we have an ethical duty to cut down on consumption in favor of donation.

Do we have less responsibility for people if we don't happen to be anywhere close to them? How much less loyalty do we owe to the children of strangers than to our own family members? How many "luxuries" can we delete from our lives before we become lots less happy -- or can we actually become more happy by increasing our sense of purpose beyond our own fun and pleasure? Do people have an ethical responsibility not to have children if they can't afford to give them what they need? What if instead of using our money for consumption, we invest it, with a plan to "probably" donate later on when the funds have grown? The field of ethics, in general, and the question of the ethics of consumption versus donation, in particular, pose many issues that are important and worth pondering.

The goal of peace and nonviolence, and cooperation versus competition

It appears to be human nature to be fascinated by competition. People who teach about writing stories emphasize that there should be conflict in order to hold the audience's interest. Sports competitions attract hugely enthusiastic crowds. Elected government officials appear to spend a good amount of time in angry conflict with those of the other party (or the other tribe). A large portion of the legal system involves conflicts between a "plaintiff" and a "defendant," someone versus someone else. Huge amounts of money, labor, and resources go to armed forces and armaments. And the possibility of nations battling with nuclear weapons is probably the greatest threat to the survival of human civilization.

In a competition-oriented culture, people tend to make heroes of those who are most proficient at defeating the enemy, often by violence. Boxing champions, military heroes, and actors who portray violent heroes, become revered. History books speak of Alexander the Great, Peter the Great, and other "greats" whose "great" deeds consisted in leading armies to build empires through killing thousands of innocent people.

In competition, the other side's loss is your side's gain. The worse the other side does, the better for your side. But in cooperation, by contrast, people are working toward the same goal, and the more proficiently the other person acts, the better for you. When people put on a play, or perform music together in a band, each of them is hoping for the others to make a good contribution so as to make the whole performance successful. When people work together to build houses, grow and harvest crops, educate children, address the problem of global warming, make a successful business, have a psychotherapeutic relationship, prevent war and crime, or have a happy family, they engage in cooperative activities. Most of the ventures that make life better for people are cooperative ones!

There have been books written on cooperative games. Some of these are derived from competitive games. Rather than playing volleyball, for example, people can see how many times they can send the ball over the net back and forth without the ball hitting the ground. When they make a record, they then can see if they can break their own record. Freecell is a solitaire game played with cards; in "cooperative freecell," two people take turns making moves, seeing if together they can accomplish the goal of the game. In the shaping game, one person (the shaper) thinks of a behavior for the other to do. The other person (the shapee) starts trying things out. The only way for the shaper to give clues to the shapee is to congratulate them for something they have already done -- for example, "I like that you moved in that direction.... That's good that you touched the window.... How nice that you touched the handle of the window.... You did it! You opened the window!"

Would the world be more peaceful and nonviolent if more people played cooperative games? It's hard to prove an answer to that. But it very much stands to reason that if almost all people valued peace, nonviolence, and cooperation more than they valued the power gained by violence, the world would benefit greatly.

Sources of meaning: work, relationships, handling unavoidable suffering

What makes life meaningful? For the word "meaningful" we could substitute "worthwhile," "worth doing," "purposeful," or "having some point." A man named Victor Frankl thought a lot about this question. He spoke of three sources of meaning: 1) work, 2) relationships with other people, and 3) handling unavoidable suffering.

The first two are not very surprising. We work to accomplish goals. We work to make things better. If we're lucky enough to work to accomplish something other than just earning money for a living, work can give us the satisfaction of knowing we're contributing something. And we are social animals -- we thrive when we have good relationships with other people. Our families and/or friends help us make life worthwhile.

The third is less surprising when you learn that Victor Frankl was a survivor of the concentration camps that the Nazis set up during World War II. Many of his friends and family members were killed, and he escaped death on more than one occasion purely by luck. He observed terrible suffering of his comrades, and he suffered himself.

If, like Frankl, we can somehow feel a sense of meaning and purpose in handling life even in the face of suffering, this will help us get through hard times. One way of looking at unavoidable suffering is that it is part of just about every life, and the more skilled we can get at handling it -- in other words, the more skilled we are at fortitude -- the better life will be. And even if we don't live through the unavoidable suffering, our use of fortitude can set an example for other people that may help them.

A key word is "unavoidable." It isn't meaningful to bring suffering upon ourselves on purpose without having a very good reason to do so. Bringing unnecessary pain upon ourselves is NOT the type of suffering that makes life meaningful. Similarly, it is not smart just to bear suffering when there is some good way of making it stop!

There are lots more possible sources of meaning and purposes in life than these three. But they are very important ones.

Orientation to "making the world a better place"

Ralph Waldo Emerson wrote about his definition of "success." Part of his definition were these words:

To leave the world a bit better, whether by a healthy child, a garden patch, or a redeemed social condition; ...
To know even one life has breathed easier because you have lived -
This is to have succeeded.

Emerson brings out the point that even small changes, even things that benefit only one person, make the world a better place.

Why should we try to make the world a better place? Why should we try to "leave the world a bit better" because we have lived? There is evidence for a capacity that most people have, to get real happiness out of having a positive effect on the world. I say a capacity, because it needs to be developed and its development can be stunted or thwarted. People do best when they have some sort of goal. People have amazing capacities to get involved in games and to convince themselves that the outcomes are very important -- for example, how many times a ball gets moved to a certain place in the course of a game can seem to be an issue of huge importance. If everyone got involved in activities where the object of the game were to make the world a better place, the world would probably become, because of that ... a better place!

Correlation of happiness with good relationships

What makes people happy? Researchers have studied this question. Is it becoming famous? Is it becoming wealthy? Is it being powerful? Well, it is good to have some people know you exist; it's good to have enough money to meet life's needs, and it's good to be able to influence people and to keep people from taking advantage of you. But what really seems to be the most connected with happiness is good relationships: having friends and/or family members that you spend time with, get along well with, feel loyal to, and love.

The art of having good relationships is a set of skills that people can cultivate. Those skills include meeting people, having good conversations with people, not being too bossy, sticking up for your own rights, resolving conflict, becoming genuinely interested in and curious about what the other person is going through, and perhaps most importantly, being able to take pleasure in making other people feel good -- feeling good about being kind.

The concept of net financial worth

Suppose that you sold off everything you own, paid off any debts you have and could pay, and counted up how much money was left. The answer would be called your "net worth." I like to think of this as "net financial worth" instead, just to make clear that it doesn't have anything to do with your worth as a person, how valuable you are to other people, or anything like that. It's just a number that says how much money you have, counting also the worth of things that can be converted into money by selling them.

Some people live "paycheck to paycheck." When they get paid, they use the money to pay rent, buy food, pay an electric bill, and so forth, and when the money runs out, they have nothing to spend. If they don't have anything they can sell for money, approximately what is their net financial worth? It's about zero. On the other hand, if someone has $20,000 in a bank account in addition to what the first person has, that person's net financial worth is about $20,000. If someone has $50,000 of debt from student loans in addition to what the first person has, that person has a net financial worth of negative $50,000.

As a general rule, the higher someone's net financial worth, the more secure they can feel that they won't run out of money when there's an emergency need for money.

What stocks and bonds are

To invest your money means that you don't spend it, but use it in some way that you hope will bring about a good result in the future -- and usually, when we talk about investment, that good result we are talking about is an increase in your financial net worth. In other words, most people invest in order to make money.

Two types of investments that are useful to understand are stocks and bonds.

When you buy stock, you are simply buying a certain fraction of a company. So for example, if there exist 10 million shares of stock for a certain company, and you buy 10 shares of that company's stock, you now own one millionth of the company! If, after you buy the stock, the company starts making lots more money, the price of your shares will probably go up, and when you sell them, you have made money on your investment. Another way of making money from stocks is that the company decides to give out some or all of the profits to the owners, and makes payments to the shareholders; this payment is called a dividend. On the other hand, the company could start making lots less money, or could start losing lots of money, in which case the company could pay no dividend and the share price could go down as low as zero! So when you buy stock, you are betting that the company will do well.

When you buy a bond, you are simply lending money to whoever issued the bond. The bond is a piece of paper, or a computer entry, that says, "I owe you." It also specifies how much you are owed, and how much interest the company pays you to be able to use your money. And the bond specifies when you get paid back the money you invested. So when you buy a bond, you know just what will happen, except for one thing: what if the company, or government, or whoever issued the bond, runs out of money itself and can't pay you back? That's called "defaulting" on the bond. If the bond issuer defaults, you can lose all your money. For this reason, bond issuers who are in very good financial shape don't have to pay as much interest to get people to lend them money, whereas companies that are in shaky financial shape have to pay higher interest rates. So when you buy a bond, you are betting that the bond issuer will not default and will be able to pay you back, with interest.

Improvement through practice

If you ever watch the Olympics, you see people doing things that would be impossible for most other people. You see marathon runners going for a little over 26 miles at a pace that most of us couldn't keep up with for 300 yards. You see skiers taking jumps that would result in severe injury if not death for most of us. You see weightlifters putting barbells over their heads that most of us couldn't get off the ground.

If you watch expert musicians performing with piano, guitar, violin, or any of several other instruments, you often see fingers moving with such speed and accuracy that it hardly seems possible that the brain is capable of directing those fingers in that way. If you start to try to learn one of those instruments, the feat may seem even more remarkable.

Writing, public speaking, playing chess, dancing, making business decisions, making medical decisions, going on long hikes, skateboarding, drawing, being a lawyer, being an engineer, playing a certain videogame ... there are so many ways in which people can get to be very skilled at something, and can eventually get to the point where they can do things far beyond what most other people can do.

How do people get to be experts? Is there a certain drug for distance running, another for piano playing, another for becoming a doctor, and so forth? Or are certain people just born destined to do heart surgery, write enlightening books, and hit 3-pointer basketball shots? No, and no. People get to be experts by starting out with easy challenges, devoting many hours of practice, and gradually working their way up to more and more difficult challenges.

Here's the wonderful fact that this "big idea" celebrates: the more we demand of our brains and bodies to meet more and more difficult challenges, the more our bodies (including our brains) adapt in order to meet those challenges. If we do as many push-ups as we can each day, the number we can do gradually goes up. If we practice "Twinkle Twinkle Little Star" on the piano, we start making our brains change in ways that make more complicated songs possible for us. If we practice running every day, eventually we get much faster than we were before. This is a wonderful thing about our bodies. It's easy to imagine an alternate world where no matter how much we practiced and trained, our abilities would stay just the same. The fact that we can get more skilled at almost anything we want to is one of the marvels of this life!

Of course, there are limits to how much practice can make most people improve. There is such a thing as innate talent. If I had trained and practiced as often and as much as a champion sprinter, I still would have been left behind in short races in a high school track meet. I'm pretty sure that I didn't inherit the types of muscle fibers that make for championship sprinting. But still, practicing sprinting made me a lot faster than not practicing at all!

Psychological skills make a good society

Let's imagine two countries. In Country 1, you can buy all sorts of gadgets cheaply; there are lots of expensive cars around; lots of people have expensive houses. But: there are very high rates of suicide, drug addiction, murder, other crimes, unhappiness, and people who are too depressed to work. Many of them have lots of money, but they tend to waste their money and their time on things that don't bring them much happiness. People tend to be angry at other people, or scared of them.

In Country 2, there are customs that bring people together to have friendly relations with each other. People tend to be kind to one another, to have fun, to take care of themselves and other people. They enjoy doing their work, partly because the work people want each other to do is really helpful work that makes life better. They know how to have fun in inexpensive ways, like walking in the woods, talking with each other, reading and writing, singing and dancing, improvising plays, growing food, and others. Murder, other crime, suicide, drug addiction, and mental health disability are rare.

Which country would you rather live in? I would much rather live in the second. People speak of the "gross domestic product" of a country -- the total amount of money that people earn and spend. People sometimes use this as a measure of how well the country is doing. But people are also now trying to measure something more important -- how happy and meaningful life feels in the country.

Happiness and meaning in the society are proportional to the psychological skills of the citizens. To what extent are the people of that country productive, joyous, kind, honest, resilient, good at decision-making, good at conflict-resolution, nonviolent, and polite? To what extent can they make friends, work for future goals, sustain relationships, not be wasteful, look after health and safety, follow the rule of law, practice good things in imagination, and be brave enough to do what's best? If you imagine a country where all the people are good at these "psychological skills," it's hard to imagine that this country doesn't score much more like country 2 than country 1 in the examples above.

The notion that happiness of a group is proportional to the psychological skills of the people in it does not just apply to countries. It applies to neighborhoods, workplaces, schools, families, and any other collection of human beings.

The skills-challenge matchup -- "Hierarchy-ology"

A large part of life involves taking on challenges and seeing if we can succeed at them. In school, we take on homework assignments, tests, articles to write. In work, we take on tasks that need to be performed well enough. In social relations, we take on the challenge of acting in ways that build friendships. In family relations, we see if we can act in ways that make the family happier. In sports, we try to win by doing certain moves as well as we can. In performing music, we try to do a certain song proficiently. In just spending time by ourselves and relaxing, we take on the challenge of seeing if we can come up with something useful or fun to do. In just thinking, we see if we can achieve whatever goal our thoughts were aimed at.

For most of the challenges of life, we can make a hierarchy -- a list of challenges in a certain area, arranged in order from easiest to hardest. A hierarchy for piano songs might have "Little Bird In Your Nest" close to the bottom of the hierarchy (it has 9 notes, playable with three consecutive keys of the piano) and a very difficult classical piece near the top of the hierarchy (one where the fingers move so fast that most observers can't even keep up with them). For people getting into better physical condition, just taking a short walk may be near the bottom of the hierarchy, and participating in a triathlon (running, swimming, and cycling a great distance for each) may be near the top of the hierarchy. For math, learning to say which of two piles of things has "more" or "less" things may be close to the bottom, and doing advanced calculus is a lot higher (I don't even know what's near the top).

Here's the idea we've been building up to: life seems to be happiest when the challenges are not too hard, not too easy, but of "just right" position on the hierarchy of difficulty. What's more, progress to higher levels of skill also seems to be stimulated the most when the challenges are in that "sweet spot," neither too hard nor too easy. When challenges are too easy, we get bored; when they are too hard, we get frustrated. The nice experience of being in the right level has been called "flow." (A man named Mihalyi Csikscentmihalyi wrote a book where he made popular the word "flow" to refer to that nice experience.)

This is an idea that seems obvious once we think about it. If Algebra 1 is the right math level for my current skills, and I go to either a kindergarten class focusing on learning to count, or a graduate school math class focusing on things I can't begin to understand, I'm probably not going to either enjoy myself much or progress any in math skills.

People ignore this principle all the time, and great unhappiness results from it. Many students in schools are being given reading to do that is way over their heads. I have seen students who were being made to take algebra when math placement tests revealed that they were at a second or third grade math level. Psychotherapists sometimes pose questions to clients that for some of the clients are way over the clients' capability of grappling with. People sometimes push people into confronting traumatic memories that are way beyond the persons' capabilities of dealing with at that particular moment. People are often asked to do the same job that they have mastered long ago, without the opportunity to gain higher levels of skill and take on higher challenges for the mission.

The moral is that it's good to try to assess how skilled people are at something, and make the challenges they are given not too hard, not too easy, but just right for the level of skill. This isn't easy to do. If you're a teacher with 25 students in your class, how do you make the challenges at just the right level of difficulty for each of the students, if they vary widely in their skills? If you are an employer, you may be looking for someone to do a certain task -- you usually can't make the task easier or harder to fit the current skill level of the employee. But the more people can be working on challenges that are at the just right level for them, the happier they will be and the nicer they will probably be to others. So the goal is worth pursuing! Because people often think of a list of challenges ordered by how difficult they are, called a "hierarchy," and life goes better when people are working at the "right place on the hierarchy," I've referred to this big idea as "hierarchy-ology."

The abstraction ladder

Suppose that someone has a job of helping parents to improve their children's behavior. They ask the parent, "What are the problem behaviors that you would like to see happening less often?"

The parent replies, "He is inconsiderate. And he can be really stubborn. And selfish."

Inconsiderate, stubborn, and selfish are abstract words. They can refer to many different possible behaviors. The opposite of abstract is concrete. What concrete behaviors might the parent be thinking of?

Let's consider child 1. More concrete examples of "inconsiderate" behavior is that he stole money from family members and hit his siblings when they wouldn't do what he wants. More concrete description of "stubborn" behavior is that he refused to leave a park to go home, until his parent physically dragged him. More concrete example of "selfish" behavior is that when he got behind in a board game, he scattered the board and all the cards and pieces all around and ended the game for everyone.

Let's consider child 2. A more concrete example of "inconsiderate" behavior is that he waited 2 days to write a thank-you note for a gift rather than doing it right away. A more concrete example of "stubborn" behavior is that he argued that the U.S. Supreme Court has too much power, despite all sorts of good counterarguments the parent gave him. A concrete example of "selfish" behavior is excusing himself and going to his room a little after supper rather than sticking around and talking with guests when the parents had a couple of their adult friends over.

What's the moral of this? More concrete language often communicates much more clearly. The abstract words seemed to suggest that child 1 and child 2 were very similar. The concrete examples made clear that they are very different. If you really want people to understand you, give concrete examples.

On the other hand, we don't want to avoid using abstract terms. They often let us communicate ideas with many fewer words than we would otherwise need. For example: Someone says, "Don't tell people you won a game when you didn't. Don't say you've brushed your teeth when you haven't. If you break something that belongs to someone else, let them know. If your experiment came out with messy results, don't change them to make them look better." The person could go on with concrete language for thousands of examples. But when someone uses more abstract language to say, "Be honest," they cover thousands of concrete examples in one sentence.

Often the best communication uses a mixture of abstract language, with some concrete examples illustrating the abstract concept.

A linguist named S.I. Hayakawa spoke of the "abstraction ladder" -- an arrangement of concepts or words in order from most concrete to most abstract. For example, one particular cow (named Bossy) might be at the bottom, the most concrete. You can point to her, and say, "That's Bossy." The concept of cattle is more abstract; livestock is still more abstract; and wealth is more abstract -- this is an example that Hayakawa gave.

Here's another example: A certain pistol is most concrete; the concept of pistols is more abstract; guns is more abstract; firearms is more abstract (includes cannons and others in addition to guns); weapons is more abstract, and implements or tools is still more abstract.

This is an even bigger idea because we use language to think as well as to communicate. If we find ourselves using a lot of words but not really getting anywhere, it's usually a great idea to move down the abstraction ladder and think of concrete examples of what we're trying to talk or think about.

Interdependence, specialization, division of labor

At some time many thousands of years ago, most human families probably had to figure out how to meet all their own needs. They found some way of getting water, growing food, building something live in that would shelter them from the weather, making clothes to wear, and making any tools that they needed. They figured out how to use fire to produce light and cook food. What if they needed advanced medical care to keep them from dying? Well, that was the end of life. What if the endless quest for food, clothing, and shelter didn't provide as much meaning and enjoyment as participating in a society where many more things are possible? Well, that was tough luck.

There are still some people who choose to live in remote regions and survive independently of other human beings. But most of us live in a society where we take advantage of the skills that other people have, that we don't have. I use electric lights; I don't know how to produce them. I get water from an amazing system of pipes that I am not expert in installing and repairing. I take advantage of roads, buildings, and countless different machines that I don't know how to build or repair. But I'm happy to help other people by using skills that those people don't have.

The more developed civilizations become, the more people are allowed to do some things well without having to do everything well -- people have specialties. They depend on other people to do the things that they don't know how to do. This specialization and interdependence ideally allow people to get into the occupation that they are best at and enjoy the most. Unfortunately, this doesn't always work out -- the person would like to work in a certain job, but there just aren't jobs available in that field. The person would like to become a specialized expert in a certain task, but the person for whatever reason doesn't get to be very skilled at it. But it works out probably much better than in primitive, unspecialized societies.

The advance of civilization with invention, artistic creation and performance, medicine, science, building, financial institutions, and so much else that we take for granted, is really made possible by the invention of specialization, interdependency, and division of labor.

Well-being of employees as part of the purpose of a business

I'm guessing that if human society gets better and better over time, one of the main ways for it to do so will be making more jobs available that are just right for the worker, even if the competitive marketplace doesn't make these jobs available. This is a complex task. For example, what if there are lots of people for whom the job in which they are happiest is as a dishwasher, but there are already enough dishwashers to clean all the dishes that are now being dirtied? Maybe the worker can be helped in some kind and very organized way to figure out other jobs that require very similar skills, that society has more of a need for. What if the worker will be happiest doing a certain job, but they can only do it half as fast as other workers, and thus they can't keep their job in the marketplace where everyone has to get the same hourly pay?

This gets us to the big idea: that businesses should exist partly in order to make their workers happy. Traditional ideas are that the definition of success for a business is that it makes money for the owners, that is, the stockholders. In order to make money for the owners, the business has to please the customers, so they will want to turn over their money in exchange for what the company offers. (If the product makes the customer happy in the short run, but causes unhappiness in the long run -- as is often true for junk food, cigarettes, alcoholic beverages, violent videogames, and others, that's usually not regarded as a problem for the business owners.) So two groups have to be happy: the owners and the customers. But what about the workers? Many people have gotten very rich off the proceeds of businesses where the workers felt scared or angry most of the time. The word "burnout" was made up to refer to workers being drained of their energy and happiness and motivation by jobs that require lots of them but don't reward them or meet their needs enough. But businesses have done worse than this, making workers work in unsafe or unhealthy conditions that have killed or disabled them.

Workplaces are where most adults spend large fractions of their waking hours. What can be done to make workers happier? Much of the answer lies in providing an effort-payoff connection: the workplace is designed so that the workers can get satisfaction of some sort from the efforts they put out. The payoff is partly in money. The payoff should also be partly in "social reinforcement": recognition of the good that the worker has done. Workers should be trained expertly to do their jobs well, rather than relying only on threats and punishment for doing their jobs badly. The match between skill levels and task difficulty, what I've referred to as "hierarchy-ology," should ideally be arranged so that each worker performs in the not-too-easy and not-too-hard zone. Workers should be able to get adequate rest, and adequate variety in the day's activities, as contrasted with doing repetitive tasks for hours on end. A positive emotional climate should be fostered. There should be some opportunity to move around rather than sit still all day. Ideally, the business really contributes to making the world a better place, and workers celebrate together their contributions. In other words, much of the same conditions for well-being of human beings in general need to be imported into workplaces.

It's important not to create so many regulations on businesses that people can't start them up. So the solution to the unhappy workers problem may not be government rules. It may be ways of measuring workers' satisfaction, and communication of this, and a change in society's customs. In some places, this change is already underway.

Being a net contributor versus a net consumer

There's lots of work that we can do in the world: we can make or deliver food, water, clothing, shelter, or other useful objects; we can perform health care, education, cleaning, information, repairs, selling, entertainment, or other useful services. And there's lots of ways we can consume the results of other people's work.

Some people contribute a lot more than they consume -- they are net contributors to the total work of the world. If someone works hard at something useful, saves their money, and gives away lots of money to charitable causes, that person is probably a net contributor. If someone uses the money someone else made, to do no work but to play videogames, that person is probably a net consumer.

What's the point of thinking about this? Does someone have a duty to contribute as much as they consume? What about the people who aren't able to work? Does "making money" mean the same thing as "making a contribution?" (It sure doesn't! People who do unpaid work, like taking care of their children, can make huge contributions, whereas people who make a lot of money selling things that do more harm than good are making negative contributions.) If we don't measure contribution and consumption by money, how do we? There are no perfect measures, or even widely agreed upon measures. There are lots of complications to this idea.

Despite all the problems, it seems that a reasonable principle of ethics is that if one is able to do so, it's good to try to contribute at least as much as you consume.

Truth-telling

Why is truth-telling, honesty, not lying, so important? The idea that it is important is one of the oldest big ideas of the human species.

In life, we are constantly making decisions. We decide what job to do, how to do everything we do on that job; whether to take certain risks or not; whom to depend on for certain things; what to do with our money; whether to get vaccinated, what to eat -- on and on. Making good decisions depends on accurate information -- understanding what is really going on. And a great fraction of our information comes, not from our direct observation, but from those of other people, who report information to us. Imagine a place where whenever you got any information, the chance was very high that the person you got it from was lying. How would you ever make good decisions (other than the decision to leave that place and find someplace else to live!)

When people make decisions based on what someone tells them, and then it turns out that the person was lying, people tend to get very mad at the lying person. And being caught in just one lie can sometimes permanently make other people not trust the lying person.

These are some of the reasons why systems of ethics -- the study of what's right and wrong -- almost always emphasize the importance of truth-telling.

I've emphasized reasons why people don't like to be lied to. But there's an important exception to this rule: lots of people like to be lied to when someone tells them what they want to hear. Lots of people seem to enjoy hearing lies like this: Your group of people is the greater than other groups; the people you already dislike have done these bad things; the people who disagree with you are bad and stupid; nothing bad that has happened to you is your fault, but the fault of other people whom you dislike; any problem that requires sacrifice on your part is just made up and faked by other people; this substance will make you healthy and happy; God is on the side of your tribe, etc. The fact that lots of people like to be lied to does not make it ethical to lie to them! When people base their decisions on ideas that are false, bad consequences usually come, sooner or later!

Ad hominem arguments versus prediction of consequences.

Suppose someone in government proposes a plan for fixing and maintaining the bridges in the country, and how to pay for this. The person's political opponent says, "Don't listen to any plan proposed that that person! He flunked a course in college; he cheated on his wife; he drinks too much alcohol; and he's way too fat!" These arguments don't have anything to do with bridges, do they? They are called ad hominem arguments -- the phrase means, in Latin, "against the person." Lots of people use ad hominem arguments, and lots of people are persuaded by them.

What makes more logical sense in trying to decide what to do? The important thing to know about whether an option is a good plan or not is what the consequences of it would be. "If we do this, there will be about this many fewer accidents of falling bridges." "If we do this, we will create jobs for this number of people." "If we do this, it will cost this much. The money will come from this source. That means it can't go other places." "My prediction is different from yours because of this calculation with these numbers." These are the sorts of points that lead to sensible decisions about what to do. Do the good consequences outweigh the bad consequences more than the other options? We should be asking this, and not "What dirt can we dig up about the faults of the person who proposed this idea?"

I have to admit, however, that ad hominem arguments are not totally invalid 100% of the time. Suppose the person cites a bunch of facts and statistics in making their case, but others present good evidence that the person is a liar and has presented incorrect statements as if they were true on many previous occasions. In that case, we should be less inclined to believe the predictions of consequences that the person makes. And if we are electing someone to be a leader, we have to think not just about the plans that the person proposes, but about the person's character -- how good a person they are, and whether we can trust them to make good decisions in choice points that haven't even come up yet.

Expected utility in decision-making

Suppose someone offers us a gambling game. The person flips a coin. If it comes up heads, we win a dollar, and for tails, we lose a dollar. If we play this game over and over a large number of times, how much money do you think we would expect to win or lose? The number of heads is going to be approximately equal to the number of tails. Let's imagine we play the game 2000 times, and it happens that there are 1000 heads and 1000 tails. Our total winnings would be $1000 - $1000, or $0. The "expected value" of this game to us is 0.

There's a formula that we can use to calculate the expected value of games like this. To use it, we take the probability of each outcome, and multiply that by the payoff of the outcome, and add up those products for all the possible outcomes. So for our game, 1/2 or 0.5 is the probability of heads and of tails. +$1 is the payoff for heads, and -$1 is the payoff for tails. (For tails, our payoff is a negative number.) So when we use our formula, we get

Expected value = the sum of the product of probability x payoff for each possible outcome
Expected value = probability of heads x payoff from heads + probability of tails x payoff from tails
Expected value = 0.5 x 1 + 0.5 x -1, = 0

So our formula tells us that the average payoff for this game is 0, even though no particular round of it has that payoff.

Let's imagine a second game room at our imaginary gambling casino. Suppose now we roll a die (one of a couple of dice) that has six sides. If the die comes up showing 6 dots, we win $60. If it comes up anything else, we lose $18. Should we play? Do we expect that on the average round of this game we win or lose money? Someone who's just thinking of the payoffs might think, "Hey, we stand to win $60. But the most we can lose is $18. Sounds like a good deal!" Someone else who's just thinking of the probabilities might think, "Hey, there's a 1/6 probability that we win, and a 5/6 probability that we lose. Sounds like a bad deal!" In order to really figure out whether the game is a good deal or not, we can use our formula, which takes into account both the payoffs and the probabilities. Let's do it!

Expected value = the sum of the product of payoff x probability for each possible outcome
Expected value = probability of a 6 x payoff for a 6 + probability of something else x payoff for else
Expected value = 1/6 x $60 + 5/6 x (- 18)
Expected value = $10 + -$15
Expected value = -$5

So if we played this game many times, we would expect to lose an average of $5 for each time that we played it!

So if we were in a gambling place, and we had a choice between playing the first game and the second (and we had to play one of them) which should we pick? Probably the first, the one with the higher expected payoff.

So let's review where we've gotten so far. There are two options. We figured out the expected payoff, or expected value, for each of them, by multiplying the probability of each outcome by the payoff of that outcome, and adding up those products. The option that is better is the one with the higher expected payoff.

If you are wise, you won't spend much time gambling in casinos, because the expected payoff for the player is almost always negative. That's how gambling casinos make money!

But the big idea of this section is that the same idea applies to every decision we make, for our whole lives!

Let's suppose we can rate our happiness on a scale of 0 to 10, where 5 is neutral, 10 is extremely happy, and 0 is extremely unhappy. We can use this when we calculate payoffs, instead of dollar amounts.

Imagine we are trying to decide between two jobs. In the first, there's a 90% chance we'll be happy 5 on a scale of 10, and a 10% chance we'll be happy 6 on a scale of 10. In the second, there's a 75% chance we'll be happy 8 on a scale of 10, and a 25% chance we'll be happy 4 on a scale of 10. If we apply our formula:

Expected happiness job 1 = sum of probability x payoff products

$$= .9 \times 5 + .1 \times 6$$
$$= 4.5 + .6$$
$$= 5.1$$

Expected happiness job 2 = sum of probability x payoff products

$$= .75 \times 8 + .25 \times 4$$
$$= 6 + 1 = 7$$

So if we want to maximize our expected happiness, we pick the second job!

Of course, in life, there are a couple of big problems when we try to use this formula to make decisions: it's hard to predict how happy we are with certain outcomes, and it's hard to figure out the probabilities of those outcomes given a certain choice! In other words, there's lots of uncertainty about all the numbers that go into our formula! Nonetheless, what good decision-makers do is to make as good guesses as they can, and usually they calculate expected happiness just with a gut feeling rather than by doing any arithmetic.

The word "utility" is sometimes used to refer to happiness, or payoff, or well-being, or whatever goodness of outcomes we want to maximize. So expected utility, expected happiness, expected value, and expected payoff are all ways of talking about the answer we get when we calculate a number summarizing how desirable a given option is.

When the utilities are very high or the probabilities are very small, sometimes the expected utility formula doesn't give us the answer that makes the most sense. Suppose a lottery has grown to where the prize is a billion dollars, and the chance of winning is one in a couple of hundred million. The expected payoff for any given ticket is about 5 dollars. So a person takes his whole life savings and invests it in lottery tickets. One problem is that the overwhelmingly most likely outcome is that he will lose everything! (Another problem is that only one of the tickets that he buys can win the big jackpot, so even if he used this strategy millions of times, he would not average winning $5 per round.) The expected utility formula, like all other guides to how to live, is not a dogma that always gives the true right answer.

The middle way or path

Some people have thought that the key to a good life is to avoid indulging oneself: to work rather than play, save rather than spend, eat only what it takes for health, not waste time on purely fun activities, to avoid sexual activity except when necessary to have a child. Such a way of thinking about life has been called ascetic.

Other people have thought that the key to good life is to get as much pleasure as possible: to eat, drink, have

112

sexual activity, do exciting and fun things, in a single minded pursuit of good feelings, as temporary as they may be. Such a way of thinking about life has been called hedonistic.

Others, notably one called the Buddha, have advised a "middle path" between these extremes. Followers of the middle path have the self-discipline to pass up a more pleasurable activity when a different activity helps them more to achieve a desired goal. But they have the joyousness skill to enjoy a pleasurable activity when that activity doesn't do any harm and when it is compatible with achieving their goals. They realize that doing fun things can sometimes "recharge the batteries" and leave them more able to work and use self-discipline. In other words, they try to have a reasonable balance in life.

Of course, one person's idea of the best balance may not be another person's idea! Some people are lucky enough to thoroughly enjoy their work, and thus they don't need nearly as much to "get away from it all" and relax and play. These people tend to be very high achievers in life.

But the point of this "big idea" is that it is up to every person to figure out the best balance between "I want to work toward my goals, whether it's fun or not," and "I want to have fun, whether it accomplishes a goal or not." There is a place in life for both attitudes at different times, and how much of each is best, is a question for every person to answer.

Autonomy, beneficence, informed consent

Autonomy, beneficence, and informed consent are three of several words that are often used in discussions of medical ethics -- what is the right thing for doctors and other health professionals to do. Autonomy means letting people decide what to do with their own bodies, unless they are too young or too mentally disabled to be able to make good decisions. Informed consent is a consequence of the principle of autonomy. It means that before giving a treatment, you tell the person about the pros and cons and let the person decide whether to consent to the treatment or not. Beneficence means doing what you think will make the person happiest in the long run. Sometimes the principles of autonomy and beneficence are in conflict with one another. For example, someone has an illness that could have very bad consequences, and there is a treatment that is very effective for it. But the person refuses to get the treatment. Should the person be allowed to make a decision that would result in their own death or long-term disability? Sometimes there is no answer about which everyone would say, "I feel good about that decision."

These principles of ethics are not limited to medical settings. If someone wants to hug and kiss someone else or do something else physically affectionate, the principle of autonomy and the idea of informed consent imply that the person should get a clear communication from the other person that they consent to this before doing it. If someone wants to offer food to someone's child, they should ask the parent if it's OK. Even if someone wants to pet someone else's dog, it's good to get the consent of the dog's guardian. On the other hand, if a child is swimming and is about to be swept by current into a situation that could kill the child, an ethical person will focus on beneficence, not worry about autonomy, and save the child from the danger.

Empirical questions, falsifiable hypotheses

An empirical question is one that can be answered by scientific methods, that is, by making observations, doing experiments, analyzing data, and so forth. Scientists tend to generate hypotheses that are "falsifiable" by the information they gather. But for some questions, it's probably impossible to think up an experiment or a way of gathering information that would answer the question.

Here's a question I'm curious about. What if my mother had had a different husband, and the exact same egg that she produced to make me were fertilized by some other guy. Would the resulting person still be "me?" Would "I" exist, or would the resulting person be like one of the billions of other people who are not me? Suppose we try to figure out some sort of experiment we could do to answer that question. Hmm. Get a handy time machine, rewind time, and this time around, make sure the egg was fertilized by a different father, then ask the resulting person, "Are you the same person that existed before we rewound time, whose memories I hope you somehow still have?" The more we ponder, the more we realize that there is no possible experiment that could be done that would answer this question.

There are lots of other questions that are quite meaningful, that can't be answered by scientific methods. What, if anything, existed before the "big bang" that scientists think was the beginning of the universe? How would the course of history have been different if Adolf Hitler had never been born? If no peace activists existed, would humanity have had a large scale nuclear war by now? Did the universe get formed by a voluntary action of some intelligent being, or not? What, exactly, does it feel

115

like to be a particular dolphin, cow, or chicken, at some given moment? For a given action that a certain person did, what were the unconscious motives that the person was not aware of, and never became aware of? Is it possible for there to be nothing, not even empty space?

Fortunately, most of the questions whose answers can make the world a better place are empirical questions. If we do a certain action, are people happier or unhappier as a result? This may be a very difficult question to answer, but at least we can gather some information that will shed light on the answer, and help us to at least make better guesses.

Fantasy rehearsal

Suppose that you want to get better at the skill of anger control. You want to use the principle that skills improve with practice. You want to experience a lot of situations that might make you angry, and practice handling them in a calm and rational way. But if you wait around for these situations to happen in real life, they may not come frequently enough for good practice. The situations may catch you unaware, so that instead of practicing a good way of handling the situation, you practice a bad way. Ideally, you would practice with the easy situations first, and then work your way up to the harder ones, but real life probably won't present these situations to you in the best order.

There's a good solution to this problem, called fantasy rehearsal. When you are ready to practice this skill, you imagine the provoking situations, and imagine yourself coming through with the sorts of thoughts, feelings, and behaviors that you have decided will work out best.

Does fantasy rehearsal work to increase people's skills? A very large amount of research gives the answer: Yes. People can improve their skills in sports by visualizing the sorts of moves they want to make. In fact, a very high fraction of Olympic athletes reported using fantasy rehearsal to help their performances. People learning to do surgical operations have in several studies benefited from practicing doing the operation in their imaginations, rather than having to do all their practice on real people. Musicians and dancers have improved their skills by practicing their performances in imagination. Fantasy practice with scary situations is one of the major ingredients of successful treatment of anxiety problems.

I believe that fantasy rehearsal is a very underrated technique in learning to live better. However, there's something that has to happen first: some good decision-making about what to rehearse. Spending a great deal of time fantasy rehearsing how to be a proficient fighter, or how to fearlessly put oneself in very dangerous situations, or how to be very obnoxious and confrontive to people in a mistaken belief that this is the best way to be "assertive," may do more harm than good.

Reinforcement, non-reinforcement, and punishment

Why do we do what we do? In another of the big ideas, I list 10 different influences on us, 10 answers to this question. But one of them is this: we do what we do in order to produce consequences that we want. This was called the "Law of Effect" by a researcher named

Thorndike, and it was studied a lot more by B.F. Skinner. The consequences that come after behavior that tend to make us do the behavior more often are called reinforcers. If the desired consequence is that something pleasant happens, we call that positive reinforcement. If the desired consequence is that something unpleasant stops happening, we call that negative reinforcement. If there is something unpleasant that happens right after we do the behavior, that reduces the chances of our doing it again, that is called punishment. If we are hoping for something desirable to happen, but we don't get that desired consequence, that's what I've called non-reinforcement. If we get non-reinforced enough for a behavior, the behavior tends to become less and less frequent and we tend to stop doing it -- that's called "extinction" of the behavior, or we say that it's being "extinguished."

When one way of trying to get something works, and another way doesn't work, we tend to use the one that works and stop using the one that doesn't work. This situation is called differential reinforcement. If a child finds that trying to start a friendly conversation doesn't work in getting the parent's attention, but screaming angrily does work, differential reinforcement is working in a direction that probably is bad for the child. If the parent starts responding enthusiastically to the child's conversation and ignoring the child's angry screaming over minor frustrations, differential reinforcement is now working in a better way.

People often think they are using reinforcement and punishment in a way that encourages good behavior, when they're doing the opposite. For example, someone asks, "Did you do that bad thing?" If the person says, "Yes," the person gets punished. If the person says, "No," they go unpunished. If they really did the bad thing, differential reinforcement is encouraging lying and discouraging truth-telling.

People make mistakes in setting up reinforcement and punishment systems. One mistake is having the consequence come too long after the behavior. Another is making the standard for getting the reinforcer so difficult that the person gives up. For example, suppose a child has a bad habit of hitting their sibling. The parent says, "If you can go for the next two months without hitting, I will get you a new bicycle." Two months is probably too far into the future. And if the child hits one time, they will have lost the reward, so what's the point of trying after that? Another mistake people often make is offering a reward, and then not delivering it when the person earns it.

There are different types of reinforcers. Tangible reinforcers are things you can touch, like a bicycle or stuffed animal. Edible reinforcers are food. Money is the most obvious reinforcer that is meant to lead employees to show up for work and carry out the work. Social reinforcement consists of things like smiles, compliments, pats on the back, applause, and other forms of approval.

The word "shaping" means reinforcing little steps toward a behavior. Each step makes the learner a little more ready for the next step. For example, suppose someone wants to teach rational conflict-resolution behavior. Maybe step 1 is paying attention when there's a model presented. Step 2 is taking one of the parts and reading that part for more examples of rational conflict-resolution. Step 3 is making up dialogues when someone gives you sample conflicts. Step 4 is reporting times in real life when you were able to do rational conflict-resolution. For each step, you get approval or some other reinforcer.

Society often has a choice, without really recognizing it, between shaping and punishment, and it chooses punishment. For example, two kids at school get into a fight, and they are punished for it. But no one has ever even attempted to teach them rational conflict resolution, using shaping as described above. The more humane societies become, the more they teach people how to do desirable things, rather than just waiting for them to do bad things and punishing them for those bad behaviors.

Intermittent versus continuous reinforcement

"Intermittent reinforcement produces behaviors that are more resistant to extinction than those that have been reinforced continuously." Let's talk about what this means. Continuous reinforcement means that every single time you do something, you get a reinforcer, or reward. For example, every time a child does some work around the house, the parent compliments the child and pays the child some money immediately afterwards. Intermittent reinforcement means that you get reinforced for a certain fraction of the times you do something, not all of them. For example, every now and then, on a random schedule, the parent sees the child doing some work, compliments the child, and gives the child some money. But lots of times the child does work without getting money.

Suppose the parent in each situation goes for a while without reinforcing the work. Which child would you predict would stop working first? The one who had the continuous reinforcement schedule notices right away that things have changed. The one who had the intermittent schedule is used to doing work without getting a reinforcer immediately. It will probably take that person longer to decide that the reinforcers aren't coming any more and to stop working for them.

If you want a behavior to get started strong but to be resistant to extinction, sometimes the best way is to start out with continuous reinforcement and then to make the schedule gradually leaner, so that you move toward more intermittent reinforcement.

If the behavior is undesirable, you want to avoid moving from continuous to intermittent reinforcement. For example, suppose that every time a child has an angry tantrum, the parents give the child what the child wants, to get the child to stop the tantrum. Once they learn about reinforcement, they try to stop giving the child what the child wants. But they are only successful 4 out of 5 times -- 1 out of 5 times they give in and reinforce the child. The tantrum behavior is now probably becoming more resistant to extinction. The moral is, if they want extinction to take place, they should really prepare themselves to reinforce the behavior 0% of the time and nothing more.

Classical conditioning

Something that happens outside us, that we see, hear, taste, smell, touch, etc., is called a stimulus. The way we react to a stimulus is called our response. There are some automatic reactions that seem to be built in to most of us: these are called unconditioned responses. For example, the smell of most types of tasty food makes us salivate. The sight and sound of mean people, or other scary or provoking stimuli, tend to make us have the "flight or fight" response, involving more adrenaline going from our adrenal glands into our bloodstreams, and increases in our heart rate, sweating, rate of breathing, constriction of the blood vessels in the skin, and tension of muscles. A puff of air coming toward our eyes brings about an eyeblink. Being around people who are kind and supportive and friendly tends to bring out a response of pleasure and security.

What "classical conditioning"means is that stimuli that don't bring about these responses can come to bring them about if they are presented around the same time as, or a little before, the unconditioned stimuli. For example, the person who became most famous for studying this, named Ivan Pavlov, observed that dogs salivated if you gave them meat, but didn't salivate if you produced a tone. But if you gave them several experiences of hearing the tone and then getting the meat, pretty soon they started salivating after hearing the tone, without getting the meat. The tone was called a "conditioned stimulus" that produced the "conditioned response" of salivation. The process whereby the tone came to start the dogs salivating was called "classical conditioning."

What if you kept on sounding the tone, without giving the dogs any meat after it? Gradually the amount of saliva they produced on hearing the tone would get less and less, until eventually the tone didn't produce any additional salivation. This undoing of the classically conditioned response was called "extinction" of the response.

How much saliva dogs produce isn't one of the most important issues in the world. But fear and anger, which can also get classically conditioned, are among the most important issues. Suppose a child goes to school and gets lots of experiences with mean, bullying people. The fear and anger that are unconditioned responses to people's meanness might get conditioned to the stimulus of school itself, so that the child might become afraid of going there or might become angry and ready to fight the minute the child sets foot inside the door. But if through some lucky event, things change, and the child attends a school where the people are kind and gentle, maybe the fear and anger responses undergo extinction and there gets to be a classically conditioned response of joy and security.

Here's another example of how classical conditioning ideas may be used in your life. People sleep better if there is a conditioned association between lying in bed and going to sleep. If someone lies in bed watching movies, being on social media, doing their homework, and so forth, they practice lying in bed without getting sleepy, and break up the conditioned association. So it's good to do those things elsewhere. With the same reasoning, if someone can't fall asleep and is lying in bed tossing and turning unpleasantly, it's better to get out of bed and do something else, like some un-exciting work.

Catharsis of anger usually does not work!

One of the biggest problems of humanity is violence -- people's hurting and killing one another. A great deal of violence, but not all of it, occurs in moments of anger or hatred. Some people have thought of anger as something that builds up until you get rid of it, like urine or feces in the body that build up until we use the bathroom. Some people have thought that when you beat on a pillow or a punching bag or yell in an angry way, or play a violent videogame or watch a violent movie, you are "releasing" your pent-up anger and making yourself less likely to do something harmful to someone else. By this philosophy, the more people "take their anger out" on punching bags and so forth, the more peaceful and nonviolent world we would have. This is called the "catharsis" theory -- catharsis means getting something out of your system.

The problem with the catharsis theory is that on average, trying to use it makes people more aggressive, not less. Families where people scream at each other are more likely to hit each other, not less likely as the catharsis theory would predict. If you give kids toy weapons to have dramatic play with, they tend to hit each other more often right after that, not less often as the catharsis theory would predict. People who are angered and punch a punching bag tend to be more likely to get revenge later, not less likely as the catharsis theory would predict.

There's a different theory, called the social learning theory, that is directly opposed to the catharsis theory. According to this theory, seeing violent behaviors tends to increase the likelihood that people will imitate those behaviors. Doing aggressive behaviors, including violent acts in fantasy, tends to increase the likelihood of being hurtful in real life. The social learning theory is much more in line with what scientists have observed than is the catharsis theory.

According to the social learning theory, what we need in order to produce a less violent world is to present people with numerous models of kind behavior and peaceful conflict resolution, and give them chances to practice these behaviors in any way possible, including in fantasy.

Psychological skills

What do you need to be able to do, in order to be mentally healthy, that is, to increase your chances of being happy and helping others to be happy? In my research on this question, I found 62 skills that were worthy of the list, divided into 16 groups. Here are the 16 groups:

1. Productivity. Working to accomplish goals, concentrating, persisting.
2. Joyousness. Feeling good about the good things you do, the good things other people do for you, and the good things that happen by luck.
3. Kindness. Trying to make other people happy.
4. Honesty. Telling the truth, not cheating or stealing.
5. Fortitude. Handling it when unwanted things happen. Trying to figure out how to make things better, and toughing it out patiently if you can't make things better right away.
6a. Good individual decisions. Thinking carefully about what to do, especially for the decisions that really make a lot of difference. Being aware of the choice point situation, deciding on what your goals are, getting information, generating options, thinking about advantages and disadvantages, predicting consequences of actions, making a choice, learning from the experience.
6b. Good joint decisions. Trying to work things out rationally when there's a decision that affects more than one person, or a conflict between them.
7. Nonviolence. Not hurting or killing, and working for a world where violence is extremely rare.

8. Respectful talk. Avoiding insulting people, interrupting, or yelling at them, but being polite unless there's a very good reason not to be.

9. Friendship-building. Developing and keeping positive relationships, including those with family members, friends, and acquaintances.

10. Self-discipline. Being willing to pass up pleasure or endure discomfort in the present, in order to make something good happen in the future.

11. Loyalty. Making good decisions about whom you want to be loyal to, and continuing to nurture the relationships with those whom you want to be loyal to.

12. Conservation. Not wasting time, money, or the earth's resources; being thrifty or frugal.

13. Self-care, carefulness. Looking after your own health and safety, and also that of other people.

14. Compliance. Supporting the "rule of law" by obeying laws unless they are unethical. Being able to take directions from an authority unless you are told to do something bad.

15. Positive fantasy rehearsal. Using your imagination to practice positive behaviors.

16. Courage. Carrying out the best choice even when it is scary or aversive.

If people simply try to carry out as many positive examples as they can, of each of these skills, they very much increase their chances of leading a good life!

Methods of Influence

Why do people do what they do? How can someone influence someone else, or help themselves, to do good things? My research on this question leads me to list 10 influences.

1. Objective formation. The person somehow gets convinced that it's a good idea to think, feel, or behave in a certain way.
2. Hierarchy. This means there is a series of steps that the person can go through, to work their way up to the behavior gradually. They don't just become a great surgeon or a great piano player because they decide to -- they go through many intermediate stages on the way toward being an expert.
3. Relationship. The person has a relationship with someone who helps them do the thing, or influences them toward it.
4. Attribution. This means that the persons attribute to themselves the ability to do the thing in question; in other words they believe that with enough effort they can learn to do it.
5. Modeling. The persons observe examples of other people doing the behavior, providing models for imitation.
6. Practice. The persons rehearse the behaviors, either in real life or in fantasy.
7. Reinforcement and punishment. The consequences of doing the behavior, or not doing it, give the persons incentives.
8. Instructions. The persons get explanations of how to do the thing in question.
9. Stimulus control. The persons are put into, or put themselves into, the types of environments that bring out the behavior.

10. Monitoring. The persons keep track of how much they do something or how well they do it, so they can see whether progress is being made or not.

Imagine, if you will, a world where from a very early age, people get all 10 of these influences working in the direction of increasing the psychological skills we listed in the previous section. Does it seem to you that the society that would result from this would be a good one?

Attachment

People are not interchangeable for us. We get attached to specific people. When we get attached to someone, our relationship with that person is more important than our relationship with strangers. We feel more secure or trusting around that person. If that person dies, moves away, or rejects us, we don't just think, "Oh well, there are tons of other people in the world." We feel bad. When the person is away, we miss the person. When we get back together with the person, we feel happy to do so. Most of us learn how to get attached to someone very early in life, when our parents are the most important people for us. Having the feeling, early in life, that the parent we are attached to is dependable and kind probably helps us to make happy attachments to other people as we grow older.

Need for achievement, affiliation, and power

Why do people do what they do? A social scientist named David McClelland, who was particularly interested in the motives of people in the workplace, in conducting their careers, spoke of three "needs" that people can have.

The need for achievement is the wish to accomplish important goals, to be an expert, to do admirable things. The need for affiliation is the wish to make friends, to have good relationships with people, to have positive interactions with people. The need for power is the wish for the ability to direct other people's actions, to be able to say what other people do. Some people are higher in one or more of these than others, and in understanding others, it helps to try to figure out how much of these they are motivated by.

There are other motives of the same sort that can be added to the list. People have written about the need for autonomy: the wish to be able to make one's own decisions without someone else controlling you. People are also different in their "needs for": privacy, fame, time alone, physical movement, intellectual challenge, excitement, performing kind acts, risk-taking, being outdoors, structured time, physical pleasure, creative expression, and various others. Figuring out what people are motivated by is fairly complicated.

Nonetheless, the three motives McClelland focused on are important enough to qualify as a big idea. Thinking about how much people are motivated by the other "needs" I listed, and some I didn't list, may make the idea even bigger.

The rule of law versus might makes right

Who gets to do what? In a very primitive system, the answer to that is determined only by power, including the power gotten by the ability to do violent harm to others. An ancient Greek historian said, "The strong do what they can and the weak suffer what they must." Have you ever seen a movie or a TV show with the following plot? A bully does mean things to people. But our hero either gets power or has a secret power. There is a showdown, usually a fight of some sort, between the bully and the hero, and the hero wins! Hooray, there is a happy ending, the good person is also more powerful. My guess is that there are thousands, perhaps even millions, of stories with this general plot. But this story still sticks to the general rule that the power to win fights, that is, the skill of doing violence to the other, is what determines who gets their way. What is right or wrong is less important than how skilled a fighter you are -- "Might makes right."

Let's imagine a society where it's totally true that might makes right. In this society, it makes sense for people to spend a lot of time learning to fight well, making better weapons, being able to use those weapons better. The time they spend working on learning to hurt and kill each other could have been used in ways that make people happy. Lots of people must get severely injured and killed while two sides figure out who is most mighty. If you're the most powerful person and can have your way, you'd better not get sick or let your guard down, because someone else wants to take your place by killing you. You'll have a problem when you get weaker as you get old, but the violence of society will probably prevent that problem -- you'll probably get killed first.

There's another option, called the rule of law. People decide what is fair and just. They make rules -- for example, when you own something, someone else can't take it away by hurting you or threatening to hurt you. Some historians believe that when people discovered and started to agree upon the rule of law, the frequency of violence went way down.

The rule of law enables people to settle disputes without having a physical fight: they can take their disagreement to court and let a judge or jury decide who gets their way on the basis of law, by which of the people is the better fighter.

What makes people follow the law? One answer is that the power to use violent force is given to the government and to the police. If you don't obey the law, you might get shot by the police or locked up in a prison. But in the better societies, people follow the rules and laws because they agree with them -- they want to do their part to make a good society. When people follow laws because they want to, rather than because they have to, the need for violence goes down to a very low level.

The rule of law is still not firmly established on this planet. Countries have not stopped invading other countries just to take them over and add to their empires. In my country, the USA, there are more guns than people, and many people own guns in order to defend themselves against other people. Many children study martial arts in order not to be dominated by bullies at school. Police often have to enter dangerous situations with their guns as their major defense; they can make deadly mistakes.

But the more the rule of law can establish itself, and people can follow rules voluntarily, the less people have to be afraid of one another, and the more they can devote their energy to figuring out how to make each other happier instead of figuring out how to hurt and kill one another.

Government with the consent of the governed.

Governments tend to make rules that limit people's behavior. You aren't allowed to drive 100 miles an hour. You have to pay taxes. You have to go to school until a certain age. And so forth.

Why do people allow a certain group of people in government to tell them what to do? There are two main reasons: 1) because the people in government have the power to punish them if they don't obey, and they are afraid not to obey or to revolt; 2) because they agree with most of the rules that the government enforces, and they consent to abide by these rules. The fact that the second situation is much more desirable was one of the big ideas of the "enlightenment" period of world history. Government with the consent of the governed is more likely to occur when the people can vote out their leaders and vote other people in, rather than being stuck with the same leader for the rest of that person's life or until people start a successful revolution.

Freedom of the press

How do people know what policies to support, and whom to vote for? Should we help a nation in their war against another, or should we stay out? Should we require that people get a certain vaccination, or let them take their choice? How many people should we allow to come into the country as immigrants each year? Is this or that candidate for office a good person or a bad person? We need information to make those decisions, and we find out that information from the news media. (Because at one time the news was produced on paper, through printing presses, the news media came to be called the "press.")

Suppose the leaders of the government have control over the press. Then they have the power to broadcast messages to the people that say, "Keep your leaders in power. The other people who want power are no good. The things your leaders want to do are all good ideas. The people who want to do something else are all wrong." If this is the only information the people can get, they can't make their own decisions well. When the government controls the press, there's a situation that tends to put the power into the hands of one person, or one small group of people.

The opposite of this situation is when the press members have the freedom to give whatever information and views they want to, without government control. This is one of the freedoms guaranteed in the Bill of Rights in the U.S. Constitution.

Freedom of the press unfortunately doesn't insure that the information given by news organizations is accurate, or that the opinions they spread are wise. If the population of the country divides itself into tribes, news organizations can cater to one of those tribes and tell the people in that tribe what they want to hear. With the Internet, thousands or millions of people can be involved in giving out information and opinions, and there is very little to insure that the content is accurate or wise.

Rights

If a group of people agree that everyone is entitled to something, that something is called a "right." If a group agrees that people can speak their opinions, even if that speech criticizes the leaders of the group, then we speak of the "right" of freedom of speech. (In some countries today, openly criticizing the leader of the country is a recipe to be imprisoned or killed.) The right to "due process of law" means that people can't be punished by the government without some sort of trial that is supposed to look at the facts and make a good decision. The exception to this is that people can be locked up when there is reason to believe they are dangerous, while they are awaiting trial. Because of this, we want to give people the right to a "speedy trial" without being locked up for a long time waiting for it. The USA officially gives people the right not to receive "cruel and unusual punishment." There is a right to practice whatever religion one wishes, or not to practice a religion at all.

For all rights, there come up special cases where people have to decide whether the right applies to that situation or not. If someone persuades and urges other people to do some violent action but does not do it himself, can he claim that he was just using his right of free speech? Does someone have a right to put false and harmful information on the Internet? Do advertisers have a right to make false claims about their product? Do people have a right to expose their children to poisonous snakes if this is part of their religious ritual? Most people would answer "No" to these questions. So for most rights, there is room for interpretation of what is reasonable and what isn't.

What should be a right? People differ about this. Some believe that all people have a right not to have to starve or freeze to death, no matter how much work they do or don't perform to earn money. Some believe that basic health care should be a right. Most believe that children have a right to free education. Many believe that old people should have a right to health care and financial support without having to rely only on their savings.

The concept of rights is part of the rule of law. This part of the rule of law has to do with what good things people should get and what desirable things they should be able to do, while other parts have to do with what actions they are not allowed to perform.

World government as an alternative to war

Suppose there were a conflict between the states Arizona and California over water rights. Do you think it likely that they would get a bunch of soldiers together and go to war with each other? Not likely! They would be much more likely to let a federal court make a decision about what happens, and abide by it. They don't need to blow up buildings and kill people to settle their dispute. This is because they have given up some of a very important thing: sovereignty. If a government says that it is sovereign, that means, nobody can tell us what to do. We make our own decisions. But since the states recognize that they have given up some of their power to the government of the whole country, they can have their disputes settled in court. The rule of law makes violence unnecessary.

In the history of the USA, there was a time after the Revolutionary War was over and before the U.S. Constitution was agreed upon, where the states were in a "confederation," but each state was sovereign. And there were some violent conflicts between states, and some people were killed. When the states gave up some of their sovereignty to the federal government, wars between states almost ended. (The "exception that proves the rule" is the

Civil War, in which a group of states decided that the federal government shouldn't have sovereignty over them, after all -- one of the bloodiest conflicts in history.)

As I write these words, there is daily destruction and loss of life in a horrible war in which the ruler of Russia is trying to make Ukraine part of Russia. There is frequent talk about the use of nuclear weapons as a result of this conflict. There is the possibility of widespread destruction and death over large portions of the world. What if there were a world government with a fairly and wisely run court system? A country who felt that another country rightly belonged to them could present their case to the court, and the representatives of the country that didn't want to be taken over could present their case. There would be a prior agreement that the countries would abide by the decision of the judges. One of the countries wouldn't like the decision, probably, but there would be no need for blowing up things and killing people.

Why don't we organize a world government, in order to put an end to warfare? Because most people are not willing to give up their country's sovereignty to a group of foreigners whom they don't trust. The world is still too tribalistic -- people see themselves as members of a tribe that needs to defend itself against all other tribes. And the customs and habits of people that allow them to run courts and legislatures wisely and fairly just aren't strong enough yet. But the opinion of some thinkers is this: if the human race is to continue surviving without nuclear weapons or other "weapons of mass destruction" being used, movement toward world government is of high priority.

Evolution

This world is full of all sorts of plants and animals (including people, as an important type of animal). How did all these different varieties of living things come to be?

Let's start with the idea that all living things pass down their characteristics to the next generation -- plants and animals inherit the way they are from their parents. Lots of their characteristics are encoded in molecules in their cells, called DNA (this stands for desoxyribonucleic acid.) The information encoded in DNA is what makes the children of pigs become pigs rather than oak trees, and the children of squirrels become squirrels rather than fish. The units of information in DNA -- for example, for blue eyes rather than brown, are called genes.

Sometimes new pieces of DNA code get created -- these are called mutations. Lots of these mutations are just mistakes in the duplication of the code, that don't do any good, or do harm. Some of the mutations make the person worse off, and likely to die sooner or not even survive birth. But some of them actually make the plant or animal that gets them more able to survive and pass on its DNA to the next generation.

For most plants and animals, life is a struggle and a competition to survive and to pass the genes on to the next generation. Among those mutations that randomly show up, those that make the plant or animal better able to survive and reproduce tend to get passed on more, with each passing generation.

Two phrases used in explaining evolution are "survival of the fittest" and "natural selection." The plants or animals that are fittest to survive in the environment they are in, get selected to pass their genes to the next generation.

What is "fittest" depends on the environment the plant or animal is in. For example, camels have evolved to survive in very dry environments. People who study the way kidneys work have found that the kidneys of camels are built so as to save water. Animals in cold environments have evolved ways of saving heat. And so forth.

One of the strong clues that evolution takes place came from the practice of purposive selection, rather than natural selection. Long ago people started producing new types of farm crops or animals by selecting the ones that they used to breed the next generation. This is how people long ago started with wolves, or animals much like them, and eventually bred poodles!

We see evolution going on around us, in ways that we sometimes strongly dislike. For example, there's a certain type of bacterium, (called staphylococcus, staph for short) that can cause infections in people. When penicillin was discovered, the strains of staph that existed at the time could be killed by penicillin. But penicillin was used more and more, certain staph bacteria mutated in ways that let them survive despite penicillin, and these strains multiplied. Evolution produced a germ that can evade the medicine we used to kill it. The same thing has now happened with some other medicines, so that there are strains of this bacteria that are quite dangerous.

Evolution helps explain certain things about why people are the way they are. For example, those tribes of people who were best able to fight off attackers and win fights for scarce resources such as food were more likely to survive; thus "fight modules" evolved in the human brain.

138

But those tribes who fought with each other and killed each other and who didn't love and care for their children were less likely to survive; thus "caring modules" and "cooperative modules" also evolved in the human brain. This reasoning may account for people's tendency to be caring about those they consider to be in their group or tribe, and to fight against those they consider to be of the competing tribe.

Entropy

The concept of entropy can be a very complicated and mathematical one. But for our purposes here, let's express the idea in several ways, and give examples. One way of expressing it is that things tend to go toward being "mixed up" rather than "separated out." It takes lots more work to get them "separated out" than it does to "mix them up." For example, someone takes some oatmeal and stirs into it a teaspoon of brown sugar. A little bit of stirring mixes the brown sugar pretty uniformly in with the oatmeal. But suppose we wanted to undo what we just did, and end up with some sugar-free oatmeal and a teaspoon of pure brown sugar. It might be possible, but it would take a lot of work (and I'm guessing the oatmeal wouldn't be as good after the process were applied). Our oceans have lots of mercury dissolved in them, which tends to get into fish and sometimes make them unhealthy to eat. It is possible to separate the mercury back out, but it takes a huge amount of work.

Another way of describing the concept of entropy is that it takes lots more work to create a system that is in "order" than one in "disorder." For example, a parent and a toddler make a tower of blocks. It takes a minute or two, plus some careful placement of each block. Then in a fraction of a second, the toddler whacks the tower and the blocks now are lying in disarray on the floor. Creating the orderly arrangement took some work; getting rid of the order takes much less work. Sadly, we see the same principle in action in the news about warfare going on. It took many people lots of careful work to build a building; explosives turn the building into disorganized rubble in seconds.

Another way of talking about entropy has to do with heat transfer. Suppose we have a glass with ice and water in it, in a chamber that's perfectly insulated from the outside; air is the only thing other than the glass in the chamber, and it's at typical "room temperature." Over time, the ice melts and the air and the water eventually get to be the same temperature. This is because heat flows from higher temperatures to lower ones. What's the chance that the temperatures would happen to separate themselves out again, spontaneously? It never happens.

When you have something hotter than something else, you can in theory turn that difference into useful work. For example, when a hot thing heats up a cooler gas, the gas expands, and that expansion can be rigged up to turn a wheel or generate electricity or push something somewhere in a useful way. So if in our perfectly insulated system, we have a bunch of hot things and a bunch of cool things, and we take the hot things and put them next to the cool things to do work, eventually we've done all the work we can do. The heat transfer has done its thing, and we can't do any more work because the temperatures have equalized.

Another angle on the idea of entropy comes from the study of probability and statistics. Suppose someone has 50 cards, each with a number on it from 1 to 50, and the deck is arranged in order. Someone (perhaps the toddler we spoke of earlier) throws the card deck into the air and the cards fly all over the floor. If someone (perhaps the adult playing with the toddler) picks the cards up in a random order, it is *possible* that the cards, after being picked up randomly, would be in order from 1 to 50. But there's only one way in which this could occur, and the number of possible arrangements of the cards other than that is an incredibly huge number. So the cards go toward disorder, and the frequency with which some random arrangement gets them back in 1 to 50 order is just about zero. The same reasoning explains why the sugar molecules don't just spontaneously separate from the oatmeal, or the mercury from the seawater -- there are vastly many more ways for the molecules to be mixed up than there are for them to be separated out. And it explains why in a closed room, you don't have the air molecules just happen to bounce around so that a bunch of faster moving ones (hotter ones) end up on one side of the room, and the slower moving molecules (colder ones) end up on the other side of the room. There are so many more ways for the faster and slower ones to be mixed up than separated out, that the separation just never happens.

Fortunately for us, we're not living in a "closed system." With the fact that entropy or disorder tends to decrease, how do we have a bunch of random carbon dioxide molecules and water molecules get turned into something as highly organized as a tree? It needs a lot of work being done from outside the system, a lot of energy invested from somewhere -- and that somewhere is the sun. The sun is working like crazy every day to take disorganized molecules and turn them into something so improbable as a plant. And then the bodies of animals take the energy from plants and use it to arrange a bunch of mixed up nutrients in our stomachs into something so organized and improbable as our bodies.

So when we try to prevent acts of violence (which are random disruptions of the organized way our bodies are put together) or destruction, or pollution, or even when we organize our rooms, we're working against the tendency of things to get more disorganized and mixed up.

Supply and demand in the free market

In a society, there are all sorts of goods and services that people put their efforts into providing to other people. How much of each of them do people provide? In other words, where do the efforts of the people go? How much should we grow of corn, black beans, kale, and squash? How many accountants do we need, how many nurses, lawyers, farmers, videogame programmers, computer repair people, psychotherapists, and so forth? How many houses and apartments should there be? How many cars, buses, trains, and planes?

There have been some attempts by governments to have committees try to figure out how much of this or that the country needs, and to dictate the amount that gets produced. Those attempts have generally failed. It's just too hard to figure out how much is needed.

There's a different way that these decisions get made, called "the free market."

One of the big ideas that allows the free market to work is that prices of goods and services are determined by supply and demand. Supply refers to how much of something is available, and demand refers to how much of it people want to buy. If you are trying to sell something that is in very low supply and very many people want a lot of it, you can hold an auction and sell it to the highest bidder, and charge a very high price for it. On the other hand, if you are trying to sell something that is in very high supply or that there is very low demand for, the price you can get is a lot lower. This is why the ticket prices for a concert by a very famous music star are usually very high, whereas the price of a concert put on by someone like the author of this book would be zero or negative (that is, having to pay people to come). The supply of non-famous and not-extremely-skilled musicians is very high and the demand to hear them is low.

What happens when high demand relative to supply drives prices up? If the price of something gets enough higher than the cost of providing it, people can make profits from getting into that business and providing it. This situation gives people an incentive to get into the business and provide that thing, or that service. So more of it gets produced -- in other words, the supply goes up. So when demand for a good or service goes up, the supply tends to go up. In other words, the types of things that people want more, get produced more! And this is what the "free market" is supposed to do: make it happen that people put their efforts into supplying more of the goods and services that people want more of!

What people want more of is not necessarily what is best for them in the long run. The markets for junk food, addictive drugs, violent entertainment, and guns create very profitable industries. The free market makes its decisions solely on the basis of what people are willing to spend money on.

The "commons" and the need for regulation

Suppose there are a few businesses located alongside a river. One of them is very careful to take the wastes that the business produces, and to make sure they are disposed of properly, even though this costs lots of money. The second business, that produces the same good, just dumps their waste products right into the river. The second doesn't spend as much money to produce the thing, and can make just as much profit as the first business while charging people less for the thing. People choose to buy the thing from the second business, because it's cheaper, and the first either goes out of business or starts dumping their waste products into the river also. Now the free market has used its "invisible finger" to result in pollution! The river is an example of an important resource that no one person is responsible for -- things like this are called "the commons."

In any given community, the amount of crime is part of the commons: no one person can buy or sell reduced crime. People can buy gates to put around their houses, bars for their windows, and guns to defend themselves with. But they don't buy police forces, courts, probation officers, jails, crime prevention programs, tutoring for children in nonviolence skills, and all the things that are meant to reduce crime in the whole community. Thus the free market alone doesn't tend to produce those things, and government must.

Because there are many goods and services that make things better for whole groups of people, but which individual people can't buy, there's need for government, in addition to the free market. The free market doesn't produce roads, armies for defense of a country, rules against pollution and people to enforce those rules, big parks for people to enjoy nature in, rules against reckless driving and people to enforce those rules, and other aspects of "the commons." For this reason, government rules and regulations are needed in addition to the free market.

One of the big differences between groups of people in the USA has to do with how much should be left to the free market and how much should be regulated by government. It would be possible for governments to get out of the businesses of education, health care, mail delivery, administration of prisons, and others, but would this have good effects? Do we want private prison companies contributing to the campaigns of judges who promise to lock up lots more people, which (not by coincidence) would produce more profits for the prison company? On the other hand, do we want governments making so many regulations that small business owners have to follow, that it's not worth it to be in business?

The business cycle

The economic activity of a country tends to go up and down, from boom times to bust times. When business is booming, the total amount of goods and services that people are wanting to buy, which is called aggregate demand, is large. This allows businesses to find it easier to sell whatever they are providing. They tend to expand their production. They hire more workers so they can produce more and sell more. The prices they can charge for what they produce go up, and to hire more workers, they increase the wages those workers are paid. Increase in prices is called inflation; if prices increase more than wages do, the average person can buy less; if wages increase more, the opposite occurs.

But now suppose that bunches of businesses, at the same time during the boom, have started to expand the goods and services they offer. Maybe after several months or years when that expansion has taken place, the total supply of what's offered becomes greater, relative to how much people demand. When this happens, businesses find that it's harder to sell; prices stop going up or even go down; businesses decide to produce less; workers are laid off; wages don't rise or even fall. So now we have a period of economic downturn, called a recession or depression. But when businesses stop producing so much, supply relative to demand goes down, and after some time, when supply has dropped below demand, we have the conditions that tend to start another boom -- assuming that people have enough money to buy what they want, and wages and jobs have not fallen to the point where demand falls further behind supply, in a vicious cycle.

What I've just said suggests that the activity of the economy would naturally tend to go up and down, largely because of the lag time that it takes for supply to fluctuate to move toward demand. However, there are so many other things that influence the economy, that it's hard to verify what I said. What are some of those things? Wars starting, tax rates changing, government programs pumping a lot of money into the economy, natural disasters like floods or earthquakes, prices fluctuating for things many people use (for example, oil), weather fluctuations influencing how much food gets produced, new technologies producing new ways of doing things (for examples computers or robots that replace some people's jobs and create jobs for other people to run them), how much the country's "central bank" charges other banks to borrow money, and probably lots more.

People tend to be happier during times when jobs are plentiful and businesses find lots of market for their production. Suicide rates and crime rates fall during those times.

Monetary policy and fiscal policy

What can government do to stimulate the economy when it's sluggish, and cool it off when it's booming too fast? (Stimulating it means making more people get employed, and more goods and services produced, and workers' wages tend to go up, often with the disadvantage of having prices rise.)

The simplest answer is that there are two things governments can do to stimulate the economy. One is for the government to spend more money -- for example on fixing bridges, fixing roads, supporting health care or education, or almost anything else. This directly increases employment and the total amount of goods and services, but even more important is the indirect effect: the people who get paid to do these things have money to pay other people to do things, and then those people have more money to spend, and so forth. (This has been called the multiplier effect.) This way of stimulating the economy is called fiscal policy. Where does the government get the money to do this? One way is by taxing people more. But this puts less money in their hands and tends to have the opposite of a stimulating effect on the economy. The government can increase spending without increasing taxes, by borrowing money from its people (that is, by selling bonds), and this tends to stimulate the economy.

The other main way that governments stimulate the economy is by increasing the supply of money more directly; this is called monetary policy. In the days when paper money was much more important, governments could just print more bills and put them into circulation. Nowadays, the increase of the money supply is done by electronic transfers on computer files. The central bank of the US, called the Federal Reserve, lends money to banks. If it decides to lend money at a low interest rate, the banks will be able to lend to other people at a low interest rate, and more people will have more money to do things with. This stimulates the economy.

So to stimulate the economy, the congress can authorize more spending and cut taxes, and the central bank can cut its interest rates. To cool off the economy and reduce inflation (the rise in prices) the congress can cut spending and raise taxes and the central bank can raise interest rates.

People tend to vote depending on how satisfied they are with the economy at the moment of the election. But the effects of government policies may take a long time to take effect. It would be good if voters could understand how the economy works well enough to vote for people who make good decisions, even it will take a while for the effects of those decisions to take place.

Tribalism

People have a tendency to be loyal to the group, or the "tribe," they consider themselves a part of, and to become enemies with other groups. Having a "common enemy" is one of the main ways that members of tribes become united and develop loyalty to one another (otherwise they tend to squabble and argue with each other, as people tend in general tend to do). What I'm calling a "tribe" can be as small as a family or even a pair of friends; it can be as large as a country. Some idealistic people (including myself) like to hope for a world where the people on the whole planet considered themselves to be in the same tribe.

There are lots of customs in our society that promote tribalism. For example, if high schools and colleges and even countries have athletic teams that compete against their neighbors, and people root and cheer for their team, they strengthen their ties to their tribe and see themselves as enemies or adversaries or at least opponents of the other tribe. When a country has two political parties that run against each other in every election, and different news shows that specialize in loyalty to a certain tribe, the country tends to get divided into two tribes that consider one another enemies.

Some people think that tribalism wound up in the human brain because of selection during evolution. Throughout thousands of years, the tribes who have been loyal to one another but have been able to fiercely defend their tribe against other tribes have had a survival advantage. Maybe something in our genetic makeup makes us tend to divide up into competing groups. Otherwise, it's hard to figure out how so many people could get so excited when a group of people put a ball in a certain place despite the efforts of other people to interfere.

Why is tribalism important? Because we're living in a world where if countries continue to fight against each other in wars (which is the ultimate example of tribalism), the weapons that people have developed are destructive enough to destroy human civilization, and perhaps all of humanity. So in a sense, the survival of the human race depends on our being able to triumph over our tribalistic instincts.

Thoughts, emotions, and behaviors all cause each other

Imagine Person 1. When Person 1 makes a mistake, they say to themselves, "This shows that I am stupid and worthless." When Person 1 has a success at something, they think, "That was just luck -- next time it will be a disaster." When someone does something that irritates Person 1, they think, "This just shows that people can't be trusted."

Now let's imagine Person 2. When Person 2 makes a mistake, they think, "How can I make things better?" and "What can I learn from this, so I won't repeat this mistake?" When Person 2 has a success, they think, "Yay! That feels good! I want to remember how I brought this about, and celebrate good decisions I made!" When someone does something to irritate Person 2, they think, "How do I want to handle this situation? If I can handle this well, I'll deserve to feel good!"

Which person do you think is more likely to be happy and successful in life? If you think Person 2, you grasp the fundamental idea of "cognitive therapy." This idea is that what you say to yourself, what you think, has a big influence on how you feel and what you do. Not only that: you can refine the skill of being aware of what you are saying to yourself, and you can pick your thoughts so as to make things better for yourself, just as you can pick your behaviors. Many people have worked at the skill of picking thoughts that help them to be kind to themselves and others, and many have greatly improved their lives in this way. This idea began to be emphasized by cognitive therapists, who measured the positive effects of training people in the skill of thought-selection, in the middle of the 20th century. But the fundamental idea was voiced by Greek and Roman philosophers a couple of thousand years ago!

The 12 thought classification

We just mentioned the big idea that consciously picking how you want to think, what you want to say to yourself, can improve your life and those of the others whom you affect. Of course, there are an infinite number of thoughts you can have. But the 12 thought classification is a way of giving ourselves a menu, a multiple choice question, regarding what type of thought we want to think in any given situation. Here are the 12 types of thoughts:

1. **Awfulizing**. This is a thought that acknowledges the badness or danger of a situation. Sometimes this type of thought helps us recognize when we need to protect ourselves, and it can be life-saving, as in: "Oh no, a car's coming my direction, if I don't move I'm going to get hit!" Or: "Uh oh! That snake that is crawling nearby is a poisonous one!" But sometimes we exaggerate or overgeneralize the badness of a situation, and in those

cases awfulizing can make us feel bad, unnecessarily. For example, someone gets teased by another person and thinks, "I can't stand this! Nobody is ever going to be nice to me!" The word "overgeneralizing" means that the person doesn't just think the present situation is bad, but concludes that many other, or perhaps all other, situations are also bad.

2. **Getting down on yourself**. This is a thought acknowledging the badness or inadequacy of something about yourself or your behavior. Self-criticism is a synonym for this type of thought. The ability to take responsibility for one's bad actions and admit to oneself that one has made a mistake is a very important skill. This skill is a crucial part of what we call "conscience." For example: "I spoke in a rude way to that person. I wish I hadn't done that." Or, "I have to watch out in this situation -- I know I have a bad habit of taking on more tasks than I can actually do."

But when getting down on yourself is overdone or overgeneralized, this thought can be depressing. For example: "I didn't do as well as I wanted to on that test -- therefore I'm stupid and won't ever be able to succeed at anything." Or: "I said something unkind -- I don't deserve to ever feel good again for the rest of my life."

3. **Blaming someone else**. This type of thought is acknowledging the badness of someone else's behavior or motives or something else about that person. This type of thought also did not evolve for no reason. It can help us recognize when someone else is trying to take advantage of us and exploit us; it tells us that we need to oppose the other person's wishes. For example: "This person is pretending to be my friend, but he's just trying to take my

money." Or: "What this person did was very bad, even criminal; I'm choosing not to vote for him!"

On the other hand, blaming someone else when overdone or overgeneralized is behind a lot of the unnecessary violence, anger, and hatred in the world. For example: "Why are you looking at me with that face -- nobody does that and gets away with it!" Or: "I can't make as much money as I want to -- it's all the fault of those people who are a different race from me!"

4. **Not awfulizing**. This is not just the absence of an awfulizing thought. It is directly telling oneself that the situation isn't so bad, or could be worse, or can be handled. For example, "It isn't the end of the world that the person turned down my invitation. I can handle it." Or, "I don't like it that the car fender got bent, but at least no one was hurt." This type of thought is very useful in turning down the anxiety that might come from awfulizing. On the other hand, it can be misleading when we're tempted to deny danger. For example, "There are bunches of soldiers and tanks assembling on our borders, but they're probably just doing a drill of some sort. There's no reason for concern." Or, "Yes, over the last few years it's been getting hotter, but that's not a big problem -- the temperature goes up and down and besides, I like warm weather."

5. **Not getting down on yourself**. This is not just the absence of self-criticism, but directly telling yourself why you don't want to punish yourself or criticize yourself too much. For example, "The stuff I cooked didn't turn out great, but at least it was edible and the other people could handle it. I don't want to punish myself; not all experiments are successes."

6. **Not blaming someone else**. This is not just the absence of blaming thoughts, but directly explaining to yourself why you don't want to behave angrily toward the other person. For example, "He really makes a mess of things. But that's what kids tend to do when they are 20 months old!" Or, "Even though she made a hurtful mistake, I'm going to choose to be kind and forgiving."

7. **Goal-setting.** This is telling yourself what you wish would happen, what result or outcome you want for this situation. For example: "We want different things, but my goal is not to defeat or dominate the other person, but to figure out some plan together that will be a good solution to the problem for both of us."

8. **Listing options and choosing.** This is trying to make a rational decision about what to do -- generating ideas of possible plans, thinking about the pros and cons of the options, and making a choice. For example: "I could quit studying this now, and relax. Or I could spend some time making up questions and answers and practicing quizzing myself, so I'll be even further prepared. Or I could go over the types of questions the teacher has made up for tests, and then skim over the material one more time thinking about what sorts of questions could be made up. I think I'll look over the teacher's test questions, and then write out some of my own, with the answers, and practice answering them some."

9. **Learning from the experience.** This is thinking about what you have experienced (your or someone else's mistake, or good decision, or anything else) and trying to learn from it something that will help you in the future. For example: "That was a really long and slow trip. But I learned from this to examine the GPS and make sure it

hasn't been told to avoid highways. That will help me in the future!" Or, "I did really well on that test! I learned from this that the technique of making up my own questions and answers and practicing answering the questions really helps me."

10. **Celebrating luck.** The first three types of thoughts acknowledged the badness of a situation; the last three acknowledge and celebrate the goodness of a situation. Celebrating luck has to do with the situations that neither you nor anyone else purposely brought about. For example, "What wonderful weather it happened to be today!" or "I'm so lucky to be living in a country that isn't at war!"

11. **Celebrating someone else's choice**. For example: "That person is holding the door open for me to walk through with my heavy bags -- that's really nice of them!" Or: "Lots of people worked to grow and transport the food I'm having in this meal. I feel grateful for their efforts!"

12. **Celebrating your own choice**. For example, "I made really good use of my time! I have gotten lots of things on my to do list done so far today!" or "My actions made that person happier. That really makes me feel good!" Celebrating your own choice is perhaps the most important "antidepressant thought." If it makes you feel good, it gives you a payoff for your efforts, and creates an "effort-payoff connection."

For any given situation, it is possible to react in any of these ways. A useful exercise is the "12 Thought Exercise." In this, you take any situation and make up an example of each of the 12 thoughts, tailoring it to that situation. Doing this exercise teaches us that it is possible to respond to any situation in any of a number of different ways. It helps us gain flexibility of thinking, and helps with the ability to choose consciously what type of thought will be most useful to us in any situation.

A healthy lifestyle

There are lots of diseases that it is possible to avoid by having a "healthy lifestyle." Not only avoiding diseases, but also feeling better, thinking better, and living longer can be results of these healthy choices. What diseases are less likely? Diabetes, strokes, heart attacks, high blood pressure, dementias, cancer, and a good number of others -- even the ill effects of infections.

What behaviors make up a healthy lifestyle? They include: not smoking; not using alcohol or other "recreational drugs"; eating fruits and vegetables, especially berries and greens and beans; not eating too much sugar and saturated fat, eating neither too much nor too little; getting enough sleep, having a regular sleep schedule, drinking enough water, getting enough exercise, finding ways to de-stress yourself (including relaxation/meditation, and making good decisions about which situations to get into and which to escape from); cultivating good relationships with other people; not taking unnecessary risks (for example driving at high speed); avoiding exposures to unhealthy situations such as very loud noises, too much sun, sports where head injury is frequent, violent people, or people with infectious illnesses (or using PPE, personal protective equipment such as masks, when doing so).

It's amazing to think of how much illness could be prevented and how much health would result if everyone even attempted to use the healthy lifestyle behaviors listed in the previous long sentence!

Modeling and imitation learning

When we discuss the 10 methods of influence, the 10 reasons why people do what they do, one of those is modeling and imitation learning. We tend to imitate what we see and hear. If it weren't for this tendency, it's hard to imagine how children would learn to talk. In passing down what people have learned about how to survive, from one generation to the next, it's much more efficient for children to simply observe what people do and learn from those examples, than for example to rely solely on a trial and error process of seeing what gets rewarded and what doesn't.

When humanity fully grasped the big idea of modeling and imitation learning, the logical thing to do next would be to collect all sorts of positive models of the skills most important for producing a good society, and show those examples to the upcoming generations in great abundance, as part of their education. Children would see many examples through stories and videos, showing nonviolence, respectful talk, kindness, rational conflict resolution, good decision-making, productivity, and other psychologocial skills very frequently. If we did this, we would probably greatly increase the aggregate psychological skill of society with each generation, and humanity would make great progress!

But there's one problem with this program. It takes a great deal of skill to make a story 1) contain positive models without negative models, or even much more prominent than negative models, and 2) be very entertaining and fun. Think about the most popular videogames; how much is devotion to nonviolence modeled? Think about the most popular movies -- to what extent do they portray good people making one good decision after another? Think of great literature, classic novels and plays. How much do the characters show us how to be rational, kind, and nonviolent?

Every once in a while someone figures out how to make a movie or novel or story that is both entertaining and very illustrative of positive psychological skills. The people who do this are doing a good job for society.

Meanwhile, the teachers, parents, government leaders, and humanitarian workers who display good real-life models for other people to consider imitating, are also making a great contribution to society.

The parts of individual decision-making: SOIL ADDLE

If you want to make a decision very carefully, how do you do it? Here are some parts to the process.

1. **S**ituation. You try to understand very thoroughly the situation you are in (sometimes called the choice point). Who is doing what, who wants what? What are the facts of the situation? What can you learn that may be relevant to your decision?

2. **O**bjectives. What are you trying to make happen? What outcomes would you like to produce? What are your goals? Are you trying to defeat another person, or are you trying to bring about an outcome where you can both be happy? Are you trying to do what will make you happiest today, or what will make you happiest years from now?

3. **I**nformation. What additional information can you get that will help you in this choice point? For example, you have an illness; you look up on the Internet the research that exists on how that illness is treated and prevented.

4. **L**isting options. You generate different ideas about what you could do.

5. **A**dvantages and disadvantages. You think about the consequences of the options -- both the good consequences (advantages) and the bad consequences (disadvantages). You think about how likely these various consequences are to take place.

6. **D**eciding. You organize the thoughts we've talked about so far, so as to decide what to do.

7. **D**oing. You actually carry out the decision you've made.

8. **L**earning from the **E**xperience. You notice what happened as a result of what you did, and you try to learn anything useful that you can, from noticing this.

SOIL ADDLE is a mnemonic for the different tasks in decision making that we listed above.

Tasks for joint decision-making: Dr. L.W. Aap

If two (or more) people, or groups, have a problem to solve or a decision to make, that will affect both of them? How should they do it? Here's how they should NOT do it: one says that one option is the only acceptable plan, and the other argues for a different option, and they have a fight to figure out who gets their way.

Dr. L.W. Aap is a mnemonic for tasks in joint decision-making or conflict-resolution that tend to result in peaceable solutions.

1. **Defining** the problem. Each person says how they see the situation, i.e. the choice point, that they are dealing with, in a way that tells what their own wishes and interests are, and avoids accusing, insulting, or bossing the other person.

2. **Reflecting**. Each person says what they heard the other person say, in order to check out whether they understood it correctly and let the other person know they understood.

3. **Listing** options. They generate options for the plan. It's good for both of them to contribute ideas and to come up with at least 4 options, so they don't each get "wedded" to only one option.

4. **Advantages** and disadvantages. They talk about the consequences of the options, and how likely they are.

5. **Agreeing**. They jointly decide together on some plan they can agree on. Sometimes the agreement is just to gather more information and postpone the final decision till later.

6. **Politeness**. They don't interrupt each other, yell at each other, or insult each other. They stick to thinking about how good the options are rather than focusing on the bad parts of the other person's personality. They are courteous.

What if children learned to have Dr. L.W. Aap conversations from a very early age, and practiced them in role-playing for many different situations over many years? Would people in general get better at conflict-resolution and joint decision-making? My guess is: yes.

The skill of conflict-resolution is very important for all human beings, but it is very seldom taught and practiced.

Higher and lower forms of pleasure

We discussed earlier the "utilitarian" system of ethics, where good actions are defined as those that increase the average or total happiness the most. In such a system, feeling good, feeling pleasant feelings, and helping other people to feel pleasure and avoid pain, are the major goals.

With only that much to go on, someone might think, drug dealers are very ethical people -- they do a job that produces pleasure in people. People wouldn't, for example, inject opiates such as heroin into their veins if the result were not pleasurable. And someone might think, the people who produce junk food are among the most ethical people in society -- ice cream, cheeseburgers, french fries and soda produce much more pleasure than kale and broccoli and water, as evidenced by the fact that no one ever made a fortune setting up a chain of "fast kale and broccoli" restaurants.

This leads us to the idea that some pleasures are better for us in the long run than others are. Some pleasures tend to feel good for a while, but come back to bite us later. Drugs that cause us short term pleasure, such as heroin, create addictions and tend to reduce our motivation toward "higher pleasures" such as those of doing meaningful work or cultivating good relationships. Junk food feels good to eat, but too much of it gives us diabetes, obesity, high blood pressure, heart disease, and other problems.

One of the higher pleasures in life comes from setting worthy goals and figuring out how to make progress toward them. What are worthy goals? Increasing the *long-term* happiness of oneself and others, not just that of the short term. The pleasure of doing good work, successfully solving challenging problems, cultivating kind and loyal relationships, making ethical choices, helping society progress (even in some small way), creating works of art that dignify humanity and life, of giving thanks for the miracles of the very existence of life and the universe -- these are some of what some people refer to as "higher pleasures."

Equality versus incentives

Imagine that two people are talking with each other. The first says: "It's not right that some people should live in poverty while other people have much more than they need. Each person should have a right to good health care, good food, clean water, good education, living in safe housing and in a nonviolent neighborhood. Each person should have these things even if they can't work in the competitive marketplace. We shouldn't have a system where some people get all the advantages of life and others don't. Equality between people is a very important principle."

The second person says, "I understand your wish for fairness and equality. But all the things that you want people to have, someone has to produce or furnish them, and that takes work. We pay people in order to give them an incentive to do work. Some people are more willing to work than others. Some know how to do work that results in a lot more productivity than others. If everyone got the same amount, we would take away the incentive for people to achieve more and to produce more goods or services for other people."

The first person says, "I understand your wish to reinforce people for doing more of the things that make other people happier. But lots of people are higher paid, not because they do more good for society, but just because they have more power. Because they are running things, they divert more of the company's profits to themselves rather than to the workers who are actually doing the work that makes people better off. And they drive their competitors out of business by lowering prices, and then when they have a monopoly, they raise prices. They get rich by being greedy, not by being super productive."

The second person says, "I understand, and I agree with you that the inequality that results from power plays is not good for society. But still, a certain amount of inequality just results from people not being willing to work as much as other people. And a certain amount results from someone figuring out a really good idea on how to meet people's needs, and making lots of money off that. Those portions of inequality are necessary, to preserve the incentives for working and for figuring out creative ways of meeting people's needs."

The first person says, "Why are some people unwilling to work? A lot of that stems from the fact that their educations have been bad, and they have experienced nothing but unpleasant experiences from trying to get work done. If our education systems really taught people to work joyously, much of the inequality you speak of could be done away with."

The second person says, "I agree with that. Even with the best educational system, though, differences in people's work capacity will remain, and thus some differences in their economic rewards will remain, and should remain, also."

This conversation illustrates the big idea that both equality and economic incentives are desirable in society, and they are in some ways opposed to each other.

By the way, the two speakers in this conversation were rather polite to one another, weren't they? People can get very angry when discussing this or any other issue.

Ways of listening

Many of the problems of the world result from people's not listening to one another. When you are talking, it feels good to be understood by another person. Understanding each other well, and letting the other know of such understanding, is a way that people can give pleasure to one another, without side effects! When they are making decisions together that affect both of them, their ability to understand the other's point of view and communicate that understanding greatly contributes to their coming up with a good solution. Good listening can literally make the difference between life and death.

Here are some ways that people can listen well to each other:

1. Reflections. In reflections, you tell the other person what you understood them to be communicating. Reflections tend to start out with phases like this:

What I hear you saying is _____.
So, you are saying _____.

In other words, the message you're giving is that _____.
It sounds like you're feeling _____.
Do I understand you correctly that _____?

Reflections allow you to make sure that you do understand the other person correctly. If you don't, the other person can say, "No, let me try again." If you do understand correctly, the other person gets to know this, and hopefully feel good that they were understood.

2. Telling about your own experience, in a way that communicates understanding. For example:

First person: I did so much work for that guy, and then he didn't pay me! He is so rich that he knows he could get lawyers to delay things forever if I sued him.
Second person: Really! The same thing happened to me when I worked for him! I lost thousands of dollars! I'm sorry you had the same experience!

The second person was listening, right? Suppose, on the other hand, that the second person's response had been:

Second person: Oh. Well, I went water skiing last week end. It was fun.

This would have been telling about the second person's experience, but NOT in a way that communicated listening or understanding.

3. Follow-up question. These are questions that prompt the other person to tell more. Examples: "What happened next? Tell me more, please. What did you do

then? How did that affect you? Did that happen more than once? How much did you lose? How did that affect your family?"

4. Facilitations. These are brief utterances like the following: "Uh huh. Yes. I see. Oh? Is that right! OK. Humh. Right." These tell the other person, "I'm still listening; keep going if you'd like."

5.Positive feedback. These reinforce the person for something. Examples: "That's an interesting point. Thanks for telling me that. I'm glad you did that. What a good decision. That really took some courage on your part. Congrats for learning from your mistake. I'm glad to hear your thoughts about this. Thank you! Wow, good job!"

To remember reflections, experience, follow-up, facilitations, and feedback, I think of the mnemonic REFFF.

Emotion mind, logic mind, and wise mind

From antiquity, observers of human behavior have realized that some actions are driven primarily by careful, logical reasoning, and others more by strong emotions. We've always known that people sometimes make very bad mistakes when they are too emotional. We've also known that emotions are a very important part of life, and we don't want to get rid of them and become robots or computers! People make a distinction between thoughts and emotions -- for example, "I'm in a dangerous situation," is a thought, and fear is an emotion. Others point out that thoughts and emotions are both things that we do with our brains and our bodies, and both can be considered behaviors. Both act like behaviors in important ways: for example, practice and models and reinforcement all seem to influence both of them.

I take the terms, emotion mind, logic mind, and wise mind from those who write about a certain type of psychotherapy, called dialectical behavior therapy.

When we are really angry and screaming at someone, not thinking about what we're saying, that's an example of "being in emotion mind." Likewise, if we are totally panicked to the degree that we can't think of much except escaping from something, that's emotion mind. But also, if we're just happy and dancing around and not trying to figure out anything but just enjoying what's going on, that too is emotion mind.

Logic mind, on the other hand, describes emotion-less calculation -- thinking about what to do, trying to predict consequences, staying totally cool.

Wise mind is defined as combining the best aspects of emotion mind and logic mind. In it, you are aware of your feelings, and you use the information these emotions give you as part of your decision-making. You also tune in to the emotions of other people as you decide. But you are still trying to use the most accurate logic and calculations and predictions you can muster, to make the best decision you can.

Dialectical behavior therapy was developed to work with people who very often were so caught up in anger or fear or feeling devastated that they couldn't make good decisions. The descriptions of different states of mind communicate that it's often useful to turn down the intensity of bad feelings, to turn up the rational decision-making part of the brain, but not to try to get rid of emotions altogether. Rather, we can be aware of our emotions and use them as important signals in decision making. For example, the feeling of worry or fear signals us to check and see whether we are in danger. The feeling of anger signals us to figure out if someone is trying to take advantage of us or exploit us. The feeling of love signals us to want to spend time with the other person and to be kind to them. Using the combination of emotion and logic in "wise mind" is a strategy that almost all of us can use, often.

The best of traditional ideas of masculinity and femininity

There have been, for a long time, traditional ideas of what men and women are "supposed to be like."

Men, according to these traditional ideas, are supposed to be brave and physically strong. They are supposed to act confident and decisive, knowing the path of action they want and being sure of themselves in enacting it. They are supposed to be willing to oppose others when necessary, to be assertive or even aggressive when they need to defend themselves or their loved ones. They are supposed to go out into the world and make a difference to the world outside the family. They are supposed to handle hardship without whimpering, to have fortitude skills. They are supposed to be very determined to reach goals, and willing to take risks. They are supposed to be good at mechanical and building skills. They are supposed to take charge and be good leaders.

Women, according to these traditional ideas, are supposed to be loving, nurturing, caretaking, and kind. They are supposed to be patient, especially with children.

They are supposed to have great intuition about how children should be raised and dealt with. They are supposed to be aware of their emotions and not afraid to show them. They are supposed to accept help graciously. They are supposed to pay particular attention to the welfare of their family members. They are supposed to have good interpersonal skills. They are supposed to be good at or appreciative of the arts -- music, literature, painting and sculpture, dance. They are supposed to be good team players, good at complying with the rule of law. They are meant to avoid violence and promote nonviolent solutions to problems. They are supposed to be experts at promoting cooperation among people.

The big idea of this section is that as humanity progresses, it becomes clearer that all these traits are useful for both men and women. A person of either gender can cultivate any of these positive abilities and use them to make themselves and others happy.

Planethood, patriotism, and being in the same boat

Some states in the US put into law that school children are supposed to be taught to be "patriotic," and several other countries apparently have adopted this goal. The meaning of the word *patriotism*, like the meaning of many other words, can be different to different people. To some people, the word means a love of one's country, a wish for the country to do good things and to have happy people. But sometimes when people disagree with the decisions that a country's leaders make, other people criticize those dissenters as unpatriotic -- as if patriotism means unthinkingly defending whatever decisions are

169

made by the leaders who happen to be in power. And sometimes patriotism is very close to what we've discussed in another section regarding the word *tribalism*: the notion that one should be loyal to the members of your own tribe and in competition with all other tribes. "Hooray for our country, we're the best, we can beat all those other countries," is the attitude that some people think of as patriotic. Volunteering to go and fight for one's country in a war is seen by some as the ultimate patriotic act.

There are other people who wish that human beings all over the planet could have a sense of loyalty to the planet, and to those who live there. "We are all in the same boat," is the sentence often used to express this sentiment -- we're in this together, it's so much a matter of who wins or loses, as whether we can work together to defeat the "enemies" that threaten us the most. What are the enemies that threaten humanity in general? They are not invaders from another planet, but problems that are nonetheless our common enemies: global warming, pollution, poverty, warfare, overpopulation, disease, violence. For all of these, the more countries can collaborate and cooperate with one another rather than fight with one another, the more likely humanity is to "win" the struggle.

Unfortunately, we have not progressed to the point where leaders of countries no longer decide to use their armies to invade other countries that haven't attacked them. They sometimes do this just because they want to take over that country and add it to their own empire. And sometimes they do this to put in a leader who will do things that the invading country likes more. When this happens, the instinct toward tribalism and patriotism in the sense of "defend your country against its enemies" feels very justified.

Figuring out how to move to a cooperative, collaborative relationship among countries who now see themselves as on opposing tribes is a major goal for humanity -- perhaps the number one goal.

Rational use of imprisonment

When someone robs or assaults or kills or otherwise commits a crime, what should be done with that person? A very common response is to put the person in prison. What purpose is served by imprisonment, otherwise known as incarceration?

For some people, the point of imprisonment is revenge. The person caused other people to suffer, therefore the person should be made to suffer, to pay for the crime. If one is only interested in revenge, the worse the prison conditions are -- the more brutally prisoners are treated, and the more vicious they are toward each other -- the better. But how does getting revenge, by itself, make anyone better off? If it doesn't make anyone better off, it's not rational -- it doesn't make sense. The revenge idea allows cruel behavior by "bad guys" to prompt and justify cruel behavior by "good guys."

There are some ways in which imprisonment might help, at least in theory. One is punishment. Psychologists use the word punishment to mean a consequence that comes after a behavior, that reduces the probability that the person will repeat the behavior. If someone finds that a certain action lands him in prison for a few years, according to this reasoning, he's less likely to repeat the crime when he gets out. But other people point out that prisoners tend to learn from each other more effective ways of committing crimes, and that any cruelty they experience and see while in prison increases rather than decreases the chance of cruel behavior when they are released.

A second justification for imprisonment is deterrence for other people. That is, when people see that someone who commits an armed robbery goes to prison for a long time, they learn from that and are less likely to commit an armed robbery themselves. It's hard to measure how much deterrence works. Some people argue that people don't rationally weigh the long term consequences of actions very well, and this keeps deterrence from being effective.

A third justification for imprisonment is rehabilitation. If we want this goal, we try to teach prisoners the skills that allow them to be mentally healthy people: to be kind to themselves and kind to other people. People would teach them skills of functioning in a job, of getting along with people, of resisting drug addiction, and so forth. Such teaching would be carried out not just by "book learning," but also by trying to arrange positive practice in real life.

The critics of this point of view would say, "Unfortunately, many people just can't or won't learn what we want them to learn. Our rehabilitation methods just aren't powerful enough to change people as much as we might like."

Other people might respond: "This is partly because we haven't really tried what we know about behavior change. What if we made almost all the rewards that prisoners get, contingent upon participating in rehabilitation activities? What if those activities included daily reading or watching of models of kind, mentally healthy behaviors, daily fantasy rehearsals of those behaviors, and daily opportunities to practice kind acts toward others and be reinforced for doing so? What if the activities included daily instruction, practice, and reinforcement of work skills, going up a gradual hierarchy toward more complex or difficult skills, keeping the instruction at the correct level of difficulty for the prisoner?"

Other people might respond: "This is a very expensive undertaking. Why should we devote all this effort toward prisoners when we don't educate very well the kids who are probably much more receptive, when they're in school?" To this, others might respond, "We waste huge amounts of time and energy on other pursuits. Educating children and educating prisoners are both worthwhile, and if we devoted a fraction of the energy we devote to violent entertainment and guns and armies to these endeavors, we'd have time left over."

A fourth justification for imprisonment is protection of the public. According to this point of view, the one thing we know about imprisonment is that people who are locked up securely are not dangerous to people outside the prison, at least as long as they are locked up, and this is the main purpose that imprisonment can serve. But this goal, and the goal of rehabilitation, do not make it necessary or desirable to be cruel to prisoners. In fact, creating an atmosphere of kindness and respect as much as possible makes both rehabilitation more likely to work and long-term residence for protection of the public much easier to administer.

The prison industry is a very big one in the USA -- a much higher fraction of people are imprisoned than in some other countries. In 2023, about 2 million US people were in prison. Thus figuring out what prisons are supposed to accomplish and how best to accomplish those goals is an important question. An even more important question is how to improve education, child-rearing, economic conditions, cultural influences, and other aspects of society so as to make the need for imprisonment drastically less than it is today.

Responses to mistakes with the four R's: responsibility, restitution, redecision, rehearsal

When we make mistakes and behave badly or wrongly, one option is self-punishment -- telling ourselves what a bad person we are, how bad our mistake was, how we deserve to feel bad, maybe even physically hurting ourselves. And when other people behavior badly or wrongly, an option is punishing them, trying to make them feel bad.

But here's an alternative set of responses to mistaken or wrong behavior, called the 4 R's. Let's imagine that the wrong behavior is that I have yelled disrespectful and insulting things to a family member.

1. Responsibility. The first step is acknowledging, to myself and possibly to the other person, "I made a mistake. I was wrong. I take responsibility for this -- I don't blame anyone else. I didn't do a good enough job of deciding and choosing." This is a step that many people can't take. They can't ever admit to making a mistake. But we all make bad

decisions at times, and being able to admit this to yourself and sometimes to others is a crucial skill.

2. Restitution. This means trying to render some benefit to the other person, to make up for the harm that one has done. Examples might be not only sitting down with the family member and apologizing for one's disrespectful talk, but also trying to do kind deeds and respectful speech to that family member for a long time afterwards.

3. Redecision. This means pondering and answering the question, "What do I wish I had done instead? What do I want to do next time such a situation comes up?" If I've spoken disrespectfully, I might imagine ways of speaking respectfully in just the situation that triggered me in the past. Sometimes redecision takes a fair amount of time and effort and perhaps doing some research or getting some advice.

4. Rehearsal. This means practicing the type of behavior that I "redecided" upon. I can practice in imagination, encountering situations like the one that provoked me, and imagine myself responding in the ways that are in keeping with my values. I can perform many, many fantasy rehearsals. I can do real-life rehearsals whenever I get the chance.

The 4 R's put the emphasis on making things better rather than on revenge or punishment or anger or self-blame.

Quality control for goods and services.

Suppose that you run a company that makes pulse oximeters. A pulse oximeter is a little device you put on your fingertip, that shines a beam of light through your finger. From how much light gets absorbed on the way through, this amazing little device can tell you whether your blood has enough oxygen in it. It can also give you a readout of your heart rate, also known as your pulse rate. Suppose the engineers who work for your company figure out a way of making the little devices very cheaply. You can sell them for much less than your competitors sell theirs, and still make a profit.

But before you get too excited about how much money you're going to make, there's one more question you need to ask: how accurately do the pulse oximeters we are starting to produce give their numbers? Suppose you test 100 of them against a different oximeter that you know works really well. Uh oh! You find that 25 of them in a very short time produce numbers that are incorrect!

Figuring out the rate of defects in what you are producing, or how good what you are delivering is, is the job called quality control. People who are involved in quality control don't just test for defects. They also try to figure out how to improve the production processes to make the rate of defects as low as it can get. Maybe this involves doing some checking at every step along the way. Maybe this involves substituting a more reliable machine for a less reliable one. Maybe it involves training the workers better, or testing to make sure the workers know how to do their jobs. It might involve looking very carefully at the things that customers return because they don't work well, to figure out what went wrong with them. The quality control department works with other departments to try to get the very best product that your company can produce.

How do you do quality control with a service rather than with a physical object that is produced? For example, how do you do quality control with teaching, or psychotherapy, or being a doctor? It's much more difficult to measure how good the service is than it is to see whether a pulse oximeter works correctly. People can ask students, "How good was your teacher in this course?" They probably give high ratings to teachers who gave them good grades. They may be more likely to give high ratings to teachers who are funny, or who are particularly attractive. But these aren't the best measures of whether the teacher did the job right. Suppose you test the students after the course, to see whether they learned what you wanted them to learn. Now it turns out that the teachers who get the best results are those who had the best and most successful students enrolled in their course; the ones who work with the more challenged students get deemed less good teachers, and that's not right. The job of figuring out how good a job the teacher did is not simple. Sometimes in service jobs, employers do quality control by asking the employees to keep records of what happened and make computer entries for what they did; the way they do quality control is to see whether the person made all their computer entries on time.

I've spoken about how quality control is a difficult job, especially in industries that provide services rather than manufacture objects. But we are very dependent upon the goods and services that other people furnish to us, so it's very important that quality control methods be done as well as we can do them. These methods make a lot of difference in having the goods and services that we buy actually be worth what we paid for them.

"Torts": good for society when not overdone

Suppose that someone advertises a university where you can learn just what you need to learn to get rich. You have to pay a good bit to go there, but the return is claimed to be very great, and the people who run it produce lots of testimonials from people who graduated and then made lots of money. So you sign up. But the courses turn out to be totally useless, taught by incompetent people who cancel most of the classes. And you find out that the testimonials you read from people about how the teaching helped them were all fake! You realize that you have been cheated out of a lot of money. So you go to court and file a lawsuit, and try to get the organization to give you your money back, plus more to make up for the trouble you went through. This lawsuit, where you are telling the court, "This person should pay me money," is called a tort.

Here's another example. You get an operation from a doctor, but the doctor is drunk at the time of the operation, and leaves a piece of sponge inside your belly, which causes an infection. You have to get a lot of costly medical care to correct the mistake. You sue the doctor to pay you for the mistake. This again is a tort.

The idea of torts is to make life more fair than it would otherwise be. Lawsuits of this sort are meant to hold people responsible for doing harm to other people's bodies, their property, or their bank accounts. Torts also give a strong incentive for quality control -- people don't want to get sued because of defective goods and services, so they work to make them as high quality as they can get them to be.

It's possible for a society to make it too easy for people to sue each other for damages. People can get so scared of being sued that good things don't happen. For example, an organization provides free tutoring to children. The people who run a school district are invited to refer people for the free service. But they so afraid that something bad will happen in the tutoring and that they will get sued, that they don't take advantage of the services the organization offers. Lots of children do lots worse than they would have, because of the fear of lawsuits.

So one of the tasks of a good society is to make torts easy enough that people get paid what they deserve when other people damage them, but not so easy that people are discouraged from doing good things because of the fear of lawsuits.

We tend to become what we admire

In another section we spoke about modeling and imitation learning -- the fact that one of the main reasons we do things is that we see other people doing them. There are various factors that make us more likely to imitate someone. When the person's actions bring success in getting what the person wanted, and something we also want, we're more likely to imitate. When the person appears generally powerful, we're more likely to imitate. When we see the person as being like us, that too makes us more likely to imitate.

And not surprisingly, when we admire the person, when we consider the person one of our heroes, we're more likely to imitate. Is there someone we want to have a picture of on our wall, or a little statue of? We'd better be careful in picking who we want to be our heroes, because we tend to become like those people.

I often think that it's better to revere specific heroic behaviors that people have done rather than the person, because for every hero, it seems that if you dig deep enough into the information about that person, you will find some behavior that is not admirable. People are human, and they make mistakes. Even people who do extremely admirable things sometimes have done very regrettable things also. In fact, some people are spurred to good behaviors out of a wish to undo or make up for some of the bad things they've done in the past.

But people tend to admire people and not behaviors. They tend to remember the positive behaviors of their heroes and overlook the bad behaviors.

At any rate, the big idea is that when we cultivate strong admiration for positive behaviors that people have done, that seems to help us do things like those positive behaviors.

Choose your enemies carefully -- you will come to resemble them

We've just said that we tend to imitate our heroes. But another worldly-wise saying is also true: "Choose your enemies carefully, for you will come to resemble them." Why would we come to resemble our enemies? Because when people do harmful things to us, there's a very human tendency to retaliate in just the same way. When someone makes up an insulting nickname for us, we might tend to make up one for them. When another country spies on us, we are motivate to spy on them. When someone gives speeches criticizing us, we tend to give speeches criticizing the person back. When the person starts a fist-fight with us, we tend to fight back in the same way. If a country blows up apartment buildings filled with our innocent citizens, we tend to do the same to innocent citizens of their country.

If we think about it, our enemies are the last people we want to become like. Perhaps if we think about this, we can figure out ways of avoiding the human tendency to sink to the level of those who would harm us.

Of course, the old saying I quoted is a joke in at least one way -- we usually don't and can't consciously choose whom we want to be enemies with. But at times we do: there are times when the choice point is whether to enter into full scale conflict or whether just to ignore a provocation and go on our way.

The tool-using animal versus the clutterer

One of the amazing things about being a human being is the tools that we invent to enable us to cope with the world. Backhoes, cranes, cement trucks, scaffolds and others allow us to build buildings we would find extremely difficult to build otherwise. Computers, cell phones, cars, thermometers, airplanes, can openers, electric lights, radios, stethoscopes, x-ray machines, saws, shovels, even cups, plates, pencils and papers -- we could go on and on naming objects we've invented to help us reach our goals and to make life better.

But we have gotten so efficient at manufacturing things that many of us have a problem called clutter. We think, "Here's something that will be nice to own. I can afford it." And with online shopping, a few clicks later it's ready to be packed up and shipped to us. But we acquire more and more things until they start getting in the way. They tend to wind up all over the floor. There gets to be so many of them that we have trouble finding any of them. They make it hard to clean up, because they are taking up space on all the surfaces we would want to clean. They make a mess. And they can be hard to sell or even give away, in a society that values making new things rather than repairing old things and making them last. So too much stuff can get to be a problem.

So the big idea here is that tools are great, but we have to watch out that we don't get so many that we make life worse off rather than better!

Joint utility versus individual utility: the prisoner's dilemma

Let's imagine a little story in which there are two people who are taken into custody and questioned because they resemble the people who performed a crime. The police take them into separate rooms for questioning. The police want to give them an incentive to give information about the crime. They tell each person: "We're going to ask each of you if the other person committed the crime. If you say the other did it, and they say you didn't do it, you go free and get several thousand dollars in expenses as a witness. If you say the other did it, and they say you did it, you both go to jail for a year. If you say the other didn't do it and they say you did, you go to jail for 5 years. If you say the other didn't do it and they say you didn't do it, you both go free."

The person thinks, "Let's see. If the other person rats on me, then I get 5 years if I don't rat on them, and only 1 year if I do. So in that case I'm better off saying that they did it. Now suppose the other person denies that I did it. If I don't say that they did it, I just go free; if I do rat on them,

I go free plus I get the money. So again I'm better off telling on them. So either way, I'm better off telling on them."

Because I like happy endings to stories, I'm going to make this one turn out that the two people were really innocent, and despite the above, both people refused to betray the other. But can you see how if they were purely trying to maximize their own self-interest, they both would have told on the other, and both would have gone to prison? And can you see that because they both chose an option that didn't maximize their self-interest, the two of them as a group were much better off than if they had made the other choice?

Situations like this have been called "the prisoner's dilemma." There are good numbers of situations like this that come up in life, where if people can trust each other, they can make things much better off for the two of them than if they can't trust each other and are both looking after their self-interest. Here's a big one. Suppose there are two countries (and to keep the story simple, they are isolated from all other countries). If one makes weapons and the other doesn't, the one that doesn't can get conquered at any time by the other. If both make weapons, they both are scared to use them on each other, but they waste tremendous amounts of money and labor on the weapons, and they also are very nervous that a war could still start by mistake. If both choose not to make weapons, all the money and labor that went into the weapons industry can be used to teach psychological skills and big ideas to people and make society better! So again, if they can trust, they come out ahead; if they can't, they both take a hit but not as big a hit as if they trusted and the other proved untrustworthy.

As difficult as it seems for people to play the "trust" option in the prisoner's dilemma situation, think of what life would be like if no one ever played that option. You go out walking and you see another human being. Because there is so little trust, everyone carries a gun. If you trust that the other person won't shoot, and they don't trust you and think you will shoot them, and shoot you first to protect themselves, you probably die. If they trust you and you don't trust them, they die but you are OK (in this unpleasant world, shootings are always thought to be in self-defense). If you both mistrust each other, you each shoot at each other, but at least you have a chance of shooting first and surviving. So maximizing your own welfare in the absence of any trust makes every person your enemy and makes you the enemy of each other person. Isn't it nice that life isn't like this, and we can usually trust our fellow human beings not to shoot us out of fear that if they don't, we might shoot them first?

Here's one more example. You and another person each run a business that makes the same product. If you are very careful not to pollute the environment, and spend money on this goal, you have to charge higher prices. If you choose not to pollute and the other saves money by polluting, they undercut your prices and drive you out of business. If you choose to pollute and they choose not to, you can undercut them and make a lot more money. If you both choose not to pollute, you can both do business. If you both can't trust the other and you both choose to pollute, you can both stay in business but the environment gradually gets poisoned.

Experimenters have gotten pairs of people to play the prisoner's dilemma game, using money. "If you both choose 'trust,' you both get a dollar. If one trusts and the other chooses 'mistrust," the one that chose mistrust gets $1.50 and the trusting one gets nothing. And if both of you choose 'mistrust,' you both get 25 cents." Again, no matter what the other person chooses, I get more by choosing "mistrust." (If the other chooses trust, I get $1.50 rather than $1 by mistrust. If the other chooses mistrust, I get 25 cents versus nothing by choosing mistrust.) But the two of us as a team get more from the experimenter if we both choose "trust." (The team gets $2 if both trust, $1.50 for a trust and a mistrust, and $0.50 for both mistrust.)

There's been lots of research on the question, what strategy for the prisoner's dilemma seems to bring out the most cooperation? The answer seems to be a fairly simple one called "cooperate, and then tit for tat." That is: you pick the trusting option on the first round, and then you play the same thing that your partner did on the previous round. So you reward your partner on the next move for being nice, and you punish your partner on the next round for being selfish.

The "tit for tat" strategy is usually researched under conditions where the partners can't or don't speak to one another. What if they can say things like, "Hey, we'll get more total payoff if we both play the trusting option. How about we make a deal: I'll do the trusting option on the next round if you promise that you will too. How about it?" Being able to talk and make promises, and (hopefully) keep them results in a lot higher payoff!

Another alternative to the "tit for tat" strategy is "I'm going to find someone else to play with." If someone is

185

regularly untrustworthy and selfish, very often it's possible not to take on the job of punishing them for their behavior, but just to avoid them and associate with other people instead.

Once I had pairs of people play the prisoner's dilemma game in which I told them that they were on a team, and I wanted to see which team could get the most total points. We kept track of how many total points each team got, not how much each individual got. What do you think happened? People chose the "trust" option much more frequently than without the "team" instructions.

This whole line of thinking has a lot to do with cooperation and collaboration versus competition, doesn't it? And with being in the same boat rather than being enemies with all other tribes? Figuring out how to get nations to trust enough to stop wasting trillions of dollars on weapons and warfare is perhaps the biggest challenge facing the human species.

Reading to remind versus reading for new learning

What's the purpose of reading? There is more than one purpose. Sometimes we read for pure entertainment. Sometimes we read to learn something useful or that we're curious about. The subject of this big idea is that sometimes we read to remind ourselves of things we already know, or to inspire ourselves to enact principles that we've already decide we want to enact, or to remind us to imagine ourselves behaving as we would like to behave. Reading as reminding is a very under-rated activity, one that probably has the capacity to improve life greatly, particularly if one makes very wise choices as to what to repeatedly remind oneself of!

Preservation of self and species as basic instincts

There are some things that we want because we have learned to want them. For example, people learn that certain types of clothes are more stylish than others. But other things most of us seem to have an instinct for. The word *instinct* refers to things we want because of a module in the brain that is built in. Two things that we (and all other animals) seem usually to want by instinct are "self-preservation and preservation of the species." Self-preservation means the wish to stay alive, and preservation of the species means the wish to have or raise children to keep the species from dying out, or at least to have the sexual activity that leads to children.

We have spoken about the big idea of evolution. Suppose that there was a species of animal that had either: no desire to stay alive, or no desire to create another generation. That species would die out fairly soon, wouldn't it? So the animal species that are still on the planet have been selected to have these two instincts.

These instincts of course don't mean that every single member of the species has these wishes. Many people decide, for example, that they don't have the energy or money to support children or the right partner. Some very correctly observe that the human species does not need them to have offspring in order for the species to be preserved -- there are probably too many of us human beings on the earth now for our own good and for the good of other animal species.

Categories of disease

There are lots of things that can go wrong with our bodies (including our brains), and cause illness or inability to function. When there are symptoms that bother us, a major task is to make a diagnosis -- to figure out what the cause of the symptoms is, in hopes that there is a treatment that we have learned will relieve the symptoms for that diagnosis. In thinking about possible diagnoses, it's helpful to think of different groups of illnesses. Some of these follow.

Toxic: If people take in too much lead, mercury, arsenic, or various other poisonous substances, these can cause illness.

Traumatic: These are the illnesses that occur from injury, for example getting hit in the head or getting a broken leg. We also speak of psychological trauma, the very bad things that happen to people that create lasting problems. Post-traumatic stress disorder is the name given to bad psychological and physical effects of having bad things happen to us.

Infectious: These are illnesses caused by viruses, bacteria, worms, or other parasites that invade our bodies. COVID, malaria, strep throat, roundworm infections, tuberculosis, and many others are examples.

Neoplastic (cancer): These are illnesses caused by certain types of cells growing uncontrollably in our bodies, and interfering with what the other cells are supposed to be doing.

Nutritional: These are illnesses caused by getting too little or too much of certain food components. Vitamin deficiencies or caloric excesses are examples.

Congenital and hereditary: These are illnesses caused by genes we've inherited or something that happened in very early life that created a condition we were born with. Some of these don't become apparent until later on in life.

Endocrine: These involve too much or too little activity of the hormones of our bodies.

Vascular: These are problems with the heart or blood vessels. Strokes and heart attacks are examples.

Immune: These include illnesses caused by the immune system attacking our own cells. Type 1 diabetes, multiple sclerosis, lupus, rheumatoid arthritis, and a certain type of thyroid illness are examples. A good number of diseases which formerly were of "unknown cause" are now known to fall into this category of autoimmune diseases. Another type of problem in the immune system is allergies: the immune response to a certain substance is so vigorous as to cause problems, sometimes even death.

Cause unknown: There are some illnesses about which much is known, but much remains to be found out regarding causes. Alzheimer's disease, Parkinson's disease, schizophrenia, sarcoidosis, and certain types of high blood pressure are examples. As research progress is made, the category of "cause unknown" diseases is shrinking. Maybe by the time you read this, the diseases I gave as examples will no longer be in this category!

Drug withdrawal

There are many drugs, particularly among those that affect the brain and nervous system, that do the opposite when they are wearing off from what they do when they are coming or staying on board. When stopping taking a drug creates bad effects, we call those withdrawal effects. Alcohol is a sedative drug, meaning that it tends to reduce the activity of the brain (although sometimes it reduces the activity of the parts that would make us think twice about what to do, and results in more impulsive behavior). Withdrawal from alcohol can result in overactive brain cells with a possibility for seizures, hallucinations, elevated blood pressure, and sometimes death. Over-the-counter medicines like Advil and Tylenol tend to lessen or get rid of headaches, but the withdrawal from these can cause headaches. The serotonin reuptake inhibitor drugs like Prozac and Zoloft tend to reduce anxiety, depression, and irritability, but the withdrawal from these drugs can result in a very great increase in those three symptoms. Opiate drugs such as morphine, heroin, oxycodone, and fentanyl are taken by many people because they produce good feelings, but the withdrawal is very unpleasant and drives people to desperate measures to get more drug. Marijuana also can have very unpleasant withdrawal symptoms. Drugs given to prevent epileptic seizures can cause seizures if people withdraw from them too quickly. The antipsychotic drugs, which are used to treat "psychotic" symptoms such as getting false ideas in the brain and believing them despite evidence, and seeing and hearing things that aren't there, have been known to cause those symptoms when the drugs are withdrawn.

The reason for withdrawal effects is that the nerve and brain cells adjust when a drug changes something; they seem built to resist changes, but to compensate by trying to make the opposite of the change the drug is making. The adjustment that they make sticks around when the drug is withdrawn and thus produces the opposite effects that the drug had on the cells.

This doesn't mean that people should never take a drug that affects the brain. But people should usually think carefully and gather reliable information before starting to use a drug that affects the brain. They should get very thoroughly informed before going off the drug, about how slowly the dose should be reduced before stopping it altogether. Ideally, there should be a plan for how to stop the drug, before the drug is even started.

Reinforcement (or pleasure) is central to addiction

Drug addiction is a huge problem. Alcohol, opiates, marijuana, cocaine, and other drugs can provide people short term pleasure, or relief from displeasure, that they don't get elsewhere. They start wasting lots of time and energy seeking the drug and using the drug. The drug often interferes with their ability to think straight and act responsibly while it is on board, and often causes very unpleasant or dangerous withdrawal effects when it is no longer on board. The rewards one experiences from taking the drug become so much more important to the person than the rewards of cultivating good relationships and doing good work and taking care of oneself, that these more worthy goals get neglected. If the addicted person runs out of money, the desire for drugs can lead the person to steal money to get the next "fix" of drug. For these reasons, using any of the drugs of addiction, even with the idea of only doing so a little bit, is not something I recommend!

What is it that makes a drug addictive? At one time the prevailing idea was that unpleasant withdrawal effects were the major factor. It's true that if a drug has very unpleasant withdrawal effects, the motivation to get it when one runs out is very high. But there are drugs with unpleasant withdrawal effects that don't have nearly the bad consequences of most of the drugs of abuse. For example, some of the antidepressant drugs, the serotonin reuptake inhibitors, can have very unpleasant withdrawal effects. The same is true for some of the drugs used for epileptic seizures. The big idea that people gradually came to is that the drugs that seem to get people in the most trouble are those that produce a rapid onset of pleasure. Our brains are designed to seek pleasure and avoid pain, and the drugs that go straight to the pleasure mechanisms seem to cause us the most trouble with addiction.

I mentioned elsewhere that at one time people actually put up posters with the slogan, "If it feels good, do it." With respect to drug-taking, the opposite slogan is probably closer to the wisest: "If it feels good [immediately], don't do it!"

Junk food as analogous to addictive drugs?

Can certain foods be addictive? I remember someone's jokingly saying that she thought that Girl Scout Thin Mint cookies should be designated as a "controlled substance," in the same category as certain drugs that can lead to addiction. It is true that when people go on binges of overeating, they tend to choose foods with lots of sugar, fat, and/or salt -- cookies, ice cream, candy, cheeseburgers, french fries, soda pop, cake, pie, pancakes with lots of syrup and butter on them, potato chips, steaks rippled with fat, and so forth. On the other hand, if what people have in their kitchens and available are beans, onions, kale, squash, spinach, lettuce, tomatoes, oats, and so forth, they probably tend not to overeat and get very overweight. If we lived in a world where food was scarce, going for the the most pleasurable food and eating all we can hold would probably be the best strategy. But in a world where overeating is such a common problem, avoiding or limiting the foods that, like addictive drugs, give us a strong jolt of pleasure, is unfortunately a good idea.

Foods like stews made from beans and kale and tomatoes and so forth can be very pleasurable to eat, provided that: you are hungry. As someone said, "Hunger is the best sauce." These healthy foods tend not to be very pleasurable when you are not hungry. The more junky foods I listed earlier, by contrast, tend to be very pleasurable whether you are hungry or not. Can you get the same total pleasure from eating, by waiting until you are hungry and eating "healthy food" that is seasoned with the "best sauce?" It's hard to know the answer to this, partly because we don't have a good pleasure-o-meter that totals up the pleasure we feel. But my guess is that it's possible to get lots of pleasure from eating healthy foods seasoned by hunger, that may compete with the pleasure from eating junk foods without that best sauce.

Effort-payoff connection, a.k.a. contingent reinforcement, as central to happiness

"It doesn't matter what I do -- nothing changes. So what's the point of trying?" This is a thought pattern that is very depressing. If the thought is correct, there is no connection between efforts that you put out, and the things you are wanting to happen. Your efforts have no effect. In such a state, people feel helpless.

The opposite of this occurs when you believe that your efforts can make things better in some way. When this is the case, there is an "effort-payoff connection." Even when things are going badly, if you believe that there are things you can do to make things better, you are much less likely to go into the "I give up" sort of depressed state. Having an effort-payoff connection not only tends to prevent depression, but also promotes feelings of happiness and meaningfulness. We want something, we think we know how to get it or at least make it more likely, and we are doing the things we think will pay off -- this is central to human happiness.

An effort-payoff connection appears to be central to the happiness of our non-human animal brethren. People who study zoo animals find that if animals such as tigers just get their meals dumped in front of them, without their having to do anything to get them, the tigers look depressed, don't want to produce baby tigers, and otherwise give signs of being unhappy. But if the zoo personnel rig up ways that the tiger has to chase and catch something or figure out how to get somewhere or otherwise put out effort to get their food, the tiger seems to be a much happier animal.

What is the reason why millions of people spend thousands of hours on video games? The programmers of these games are experts at setting up effort-payoff connections. Imagine a game programmed so that you accomplished the goal of the game without even doing anything. No one would want to play it. Or imagine a game where no matter what you did, you lost the game as soon as you started playing. In both of these situations, there is no effort-payoff connection. But if the challenges you face are in the right level of difficulty and the efforts you put out can pay off, the game becomes fun.

The effort-payoff connection depends on two things: the external environment that you are in, and the way you think about things. If someone is in a class in school where the work is so far over his head that he doesn't have a chance of learning, understanding, or succeeding, the nature of that class is preventing the effort-payoff connection. If someone is in a class where the work is at the right level of difficulty, but the person strongly believes, "I'll never use this, it makes no difference whether I pass or fail, whether I learn it or not," then the person's thought patterns are getting in the way of an effort-payoff connection. Even if someone is imprisoned and there is nothing the person can do to make the environment better, if the person thinks, "I'm going to plan out a book that I want to publish if I'm released. I want to make progress on these plans every day," then the person has a chance of creating an effort-payoff connection even so. (Victor Frankl, whom I mentioned earlier, did this while imprisoned in a concentration camp.)

Many of the payoffs involved in the effort-payoff connection are the type that we deliver to ourselves, in the form of celebratory thoughts. "Hooray, I made some more progress in planning out my book!" could be the types of thoughts that help our fictitious prisoner to have an effort-payoff connection. "Yay, I did well on the test! My studying and practice really helped me!" could be the types of thoughts that help a student have an effort-payoff connection. Of course, it's much easier to celebrate bits of progress toward goals if we have goals in the first place; this is one of the reasons why goals are so important. And "worthy" goals, that is, the type that really make a contribution to the happiness of oneself and/or others, are the type that make the effort-payoff connection more lasting or attainable. If I'm correct on this, having goals of being very physically fit, cultivating very positive relationships, getting skilled at reading, writing, and math, or learning to be successful in a workplace, may create more lasting states of effort-payoff connection than "Let's see what happens with one more video game." What do you think?

Focus on future, present, and past – all good!

The big idea of this section is that thinking about the past, the present, and the future are all quite useful. We've spoken earlier about how very useful and important it is to think of our goals, which are the things we want to happen in the future. When we make decisions, a crucial part of the process is predicting the consequences of the various options, and of course, these consequences happen in the future. It's also very useful to learn from the past. Past experience, of ourselves or others, is all we have to go on when we make predictions of what will happen with different options. People of course can worry too much about what will happen in the future, and they can get down on themselves or blame others too much for things that happened in the past. But these are reasons to think about the future and the past in more constructive ways, not to ignore them. The word "mindfulness" has been used to refer to directing attention to what is happening in the present, particularly with an observing spirit and not a criticizing or disapproving one. Noticing what is happening in the "here and now" has been a helpful way to direct the attention for many people. One of the great things about our minds is that there is plenty of opportunity for learning from the past, being aware of the present, and planning and deciding for the future -- we can focus on all of these at different times, with great benefit. There is no reason to try to shut out thought about any of these. (This big idea is in disagreement with some gurus who preach that you should focus only on the present, or the "here and now.")

Behaviors that create good relationships

We've discussed earlier the idea that happiness is greatly influenced by the quality of relationships. Those who get along well with friends and family members -- those who very much like and are liked by the others -- tend to be happier people.

What behaviors do people do that create good relationships? A fairly short list, I think, can cover the bases fairly well!

1. They are kind to one another. This means they each do things they hope will make the other one happy.

2. They do "mutually gratifying activities" together. This means that they do things together that they both enjoy, that both get pleasure from. Mutually gratifying activities are more likely if the two people have some overlap in what they think is fun and good, what their values and goals are. If members of a couple both feel that raising one or more children is a very important thing to do, they are much more likely to enjoy doing this job together than if one values the goal and the other doesn't. If

two people both find a lot of meaning from working for peace and nonviolence, they are more likely to have enjoyable times together doing these things than if one is into peace and nonviolence and the other is into guns and warfare.

Mutually gratifying activities are all made more pleasant if the two people enjoy chatting with each other.

3. They make "joint decisions" well. This means that they communicate well together to make good decisions on the types of plans that will affect both of them. This includes good conflict-resolution: handling well the situation where one person is incline to want one thing to happen and the other is inclined to want something else. This implies that they do not yell at each other, insult, threaten, hit, shove, etc. It also implies that they don't get too bossy or controlling with the other person.

4. They are honest with each other.

5. They spend enough time with each other to keep up the relationship.

We could go on, and list a lot more behaviors, but if these five things are going on in a relationship, the chances are good that it's the type of relationship that tends to increase happiness and mental health.

Avoiding standard bad decisions.

Other big ideas have discussed the expected utility formula as an aid to making decisions, and SOIL ADDLE as a mnemonic for steps in making good decisions. But if people can just avoid making any of a standard list of bad decisions, they are probably ahead of the game relative to most of humanity.

There are exceptions to each of these. But to a first approximation, these are good rules.

1. Don't use violence.

2. Don't use addictive drugs (including alcohol).

3. Don't create a pregnancy without planning very carefully first.

4. Don't do dishonest or illegal things, including stealing, cheating people out of money, and lying; don't do things you need to lie to cover up.

5. Don't neglect your own education in favor of other activities (e.g. video games)

6. When you have a job, don't be satisfied doing anything less than a very high quality job.

7. Don't neglect reading and studying how to do better whatever job you have.

8. Don't drive too fast, too recklessly, or under influence of drugs, and don't ride with anyone else who does any of those.

9. Don't spend as much money as you earn. In other words, save or invest a portion of the money you earn.

10. Don't become part of a couple with someone who has bad anger control problems, uses abusive language to you or other people, or is physically violent.

11. Don't gain a lot of fat tissue without reexamining your diet and exercise habits, but don't try to get to an unhealthy level of thinness either.

13. Don't neglect medical care for conditions that could be dangerous; don't neglect routine checkups.

14. Don't invest all, or nearly all, your money in one investment.

15. Don't marry someone you don't know very well.

16. Don't marry someone with the intention of changing them for the better or the hope that they will change for the better.

17. Don't waste your time.

18. Don't be afraid to try to make connections and friendships with other people; don't neglect the good friendships you already have.

19. Don't give yourself unnecessary exposures to infectious diseases (including sexually transmitted diseases)

20. Don't commit yourself to more responsibilities than you have time and energy for. (This includes, but is not limited to, job tasks, children, pets....)

Kindness versus "enabling" and creating entitlement

One of the big ideas that has come up several times is the desirability of kindness -- of doing the sorts of actions that make someone else happy, that meet their needs or wishes. However, sometimes doing what people want us to do is not good for us (because it demands too big a sacrifice) and/or not good for them (because it interferes with their being able to take care of themselves well, or tolerate frustration well).

Here are some examples. A man is so drunk in the morning that he can't go to work. His wife calls his employer and makes an excuse for him to help him avoid consequences for doing what he did. Another time, he is so drunk that he wrecks a car. She dips into the money she's earned, to buy a new car. The problem with examples like these is that sometimes people need to experience the bad consequences of their bad behaviors, so they can learn not to do those bad things. When someone protects someone from the bad consequences of bad behaviors, that has been called "enabling" the bad behavior.

Here's another example. A child orders a caretaker, "Get me this thing to eat." When the caretaker gets it, the child says, "No, not that type. Get this other type." If the caretaker continues letting the child act like a tyrant and continues acting like the child's servant, the child gets the idea that this is how life is supposed to work. The child is getting a bad lesson in how to get along with people and what to expect and not to expect from people.

When people get what they want from other people, they tend to think that they "deserve" what they are getting, or that the other person "should" continue to give it to them, or that they are "entitled" to keep getting it. Being "too entitled" is a big problem for some people. "Too entitled" is a more gentle way of talking about this, whereas saying, "The person is a spoiled brat" is more insulting. No matter how it's expressed, the fact is that sometimes giving people what they want constitutes "overindulging" them and is not good for them.

Appointmentology

Someone said, "80% of life consists of showing up." Many, perhaps most, of the important things we do involve keeping a promise to be somewhere at a certain time. If you have a job, it's very likely that you're expected to start work at a certain place and a certain time. Do you see a doctor, a dentist, an accountant, a car repair person, or anyone else whom you want to do something for you? Chances are that things begin with your making and keeping an appointment. Do you want to cultivate a relationship with someone? Chances are that very soon, you'll plan to meet the person at a certain time and a certain place. (The "places" for appointments these days can be online locations or answering a phone call!)

Some people are in the habit of being "no-shows" for appointments. They promise to meet someone, but they don't. And many of them think very little of this, that it's not a big deal. But the people who are not good at keeping appointments tend not to be as successful in life. They tend to lead other people to the conclusion that their promises can't be trusted. They tend to be rejected from relationships and fired from jobs.

Two of the major ways to get good at "appointmentology" are to have a place where you write down appointments, and to get into the habit of checking frequently to see what appointments you have. Another important appointmentology rule is that about the only way to avoid being late for an appointment is to plan to be early (you will hardly ever be exactly on time). If something comes up that means you have to cancel an appointment, do it as far ahead of time as possible. Try to make sure the message gets through, even if you have to call, leave voice mail, text, and email. Apologize when you have to cancel, and especially apologize if you forget an appointment. If you do no-show an appointment, contact the person as soon as possible to apologize and figure out what the revised plan is. Shoot for a very low rate of cancellations ahead of time, and a much lower rate of no-shows. If you have a cell phone, use the alarms on the cell phone to remind you of appointments.

Categories of kind acts

How do people try to make each other happy? If we are wanting to do something kind, what types of kind acts are on the menu? Having a list in mind may make it easier to fantasy rehearse these and to carry them out. Here's a list:

1. Helping. Someone has something they want to do, and you help them do that. For example, you help them harvest the kale from their garden.

2. Teaching. Someone wants to get more knowledgeable or more skilled, and you help the person learn. For example, you teach someone to read better.

3. Having fun with. Doing "mutually gratifying activities" is kind to both oneself and to the other person.

4. Listening. Being a good listener, trying to understand the other person and communicate that understanding, reinforcing the person's telling what's on their mind.

5. Consoling. When the other person feels bad, trying to be sympathetic or helpful or to communicate support.

6. Giving. Giving the person something they need or want or will make them happier.

7. Working on behalf of. For example, doing some work so that the other person will not have to do it. Or doing some work to make money to support the person.

8. Complimenting, congratulating, reinforcing, thanking. Saying, "Thanks for doing that," "I'm happy that you did that," "You do that very proficiently," or other things that convey approval and appreciation for the good things the other person does.

9. Protecting. Doing things that tend to keep the other person from injury, illness, or psychological trauma.

10. Healing. Helping the person to be healthier.

11. Spending time with. Devoting time to being with the other person.

12. Caring for needs, for example feeding, cleaning, helping with transport. This is a special case of helping. You help someone meet their basic needs when they are too young, too old, or too sick to do so themselves.

13. Entertaining. You participate in some type of performance that gives pleasure to the other person or people.

14. Advising. You help the other person to make a good decision. (This can be kind, if you know enough to give good advice, and the other person really wants to hear it. Otherwise, please refer to "listening.")

15. Not spoiling. You make a decision not to do what the other person wants, because you believe that letting the other person handle not getting their way will be best for their own happiness in the long run.

Harmony in music

If you sing a song, with no instrument or no other singers accompanying you, the song is heard one note at a time. If the singer and the song are good enough, this can be all that's needed.

But more often, people take advantage of the fact that it sounds better to have other notes sounding at the same time that the melody notes of the song are. If a person strums a guitar while singing a melody, the notes of the guitar are chosen so as to "harmonize" with the notes in the melody -- that means they sound good together. People speak of "the chords" that go with a song. Chords are combinations of notes that harmonize with each other, that sound good when played at a certain point along with a melody. Sometimes two people sing together, with one of them singing a melody, and the other singing a "harmony part" -- that means the second person is singing notes that sound good when sung with the other notes that are sounding, and make the two parts together sound better than either one of them separately. You can have three or four or sometimes even more parts sung together, in ways that harmonize. There are various rules that predict which notes are going to sound good together, and which are going to sound "discordant" or clashing with one another. Sometimes discordant combinations of notes are used in music to create a feeling that something isn't right; sometimes discordant harmonies are used to create an incomplete feeling that will be "resolved" by a harmony that sounds like "all is well" the way the sounds go together.

One of the most basic forms of harmony is called a triad, a combination of three notes that sound good together. The white key that is in the middle of a piano is the note C, called middle C. The notes on the white keys going from there to the right are D, E, F, G, A, B, and then back to C again. If you play C, E, and G together, you hear how they harmonize. This chord is called C major. Any two of those notes tend to sound good together. But whether the chord sounds good in a song depends on what the rest of the notes in the song are doing. Music theory is an interesting subject, and harmony is a big idea that is dealt with a lot in music theory.

"Stultifying" conditions versus "smartifying" conditions; initiative versus passivity

Let's imagine different workplaces. The type of work could be anything. To pick one that I'm very familiar with, let's imagine the work is to try to help people to become mentally healthier – to be happier, and to be better at helping others to be happier.

Let's imagine workplace A. The main way to be successful in workplace A is to fill out a bunch of forms, without leaving any of the boxes blank, and without being late on getting your forms in. No one really talks about how to do the job better, or what ideas help to do it more successfully. It someone does bring up that topic, people don't really respond one way or another. No one measures how much better people get.

Now let's imagine workplace B. In this workplace, people are frequently talking with each other about how to accomplish the job better. People are measuring the effects of what they do. If something new seems to produce good effects, people are enthusiastic about learning the new idea, and people are enthusiastic about teaching it to one another.

Which workplace do you think will accomplish the most? And which workplace do you think brings out the smartest brain activity from the workers? Workplace B rewards people's doing smart things, and workplace A doesn't.

The word "stultifying" refers to conditions that tend to make us act less smart. They tend to reward us for being passive – for just not making ways, versus for taking initiative – or getting new ideas and trying them out. I don't know of a word in the language that means the opposite of "stultifying," so I use "smartifying."

Schools and families can be stultifying or smartifying. There have been schools where if a student was enthusiastic to talk about ideas in class, the classmates would taunt and belittle that student afterwards. There have been other schools where the students who came up with interesting ideas and explained thing well to other students became admired by their comrades. In some families people hardly converse with one another, but plug into video games upon arriving at home. In others, family members discuss things often, and reinforce one another both for having interesting things to say, and for being good listeners to what others have to say.

Variables

A variable is something we can measure or count that can take on different values -- in other words, it can be different numbers. What's your rating of how happy you feel, right now, on a scale of 0 to 10? This number probably goes up when good things happen and down when bad things happen. It varies over time. You could measure this number over time and get a bunch of different values for the one variable, your happiness rating. Another example is your heart rate. It goes up when you feel nervous or angry, and goes down when you feel calm. It goes up when you exercise, and goes down when you take it easy. Again, you could measure it lots of times, and get lots of values, in the same person, over time.

You could also take a whole classroom of people and measure the heights of each person. For the whole group, the number you get for the variable, "height," would vary from person to person, even though it may not vary for any one person in the short run. Variables can be measured repeatedly in different people, rather than in the same person over time.

Variables don't have to have anything to do with people. If you have a bunch of rock samples, and you measure the hardness of each rock, the hardness is a variable. If you have a bunch of foods and you measure how much sodium is in each one, that's a variable. When you measure the temperature outside in one place repeatedly, or measure the temperature of various cities at any given time, temperature is a variable.

We can have variables for which we don't actually measure or count to get the numbers -- we just imagine the variables taking on different values. For example, if we imagine that $y = 2x$, we are imagining two variables, called y and x. Whatever x is, y is twice that much. If x is 5, y is 10. If x is 1, y is 2. And so forth.

Goldilocks variables

There is a story called Goldilocks and the Three Bears. In it, a girl named Goldilocks goes into the house of the three bears and helps herself to different parts of the bears' property -- their oatmeal, their chairs, their beds. Each of the things that she takes comes in a set of three, where one is too much of something, one is too little of something, and one is just right. For example, one bed is too hard, one is too soft, and one is just right. (For those of you who haven't heard the story and don't mind a "spoiler," it ends up with Goldilocks being awakened to find the three bears gazing at her in the bed, and her running off, presumably escaping without being prosecuted for her trespassing and petty larceny.)

The hardness of the bed is an example of what has come to be called a Goldilocks variable. If the hardness is too much or too little, the bed is uncomfortable, but at a certain level for any person, it feels just right. Many of the variables we think about in life are the same way. We want not too much or too little, but just the right amount.

Here are some examples: When you speak, it's good for the loudness to be not too much, not too little, but in the middle. So loudness is a Goldilocks variable. When someone drives a car, they shouldn't go 95 miles an hour, but they usually shouldn't poke along at 5 miles an hour -- driving speed is a Goldilocks variable. Some people have said, "It's impossible to be too thin." That is totally wrong -- people have died from starving themselves in an effort to make themselves too thin. It's good to have an amount of fat on our bodies that is not too much nor too little, but somewhere in the right range for the person. If the temperature of a place is either too high or too low, the place gets to be a dangerous place for us humans; temperature is a Goldilocks variable for us. (This is why we have thermostats that are usually set for temperatures in the 60's or low 70's Farenheit.)

Other Goldilocks variables: how much work we do in a day; how much we relax or play in a day; how much water to drink in a day; how much to sleep per night; how much exercise to get in a day; how many layers of clothes to put on given a certain temperature when we go outside; how hard to come down on someone when the person has done something we don't like; what fraction of our incomes we should save; how many times a day we should wash our hands; how long we should talk in a conversation when it is our turn; how entitled we should feel that other people should care about us and be nice to us; how much we should feel inclined to take risks versus play it safe; how much we should get dependent on any one person for our happiness; how hard or easy the challenges should be that we give a student to practice with when we are teaching that student; how much responsibility any given person should take on. You can probably think of lots more.

Goldilocks variables are important because a lot of the important decisions of our lives involve figuring out the right place to be, with respect to Goldilocks variables!

Statistical distributions

We've said that a variable is something that can take on different values, for example in one individual over time, or in lots of different individuals at one time. The distribution of the variable is an account of what values the variable took on, and how frequently it took on each value.

For example: Suppose I know 5 people. I rate each one of them on a scale of 0 to 10, according to how nice they are. Here are my ratings:

1 person gets a rating of 3
2 people get a rating of 7
2 people get a rating of 8

That's the "distribution" for the "niceness" variable among the 5 people I've met!

Here's another example:

Someone measures the speeds of a bunch of cars on a highway (where the speed limit is 55). The person takes

210

100 measurements. (We're going to assume that the speed measurement is so accurate that all the measurements are a little different from the numbers that are the boundaries for the categories below.) Suppose that this is what they find:

Speed	Number going that speed
Under 40 miles/hour:	0
Over 40, under 45 miles/hour:	1
45-50 miles/hour	4
50-55 miles/hour	18
55-60 miles/hour	25
60-65 miles/hour	20
65-70 miles/hour	10
70-75 miles/hour	8
75-80 miles/hour	6
80-85 miles/hour	6
85-90 miles/hour	2
Over 90 miles/hour	0

This table would describe the "distribution" of the speeds that the person found!

We can take data like that in the tables above and use it to make a graph that gives a picture of the distribution. Such a picture is called a histogram. You have a bar for each interval of values; the height of the bar pictures how often values in that range were found.

Correlation and causation

What do we mean by saying that two variables are positively correlated? We mean that when we observe both variables for a good number of cases, we find that when one is higher, the other tends to be higher too. If we look at a bunch of people, weight is positively correlated with height – taller people tend to weigh more. If we look at a bunch of students, those who study more tend to make higher grades – study time is positively correlated with grade point average. If we look at a bunch of basketball players of different ages, the ones with the higher shoe sizes tend to be better at basketball (because the ones with the bigger shoe sizes tend to be older and taller). If we look at a bunch of people, the more they have smoked cigarettes, the more likely they are to get lung cancer.

Finding that two variables are positively correlated does not mean that increasing one of them *causes* the other to increase. If we take some adults and lead them to gain weight, we don't cause them to grow taller. If we take some kids and put bigger shoes on them, that doesn't cause them to play basketball better.

However, sometimes the reason two variables are correlated is that one causes the other. Smoking cigarettes really does cause lung cancer, and studying more really does cause people to do better in school.

It's a lot easier to notice that two variables are correlated than to prove that one causes the other. All we have to do to document correlation is to collect a bunch of cases where we measure both variables and do some calculations on how they are related to each other. But proving a causal relationship is most convincingly done by a study where some cases are randomly assigned to get something done to them and others are not. But sometimes we can't do that, or it isn't ethical to do so. (For example, it wouldn't be right to randomly assign some people to get hit in the head lots of times to see if this causes them problems with thinking and emotion.)

A negative correlation means that the more one variable goes up, the more the other tends to go down. For example, the more exercise one gets per day, the lower the amount of body fat the person tends to have. The higher the person's positive emotional climate in their family is, the lower their depression score tends to be.

A zero correlation means that knowing one variable doesn't help you at all in predicting the second. The number of hostile acts per day during the month of October in a certain high school in New York is probably correlated about zero with the rainfall that day in a town in Ecuador. How long someone lives is probably correlated about zero with the day of the month in which they were born.

Central tendency and variability

Suppose we measure one variable for a bunch of different cases. For example, we measure the heights of a bunch of different 5th graders. Or we measure the time it takes to run a mile, for a bunch of high school students. Or we measure the yearly income of a bunch of different families.

There are two things we might want to know right away about the distribution of the variable. One is, what is the "central tendency." This has to do with what the typical case is like. One way of answering this question is to compute the average, or mean – to add up all the scores and divide by the number of them. The answer gives you a number, so that if everyone in the sample had that value, the sample would have the same total score that it actually has in real life. Another way of answering the "central tendency" question is to look for the median score. This a number such that half the numbers in our sample are above that, and half are below that. It's a number right in the middle of the numbers we found.

Another thing we might want to know is the variability of the numbers we found. One way of answering the "how variable" question is just to state the largest and smallest value that's in the sample. But this measure just depends on two values. A different way of communicating the variability is by averaging, in some way, how far away the different values are from the mean score. The "standard deviation" is a measure that does this. The variability is also called the "spread" for the group of numbers – how spread out they are.

Another way of communicating the central tendency and the variability of a bunch of numbers is to tell which number is at the 25th and the 75th percentile. For the number at the 25th percentile, 25% of the numbers are lower; for the number at the 75th percentile, 75% of the numbers are lower. The higher those numbers are, the higher is the central tendency; the farther apart they are, the greater is the variability or spread. For example, suppose there's a test for which the scores can fall on a scale from 0 to 36. For one college the 25th and 75th percentles are 31 and 35; for a second one those percentiles are 19 and 27. The scores for the second college are lower in their central tendency and more spread out.

Maslow's hierarchy of needs

What motivates people? What do they want? What are they trying to get, by doing the things they do?

One of the most well-known answers to this question was proposed by psychologist Abraham Maslow, in the mid twentiethy century. Maslow originally proposed

5 sets of needs; later on, he expanded the list to 8. Here are the 8 sets of needs that made up the revised list.

1. Physiological and biological needs. Examples are the need for air, water, food, being not too hot or too cold, being able to sleep.
2. Safety needs. Examples are freedom from violence, protection from accidents or disasters, not being lost, not being poisoned.
3. Needs to belong, to be included, to be loved. Examples are being accepted as a member of a family, a friend group, a couple, a social network.
4. Needs for esteem. These are the desires to be admired, looked up to, approved of, both by other people and by oneself.
5. Cognitive needs. These include wishes to find out things, to learn, to understand, to satisfy curiosity.
6. Aesthetic needs. These involve a wish to perform, create, or appreciate the beautiful in life: music, art, literature, nature, dance, any of the arts, the beauty of the universe.
7. Self-actualization. This means becoming all that you can become, growing as a person, achieving personal growth, realizing your potential.
8. Transcendence. This has to do with values that go beyond yourself, to humanity or the planet; altruism, or the wish to make others happy without expecting anything in return, is probably an example of this. The wish to create a better world for future generations is probably another example.

The same behavior can be motivated by the wish for different needs. For example, a doctor performs an operation. If she needs the money to buy food, her motive is physiological. If she wants money to live in a nonviolent neighborhood, the motive is safety. If she wants to cement her place in a group of doctors, her motive is belonging. If she wants to prove to herself or others that she is competent and smart, the motive is esteem. If she has been curious about the best way to treat a certain condition and is operating as part of an experiment, her motive is cognitive or curiosity. If she gets pleasure from the artistry of an operation well performed, her motive is aesthetic. If she is motivated by a wish not only to be the best surgeon, but also the best person she can become, her motive is self-actualization. And if she is not focused on herself at all, but is thinking about the welfare of the person she is helping, she is meeting transcendence needs.

The word *hierarchy* refers to an ordering of the needs on the list, so that some are more urgent than others. The original idea was that the needs lower on the list have to be fulfilled before you can free yourself to move up to the next level. The more Maslow observed, the less rigid he felt the order of needs was. We sometimes, perhaps often, see people motivated by needs higher on the list at the expense of those lower on the list. For example, someone altruistically risks their life to save a stranger. Or people do dangerous or painful things to get acceptance by a group. But the notion of hierarchy with needs still is valid to some extent. If you can't breathe, it is much higher priority to get to where you can breathe than to make people like you. If you think people are going to hurt or kill you, it's usually of much higher priority to get away from them than to figure out the answer to the intellectual problem you may have been working on.

Stabilizing feedback loops, for example the thermostat

Here's how a thermostat works in winter. You have a heater that can be turned on and off. The thermostat has a thermometer in it that measures the temperature in the room. You make a setting with the thermostat that tells what temperature you want the room to be. When the temperature gets higher than that, the thermostat shuts off the heater. When the temperature gets lower than that, the thermostat turns the heater back on. So the thermostat makes the heater come off and on in a way that keeps the temperature of the room close to the temperature at which you set it.

The thermostat uses a stabilizing feedback loop, sometimes called a negative feedback loop. The signals from the thermostat increase the heat from the heater (an effect of positive direction); the heater increases the temperature in the room (positive direction) but a higher temperature in the room *decreases* the signals from the thermostat to the heater (a negative direction). The loop has one effect of negative direction between the variables in it, and this makes it tend to keep something steady and unchanging. A feedback loop of this sort has been called a "deviation reducing" one -- the thermostat reduces to a low number the deviation of the temperature from the one the thermostat is set at.

Suppose there were nothing but effects of positive direction. Let's imagine a defective thermostat where the higher the temperature got, the more the thermostat would tell the heater to generate more heat. The more heat gets generated, the hotter the room gets, and the more strongly the thermostat fires up the heater. The room would just keep getting hotter and hotter. This type of feedback loop has been called a "vicious cycle" if we don't like the results, or a "virtuous cycle" if we do like them. The loop is a "deviation amplifying" loop -- it makes a certain variable get farther and farther from where it started.

Here's an example of a vicious cycle. Someone gets behind in learning to read. This makes the reading tasks at school more unpleasant. The unpleasant feelings about reading make the person avoid reading. The avoidance of reading makes the person more behind.

Here's an example of a virtuous cycle. Someone has lots of unwanted and unrealistic fears. The person learns to use fantasy rehearsal to reduce one of the fears. This increases the person's confidence, and it also gives them practice in the skills of fear reduction. These make it easier to reduce the next fear.

Our bodies use all sorts of thermostat-like feedback loops, to keep all sorts of things in just the right range – not too high or too low. Several glands sense the levels of certain hormones and release more hormone if the level is too low and shut off production and release if the level is too high. There are sensors in our brain that test for the amount of carbon dioxide in our blood, and tell us to breathe faster if there is too much, and to breathe slower if there is too little. And our bodies have actual thermostats in them, to keep the temperature of our bodies at just the right level. When we haven't slept enough, our sleep-o-stat makes us sleepy; when we've slept enough, it tends to wake us up. When we haven't drunk enough water, we get thirsty; when we've drunk enough water, the thirst drive turns off.

Awareness of emotions, and "feeling words"

Sometimes we're happy, sometimes sad, sometimes angry, sometimes proud – we experience different feelings, different emotions. The big idea of this section is that it's useful to be aware of our own emotions, and those of other people, and that words for emotions are useful to have in our vocabularies.

What is an emotion, anyway? I think it's more useful to think of emotions as things that we "do" than as things we "have." Fear, anger, love, joy – all of these are ways of doing something with our brains and the rest of our bodies. Many psychologists have considered emotions to be a class of behavior.

Why did we evolve the capacity to feel emotions? One reason is that they are signals to us that give us clues about how to react to what's going on in our lives. If we feel joyous, that's a signal that we're in a good situation. If we feel angry, that's a clue that someone is doing something we need to oppose. If we feel scared, that's a clue that we need to protect ourselves from danger. Feeling guilty clues us to examine our own actions and apologize for doing something bad or stop doing it. And so forth. All these clues can from time to time be incorrect! We can feel scared when we're not in any danger at all. We can feel angry when no one has done anything bad to us. But the feelings give us very important signals to consider something or another.

Here's another reason why we evolved emotions: trying to get good feelings, and to avoid bad feelings, gives us a reason to do what we do! If we were built to feel exactly the same, no matter what happened, it's hard to figure how we would get motivated to do anything. (Some people consider the word "motivated" itself as a feeling word.)

Why is it good to be aware of how other people are feeling? Because this gives us very important clues about how to act toward them. If we've been talking for a good while about something interesting to us, but we notice that the person we're talking to seems impatient and bored, that gives us a clue about what to do: stop talking! If we see someone who appears bewildered and confused and worried, we might want to offer help. If someone seems to greatly enjoy what we're doing or saying, we get a clue to do that more. Again, the clues we get can be incorrect, but they are lots better than no clues at all.

People have made various lists of feeling words. You can find lots of them on the Internet. Here's a list I made, that is not the longest, and also not the shortest. The big idea is that the acts of asking yourself, "Which of these am I feeling?" and "Which is this other person feeling?" are often useful.

List of Feeling Words

Usually pleasant feelings: accepted, appreciative, amused, awed, attracted, calm, cheerful, compassionate, curious, close, confident, contented, elated, excited, free, friendly, fun, glad, glowing, grateful, happy, hopeful, interested, jolly, joyful, lighthearted, liking, love, moved, playful, pleasant, pleased, proud, relaxed, relieved, satisfied, self-assured, serene, silly, slaphappy, sympathetic, tenderness, thankful, tickled, wonder

Usually unpleasant feelings: afraid, angry, annoyed, ashamed, bitter, bored, bothered, burdened, disdainful, drained, brokenhearted, confused, impatient, disappointed, disgusted, displeased, disturbed, embarrassed, energized, envious, startled, fearful, frazzled, frightened, frustrated, guilty, harried, hate, hopeless, horrified, hurt, impatient, irritated, jealous, lonely, low, mad, mortified, pain, rage, regret, resentment, sad, scared, self-critical, shocked, terrified, threatened, tormented, troubled, uncomfortable, uneasy, unfriendly, unpleasant, upset, worried

Could be pleasant or unpleasant: amazed, astonished, bewildered, concerned, flabbergasted, indifferent, excited, pity, worn out, suspicious, stirred.

Perspective taking.

We've mentioned that it's useful to be able to figure out some good guesses about what other people are feeling. It's also good to understand what they are wanting, what their thoughts are, what they're likely to do, and in general, what it's like to be them. When we do these things, we are trying to see life from the point of view, or perspective, of the other person. The skill of putting yourself in someone else's place and making some fairly accurate guesses about what life is like for them is called perspective taking. It's also called having empathy for the other person.

It seems reasonable to guess that people who are better at understanding other people's points of view would be less hostile and violent toward other people, and indeed, some research tends to confirm this idea.

In a book called *The Better Angels of Our Nature*, the author looked for the things that might have made societies become less violent over time. One theory is that reading stories tends to exercise our minds in the skill of perspective-taking: we put ourselves in the place of the characters, and we enjoy the story more, the more we can do this. Songs, poems, movies, and other works of art can challenge us to understand someone else's perspective. It could be that such experiences tend to make us less violent. It probably also helps if any of the characters we admire, model for us kindness, forgiveness, rational solution of conflicts, and other nonviolence-related skills.

Degradability of waste

Let's suppose there is a piece of paper that gets dumped into the ocean. It's not good to have trash paper in the ocean, but there's a consolation. Paper is mainly made out of the elements carbon, hydrogen, and oxygen. Bacteria and other "decomposers" go to work on the paper, and eventually it gets broken down into substances that can be used by plants and animals – things like carbon dioxide and water. We say that paper is "biodegradable."

Now let's suppose that someone dumps something into the ocean that has mercury or lead in it – say a car battery, with lead in it, or some fumes from burning of coal, with mercury in them. Lead and mercury are poisonous to people's bodies. How long will it take before the mercury and lead break down into something that can be used well by animals and plants? The answer is pretty close to "forever." Mercury and lead are elements, and they are broken down as far as they can get. They can be concentrated into a small space or diluted into a bigger one, but they don't break down into anything else.

Some plastics can be broken down into simple compounds, and some of them just get dispersed into tiny particles of chemicals that get into the bodies of animals, including humans. Scientists are still trying to figure out how harmful this is – there's evidence for various types of harm.

For this reason, it's very desirable that when people make things, they make them out of things that can be degraded down into elements and compounds that are friendly to life. This is an area where government regulations are a useful addition to the "free market." The fewer things we make, that we will eventually try to "throw away," that are not degradable into life-friendly elements and compounds, the better!

Nonviolent resistance

Lots of wars have been fought, and lots of people have lost their lives, because one group of people wanted to control and govern, or be in the same country with, another group, but the second group wanted to govern themselves. The US war for independence was fought for this reason, and tens of thousands of people died. The US civil war also was fought for this reason, and several hundred thousand people died.

But in the middle of the twentieth century, India, under the leadership of Mohandas K. Gandhi, became independent of Britain, ending about 200 years of British rule, without fighting a war. Some Indian people were killed, but even so, Gandhi preached nonviolence.

Independence was won with many, many fewer people hurt or killed than in wars of independence.

How did they do it? Under Gandhi's leadership, the people in India remained nonviolent, but they simply refused to accept and abide by the rules that the British imposed upon them. For example, there was a tax the British had imposed upon salt, and Indians were prohibited by law from making their own salt, for example from ocean water. The British ran many clothing factories in India, with Indian workers. The Indians simply stopped cooperating with all this. They held public demonstrations of their unified wish for independence. Some were imprisoned and some were killed or injured, but their nonviolence in response made them look more admirable in the eyes of the world, and the violent acts against them looked more undesirable. Independence was won, without a war.

Gandhi was a big influence on Martin Luther King, who mobilized African American people to use nonviolent civil disobedience to oppose US laws that made them second class citizens. They held marches and sit-ins and resisted laws that said they were not allowed to eat at certain places or ride in certain seats on a bus. Some people were hurt and some were killed in the whole struggle. But the nonviolent strategy eventually paid off in a major way.

Some recent research has looked at many examples of nonviolent resistance and has concluded that it works better than violent struggle. Of course, it tends to work better if the group you are resisting has some semblance of conscience, or even a wish to be seen as decent human beings. If the people being resisted possess neither of these, and there's no one else to influence them in the right direction, they can just gun down the nonviolent resisters and go on about their business. But fortunately, there are very important exceptions to the condition of authorities without conscience or shame! The growth of nonviolent strategies for resolving conflicts is one of the major advances of human society.

Acidity and alkalinity

Some substances are strong acids, and others are strong alkalis, otherwise known as strong bases. Both of them are not good to get on your skin, and especially important not to get in your eyes. If you take an acid and mix it with a base, in the right amount, you can get a substance that is neither acidic or basic, but "neutral." What's going on with these?

The water molecule is composed of two hydrogen atoms connected onto one oxygen atom. A very small fraction of water molecules (about one in 10 million) split apart into a hydrogen ion (with a positive electrical charge) and a hydroxide ion (with a negative electrical charge; the hydroxide ion has one oxygen but only one hydrogen attached to it). The two types of ions that water can split into are called $H+$ for hydrogen ions, and $OH-$ for hydroxide ions. (Hydrogen ions tend to connect up with water molecules to form what's called a hydronium ion, $H30+$.)

The hydrogen ions or hydronium ions, as well as the hydroxide ions, tend to be very reactive with other substances, including the substances that make up our bodies. But in pure water, the number of these ions is so small that they make no difference.

However, some substances, when dissolved in water, result in lots of hydrogen/hydronium ions being present. Hydrochloric acid, for example, whose chemical formula is HCl, splits into a hydrogen ion and a chloride ion for each molecule. When all those hydrogen ions become available to react with our skin, they can burn it. Sodium hydroxide, whose chemical formula is NaOH, splits into a sodium ion and a hydroxide ion. The hydroxide ions are very reactive.

But what happens if you mix a solution of HCl, hydrochloric acid, with a solution of sodium hydroxide, NaOH, measured so that there are approximately equal numbers of molecules of each? The hydrogen ions and the hydroxide ions join up with each other to make more water. The sodium and chloride ions keep floating around in the solution, to make salt water. So the strong acid and the strong base have made a solution of salt, that is neither acidic nor basic!

There's lots more that can be learned about acids and bases, but what was said in the paragraphs above will give you the "basic" idea (as well as the "acidic" one).

Logical fallacies

Some of the ways that lots of people think are not really logical -- they lead to mistakes. People have made up various lists of "logical fallacies." They've also spoken about sources of "bias" in our thinking. Here are some of them.

Ad hominem reasoning. We discussed this one in a separate section. Ad hominem is Latin for "against the person." Someone says something you disagree with, and you argue against it by insulting the person who made the statement.

Bandwagon. This is something like, "All sorts of people are hurrying to do this, so you should do it too!"

After this, because of this. For example: "When I used that pen, I did well on the test. Therefore I should always use that pen if I want to do well on a test."

The sunk cost error. Keeping on doing something you think it a bad decision, because you've already sunk money or something else to be able to do it. For example: "Starting this war was a mistake. But if we stop fighting now, the lives that have been lost will be in vain." For another example: "I don't like this movie. If it were a free movie, I'd walk out. But since I spent a lot of money to see it, I need to stay and not waste the money."

Overgeneralization: For example: "A man with a beard and a foreign accent stole money from me. So I should stay away from all men with beards and foreign accents -- they're all dangerous."

Appeal to ignorance: For example: "Nobody has ever disproved the idea that when we die, we go to a different dimension where we get born again as dragons. Because there's no evidence against it, it must be true."

Authority: For example: "The president says that we should go to war. Therefore it must be true."

Straw man: Making up a proposition that is easy to argue against, even if no one is really arguing for it. For example: "My opponent in this election wants to reduce gun violence. Do you want people showing up at your house at all hours of the day and night to search all your drawers and look for guns? If not, vote for me! (The opponent didn't propose what this candidate is opposing.)

Appeal to tradition: For example, "My grandfather played football, and so did my father. I'm proud to have played football right on this field, and to have heard the same fight song every game. And now somebody says that football hurts your brain?"

Correlation equals causation: For example: "Children who live in apartments with roaches in them do worse on achievement tests. Therefore using more pesticides to get rid of roaches should raise achievement test scores." (It could be that roaches in the apartment don't cause low achievement, but that they are a marker for poverty, which comes with all sorts of other factors that might cause low achievement.)

For a second example: "Shoe size is very much correlated with skill in basketball. Therefore, if we give bigger shoes to the fifth grade girls' basketball team, they'll win more games." (Probably shoe size is a marker for height, which is what is really helping with basketball achievement.)

Confirmation bias: We get convinced of a certain opinion, and then we look for facts that back up that opinion, and ignore or discount the facts that do not support it.

All or none thinking: Otherwise known as black and white thinking, we ignore the shades of grey. For example, if someone told one thing that isn't true, the person can never be trusted for anything for the rest of life. If I made a mistake in how I acted with someone, I'm no good at getting long with people and will never be worth people's friendship. If someone I meet is nice and attractive, that person can do no wrong. When that person acts grumpy and irritable, oops I was wrong, the person is a horrible person.

Emotional reasoning. This is judging some person or circumstance based on emotions that do not give accurate information about the person or situation. For example, I conclude that someone I'm interviewing is not a good person for the job, because I feel bad during the interview (when I happened to have a headache that started before the interview). For another example, I feel guilty, and I conclude that I must have done something really bad. I feel hopeless, and I conclude that there is no way to solve the problem I have.

Mind reading. This is thinking that you know what someone else is thinking, when you don't have enough evidence. For example, someone sees some people laughing, and one of them gives a quick glance at him. He concludes that they are laughing at him.

One option only. Someone has a decision to make. The person gets in mind an option for what to do, and stops thinking about any other possibilities. The person does not benefit from "brainstorming options" so that the person can try to pick the best one.

The compound probability error. Suppose people hear a story of a young woman who went to a very liberal college and studied sociology. Then they are asked to guess the probabilities of different circumstances that the young woman might be experiencing now. Suppose they guess that the probability that she's a bank teller is 3%. But then they guess about the probability that she is a bank teller who is active in the movement for women's liberation, and they rate that scenario as more likely, 6%.

This couldn't be right, could it? The set of bank tellers who are also into women's liberation can't have more members than the set of bank tellers, can it? The probability that both of two things are true has to be less than or equal to the probability that either one of them alone is true. But even doctors have made the compound probability error when thinking about how likely certain physical conditions are.

The wisdom in proverbs

People have made up lots of one-sentence summaries of wisdom, known as proverbs. It's good to take in and make use of this wisdom.

Don't bite off more than you can chew.

Many proverbs make use of symbolism. They refer to some concrete example, but they are trying to communicate and idea that is much more abstract. For example, "Don't bite off more than you can chew," does mean, don't fill your mouth so full of food that you can't chew it and end up choking on it or spitting it out. But it means much more than that. It means don't sign up for so many college courses that you end up doing poorly, or stressing yourself too much. It means don't accept a promotion to a job that you don't know how to do well enough. It means don't volunteer for so many things that you don't have time to do any of them well. It means don't host a party and invite a lot of people when you don't know how to do it up right. It means don't commit yourself to a very long hike when you're not in good enough physical condition. The proverb has to do with the abstract idea: take only those challenges that your skill levels and resources have prepared you for, where there is a reasonable chance of success.

You can't have your cake and eat it too.

When we have some good food, we can either save it, or eat it. But each of those options has a disadvantage. If we save it, we don't get to enjoy it and be nourished by it. If we eat it, we don't have it any more. So there's no way to avoid both of those disadvantages -- we have to put up with one or the other of them.

The abstract meaning of this proverb applies to all sorts of other choices -- nearly all options have at least one disadvantage. When we choose, we usually can't avoid all disadvantages. There's a high paying job, but it's very stressful. There's a safe neighborhood to live in, but it's more expensive. It will be fun putting on a performance, but it will also make me nervous. Often we have to choose the better option, even though it is not a perfect one.

An ounce of prevention is worth a pound of cure. And: A stitch in time saves nine.

Both of these proverbs mean, don't wait until a problem has gotten really bad, before you do something to solve it. If we can teach children to be nonviolent starting when they are very young, we save all sorts of money and misery that comes if we wait till they are violent criminals to do anything constructive. If we get vaccinations, we save lots of suffering that would come if we waited until we got sick to to anything. If we have a seam in our clothes that is starting to come apart, we can fix it with very few stitches of thread, whereas if we wait until the tear gets really big, we need lots more stitches (approximately 10 times as many, if the proverb is correct!)

Don't judge a book by its cover.

This refers to books, but the more abstract meaning refers to anything that has both an appearance and some sort of worth that is more important than the appearance. For example, regarding people: the proverb means, don't decide whether a person is a worthwhile, good person, worthy of hiring or marrying or befriending or lending money to, just on the basis of how good-looking they are. If we're buying a house, it's nice if it looks pretty from the curb, but we want to make sure on the inside, the plumbing works, lead paint isn't peeling off, and water doesn't flood the place every time it rains. A college may have a very pretty campus, but not be at all right for the student in other ways.

It's better to light a candle than to curse the darkness.

The abstract meaning is, if there's a problem, it's better to try to solve it than just to complain about it. For example, rather than just complaining about the residents of an apartment being lonely and isolated, someone invites them to a get-together. Rather than just complaining about how hot it is, someone wets their clothes and sits in front of an electric fan. Rather than just complaining about how someone left a piece of litter in the hallway, someone picks it up and throws it away.

Don't put all your eggs into one basket.

This proverb is about having a "diversified portfolio." It means don't risk everything on the success or failure of just one venture. It means don't risk all your money on just one investment that could fail. But suppose you risk money on a bunch of different investments, each of which has a good chance of success, despite some chance of failure. Also suppose the investments are different enough so that it's very unlikely that all of them would fail. Then you are probably being a wise investor. The proverb has to do with things other than money. If you invest all your chance of happiness in a relationship with one person, and think, "You're my everything, I can't live without you, you're the reason I'm living," (which are sentiments often found in popular songs), then you're very vulnerable if that relationship goes sour or if the person dies. On the other hand, if you have several different friends that you like and feel supported by, you still won't like losing a special relationship, but it won't be as devastating.

Practice makes perfect.

It's an exaggeration to say that by practicing, you become perfect at something. But practicing is a great way to get better at it. If people spent more time practicing the skills that are really important to get better at, the world would be much improved.

Sometimes people alter this to say, "Only perfect practice makes perfect." This isn't really correct either -- for example, everyone who puts on a "perfect" piano performance has probably played the song imperfectly plenty of times while practicing. But there's some truth in the saying, nonetheless: if you practice performing a song, over and over, but each time you are doing it incorrectly (let's say without the right rhythm, or off pitch) then you are just getting yourself deeper into a bad habit that you'll have to undo if you want to perform the song well. If you practice handwriting, but you're making the letters incorrectly or illegibly, you make be making your handwriting worse, not better.

Practice what you preach.

It's so easy for people to give good advice to others. "Don't eat much sugar. Get lots of exercise. Write down your important goals and work toward them daily. Go to bed and get up at a regular time. Don't raise your voice in anger at anyone. Always tell the truth, and don't deceive people. Don't cheat on your spouse. Save a good part of all the money you make...." Lots of people "preach" these ideas. If those people aren't following this self-discipline oriented advice themselves, people can legitimately think that they should "practice what they preach." People who preach what rules other people should follow, while trying to hide the fact that they break those rules themselves, tend to be called "hypocrites."

A proverb that means almost the same thing is, "Doctor, heal yourself." It's not very inspiring to hear advice from a doctor to stop smoking, lose weight, and get exercise, when you're pretty sure the doctor doesn't do those things.

Rome was not built in a day.

The concrete meaning of this is that it took a long time, much more than a day, for a bunch of folks to build the city of Rome, Italy, centuries ago. (The same thing can be said more recently about Rome, Georgia, Rome, New York, and several other Romes, but these cities are not what the proverb-makers were thinking of!) The abstract meaning is that almost any big or important goal takes a lot of time and patience to achieve. You don't get to be an expert guitar player, a doctor, head of a useful business, or expert psychotherapist in a short time. The world doesn't solve the problem of global climate change, warfare, extinction of animal species, or crime in a short time. A very long time of working at it very steadily and vigorously is how most big goals get achieved.

A journey of a thousand miles begins with a single step.

This proverb goes along nicely with the previous one. Sometimes when there's a big goal, and people realize how much time and work it requires, it's hard for them to get started. But this proverb reminds us that for every big goal, it's important to just go ahead and start. By taking that first step, and then continuing steadily with more and more bits of progress, the goal may eventually be achieved.

Two wrongs don't make a right.

Suppose that neighbor #1 plays a lot of loud music some night when neighbor #2 is trying to get to sleep. Neighbor #2 has to get up early to go to work, so it makes him really mad that his sleep is disturbed. So the next morning, neighbor #2 gets up early for work, and blasts loud music right in the direction of neighbor #1, who at this time is sleeping in after his night of partying.

When neighbor #2 tells his wise mother about what he's done, his mother points out, "Two wrongs don't make a right." She's making the point that getting revenge usually doesn't solve the problem. She might also say to her son, "Did you ever think about asking him politely to turn it down?"

Look before you leap.

The concrete meaning is that if you are leaping into a lake, or leaping into a hole, be careful! Look first to see what you might land on. If you could get hurt, don't take the leap. Many people have been seriously injured or killed by jumping or diving into water that had rocks or a fallen tree invisible below the surface.

The abstract meaning is before you do anything that might be risky, investigate to see how big the risk is. Before you take a long hike, look to see whether a heat wave is coming in during the time you would be out. Before you become a football player, look up the statistics on CTE (chronic traumatic encephalopathy), the brain disorder that can come from getting hit in the head too many times. Before you get married, find out all you can about the person you're thinking of marrying. Before you have a child, find out all that you would have to do to raise that child right, and figure out whether you will have the time, money, and ability to do those things.

The pen is mightier than the sword.

The concrete meaning of this one is not true if we judge "might" by who wins in combat. Suppose two guys go into a fight with one another, and one has a sharp sword, and the other just has a ball point pen. All other things equal, we would advise the one with the pen to wear his running shoes and scoot away from this competition as fast as possible.

But the abstract meaning is that by writing about things and persuading people with your words, you can often accomplish more than by just fighting for it.

Back in the early 1500's a professor of "moral theology" named Martin Luther had some complaints about how the Catholic Church was doing things. He wrote something called "95 Theses" which were a list of arguments against some things the church was doing. This got things started in ways that ended up with the formation of the Protestant Churches. People are not sure that this is what Luther originally wanted. But the point is, he had a "mightier" effect by writing than he would have, say, by going over and challenging the pope, the head of the Catholic Church, to a fist-fight or a sword fight!

In 1852, a woman named Harriet Beecher Stowe published a book called *Uncle Tom's Cabin*, which influenced many people to end slavery and to act humanely toward former slaves. Her pen made a mighty contribution to the ending of slavery in the USA.

Birds of a feather flock together.

The concrete meaning is that birds in a flock are usually of the same species -- they look pretty much alike. The more abstract meaning is that people tend to seek out others that they have important things in common with, to be with.

Colleges in the USA are very interested in getting diversity of students -- representatives of different races, different hobbies, different backgrounds. But suppose after all these efforts toward diversity, one walks into the college cafeteria and sees a bunch of black kids sitting together, and a bunch of kids of East Asian descent sitting together, a bunch of athletes or "jocks" sitting together, and a bunch of theater and drama enthusiasts sitting together, and so forth. The observer might say that at least part of the time, "Birds of a feather flock together."

A leopard doesn't change its spots.

The concrete meaning is that a spotted leopard doesn't all of a sudden show up without spots, or with spots of a different color or pattern. The abstract meaning is that people (and other animals) tend to keep doing the behavior patterns that they have been doing.

A young lady is contemplating marrying a guy who has abused alcohol and drugs, stolen things, cheated on girlfriends, and gotten fired from several jobs. He says over and over again that because he loves the woman so much, he is a new man, is putting the past behind him, and from now on out will be a model citizen.

The woman's mom says to her, "I know it feels good to think that you are powerful enough to turn someone's life around. But be careful: you know what they say, that "A leopard doesn't change its spots."

Better safe than sorry.

This proverb simply means, "Be careful." It's better to avoid unwise risks and be safe, than to take them, suffer the consequences, and be sorry.

A ship staying in the harbor is safe, but that's not what ships are for.

Some proverbs have meanings that run counter to other ones. "Better safe than sorry" tells you to avoid unwise risks. But the proverb about the ship in the harbor tells you that you don't get far if you don't take at least some risks. Whenever you go out into the world and take on challenges, there's a risk of failing. Whenever you make efforts to develop a friendship, you run the risk of getting rejected. When you invest money, you can lose it. When you invest time into a project, you run the risk of concluding your time has been wasted.

So we should avoid unwise risks and take on wise risks. How do we tell the difference? By making good estimates of the probabilities of the different consequences of our choice, and good estimates of how good or bad the various consequences are. How do we do that? Well... you gain a lot of knowledge and experience, and try to learn from other people's decisions as well as your own. Making good decisions is an important skill, requiring lots of effort to become expert. But that effort is worth it, because our decisions determine how our lives go!

Don't cry over spilt milk.

The concrete meaning is that if you spill milk, crying about your misfortune doesn't accomplish much. The abstract meaning is that you want not to make yourself too unhappy about the mistakes or misfortunes of the past -- instead you want to make the present and future as good as you can make them.

A therapist I met wrote a book called *Woulda, Shoulda, Coulda*. It was about people's tendency to think, "If only I would have done this. I should have done that. I could have done this, but I neglected to do so," and how they can substitute more constructive thoughts.

One more constructive thought is "Learning from the Experience." For example, "I learned from this that in the future, when I transport milk, I'm going to make sure the top is fastened securely."

Another constructive thought is "Listing Options and Choosing." For example, "I can clean it up with a sponge, with a washrag, with paper towels. I can go to the store to get some milk to replace it. I can grind up some

239

oatmeal in a blender and make oat milk instead.... I think I'll use the washrag and then make the oat milk."

Most general statements aren't true 100% of the time. It may sometimes be useful to think back upon past traumas, even if doing so brings out some tears. This may make more sense when we think about larger tragedies and traumas than a milk spill!

Don't miss the forest for the trees.

The concrete meaning of this one is, you won't be able to appreciate the beauty and magnitude and importance of a whole forest if you focus your attention on the details of one or two or three trees. The abstract meaning is, don't get so wrapped up in the details of something that you overlook the important part of the whole thing.

Suppose someone is reviewing a children's movie. They comment on the quality of the animation; they point out that in one of the songs, the singer was off pitch on a note or two, they talk about how the coloring of one of the characters is not totally consistent from one scene to the next. Someone might say to this reviewer, "You're missing the forest for the trees. The point is, kids love it, and the movie contains good models of behavior from start to finish." The second person is trying to look at the overall effect.

Too many cooks spoil the broth.

The concrete meaning has to do with cooking soup. If you have several people all in charge of the cooking project, it's likely that they will disagree on what should go into it. If they discuss every ingredient and have to vote on each one, they will probably produce a worse soup than

240

they would have if they had just let one person be in charge of the project.

The abstract meaning has to do with all sorts of projects other than soup-making. Running a country, running a business, designing a building, writing a novel, being the doctor in charge of treating a certain problem -- these can benefit from the input of other people, but it's almost always most efficient if there is one person who has the most decision-making power. Otherwise people tend to waste too much time arguing with each other about how it should be done.

Two heads are better than one.

This definitely doesn't refer to a beast with two heads, like a dog in ancient mythology. It refers to the fact that when two (or more) people both put their minds to a project, they can often come up with something far better than any one person could have done on their own. They both bring important ideas to the table, and make their contributions to the final outcome of the project.

But wait -- this wisdom is just the opposite "big idea" from that contained in "Too many cooks spoil the broth."

I think that the answer to this contradiction is that "It depends." If the people involved in the project are able to cooperate, supporting the other person's expertise and contributing their own expertise, keeping their eyes on the goal and not needing to control everything, then two (or more) heads can be much better than one. When the people don't have time to communicate, have different philosophies, have an argumentative streak about ideas at variance with their own, or when the job can be done

241

perfectly well by one person, then it's probably "Too many cooks spoil the broth" time.

When the going gets tough, the tough get going.

This proverb is similar to "It's better to light a candle than to curse the darkness." It means, when there are problems, use your energy to solve them. Don't get immobilized by depression or run away from the problem or escape to drug abuse etc. -- get to work on making things better.

You catch more flies with honey than with vinegar.

The concrete meaning of this is kind of strange, because most of us never form the goal of catching a bunch of flies. Maybe for a biology experiment, or something? The concrete meaning is that flies like sweet stuff, and you'll attract more of them with sweet than sour. But the more abstract meaning is that when you are trying to accomplish something with people, you have more success with kind words (being sweet) than with being hostile and critical (being sour).

You can lead a horse to water, but you can't make him drink.

The concrete meaning of this is clear. Although you may know the horse could use a drink of water, when you take the horse to the nice trough of clean water, the horse may just stand there. Of course, this isn't really about horses. It means that lots of times you can give someone the opportunity for something, but you can't force them to take it. For example, a teacher can make books available, can give explanations, can assign homework, etc. But the teacher can't force the student to read the books, listen to the explanations, or do the homework. As another example, a political party can pick a really wise and good person to be a candidate for an office. But lots of voters may pass up the opportunity to vote for that person, and instead vote for someone who is selfish, dishonest, and not very smart. You can lead those voters to water, but you can't make them drink.

A fool and his money are soon parted.

This means that when unwise people have money, they tend to lose it. Sometimes they gamble it away; sometimes con men swindle it away from them; sometimes they buy a bunch of stuff they don't need; sometimes they lose it in unwise investments.

Even smart people are often parted from their money fairly quickly sometimes. Many people have the ability to be foolish when it comes to wasting or losing money.

Use it or lose it.

This means that if you don't use your skills and abilities, they tend to vanish. For example, someone works very hard to learn to play the piano. Then the person stops playing for years. Sadly, they find that they have to do a lot of work to get their skills back. (However, it probably won't take as much work as it would to learn the piano from no previous experience.) Somebody works out every day, and gets into great shape. But if the person stops working out, out of shape they get! Someone is good at math, but if they don't use those skills for a long time, they tend to lose them. This is the other side of "Practice makes perfect": it's saying that "Practice also keeps you from getting worse."

Waste not, want not. A penny saved is a penny earned.

Both of these proverbs are telling us to be thrifty, to be frugal, not to be wasteful. In "Waste not, want not," the word *want* is used to mean "fail to be able to get the things you need." It's telling us that if we don't waste our time and money, we'll have more money to get what we want if we need it.

The concrete meaning of "A penny saved is a penny earned" is that if you have a penny (or a dollar, or a thousand dollars) because you didn't waste it, that's just as good as having the money because you earned it. Actually, it's better. You have to pay income taxes on the money you earn, but you don't get taxed on "not spending" money. Suppose your income tax rate is 20%. Then $100 dollars saved adds $100 to your net financial worth, whereas $125 earned adds the same amount after 20% of it goes to taxes.

"A penny saved is 1.25 pennies earned (depending on how much tax you are charged)" doesn't quite have the catchy ring to it. That's why people hang on to the original proverb!

I have read advice that you should use 75% of your income for expenses, 15% for investment, and 10% for saving. But it's more complicated than that. If you make a lot of money, you can save and invest a lot more, because you have more left over after paying for the necessities of life. And how much you expect to earn in the future has something to do with it too. Anyway, these proverbs are telling us things like: don't buy a new car when the old one works well; don't buy a bunch of new expensive clothes just because styles change; don't blow money on fancy restaurants; don't get a house that is more than you need; don't waste any money on addictive drugs, don't waste money and time on video games, and so forth!

Measure twice, cut once.

The concrete meaning of this is that when you are doing carpentry work, before you saw a board, you want to make very sure you've measured accurately, so that you are cutting at the right length. Otherwise you might end up with a board that you can't use and have to throw away.

The abstract meaning is that in any project, you save a lot of effort and expense and unpleasantness if you try to plan carefully enough to do the job right the first time, so you don't have to do it over again or spend a lot of time correcting the problems that come from doing a sloppy job the first time.

You have to be careful not to let this idea make you too perfectionistic to even start the project. If you feel that you have to do it perfectly the first time, this can sometimes keep you from doing it at all. And the next proverb has to do with that.

The best is sometimes the enemy of the good.

Suppose I'm writing a section of a book, for example a book on big ideas. Suppose I really go to the extreme on the idea that it should be done right the first time -- and I come to think that it should come out *perfect* the first time. I imagine a sentence to write. But I realize that it's not the best possible sentence. It could be improved in lots of ways. And I don't want to write down an imperfect sentence. I get so critical of any sentence that comes to mind that I reject each option. This is a recipe for not writing anything at all.

So what this proverb means is that trying for the absolute best, right from the start, rather than creating a first draft and improving it and gradually making it better and better, sometimes keeps you from doing something good.

Maybe this is why the previous proverb said, "Measure twice and cut once," rather than "Measure all day and never get around to cutting."

No one is an island.

The original proverb was "No man is an island," but we no longer use the word *man* to refer to human beings in general.

An island is alone, not connected, something that exists unto itself. The proverb is saying that human beings aren't like that -- we're meant to socialize. Another way of putting this is another saying, "Humans are social animals." (This saying at one time also used the word *man* instead.)

I think that this is a little more complicated than these proverbs communicate. Different people have different needs for socialization versus aloneness. In fact, for any given person, there may be an ideal ratio of time spent alone to time spent with someone else; some people like being with others almost all the time; others like being alone almost all the time, and most people are somewhere in the middle. But even the ratio we're talking about is more complicated -- it probably depends a lot on how nice and how much fun the people are whom we get to socialize with. If they are fun, we choose a lot less time alone; it they are mean, we would probably choose a lot more time alone.

These complications aside, this proverb reminds us of a big idea mentioned earlier in this book: if we want to be happy, cultivating good relationships with people is usually one of the most important things we can do to achieve that.

Honesty is the best policy.

This simply means that being honest is a smart way to be. Why should we tell the truth, not cheat, not steal, not make promises and then break them? One reason is that people who do these things almost always eventually get caught. And the consequences of being caught in dishonesty usually include a loss of people's trust for a long time after that, if not permanently. And consequences can also include being fined or imprisoned or fired from one's job or kicked out of one's marriage, and others.

What if you *know* you won't get caught? Even if we imagine that it's possible to be certain about this, being dishonest and getting away with it strengthens the habit of dishonesty, and makes it easier to lie, cheat, or steal again. It's important to keep the precedent of honesty.

A friend in need is a friend indeed.

This means, "Someone who is your friend and sticks by you when you are in need is indeed a true friend." Lots of people are willing to jump on the bandwagon for someone who is totally successful and triumphant. Many of them are acting out of selfish motives, hoping to get something from the relationship -- money, fame, high regard, or just the chance to say "I know ____ (hot-shot person)." But when you are in need and the other person has to sacrifice some to help you out, that's when you get some evidence that the other person isn't purely selfish. (Unless, of course, the person is figuring that you'll soon be out of need and their investment in you will be richly rewarded.)

Variety is the spice of life.

Thyme, rosemary, cinnamon, garlic, turmeric, ginger, and other spices keep food from being bland and uninteresting and monotonous. They make eating more fun. In the same way, doing different activities, meeting different people, going to different places, and being exposed to a variety of ideas, keep life interesting and make it more fun. (This assumes that the activity isn't fighting, the people aren't muggers, the places aren't in a war zone, and the ideas aren't hateful -- just as we assume that the spice isn't a bunch of very hot pepper spilled on ice cream!)

Work expands to fill the time allotted.

This is one proverb where there isn't a separate abstract and concrete meaning. It simply means that if you are given 3 hours to accomplish something, you often can stay busy the whole time; if you'd only had 30 minutes to do it, you (maybe) could have done the job just as well. On the other hand, maybe you do the job lots better in the longer time; maybe you do more of it -- it's not always true that working the shorter amount of time is better. But the proverb simply points out that when we have a longer time that we can do a task, we tend to take longer at it.

Some people get in trouble by applying this reasoning to think that tasks can be done well even if the time allocated to them is way too short. Those people should refer to "Don't bite off more than you can chew," and "Rome wasn't built in a day," rather than to this one.

Time is money.

This proverb, taken literally, is false – time is something very different from money. But what this proverb is getting at is that when you spend time working at a job, you make money. When you waste someone's time, you take away time that they could be earning money. When you waste your own time, you avoid using the time to earn money. The number of hours spent in playing videogames doing other entertaining things with "screens" in the USA represents a staggering amount of money that people could have made in the time spent.

I suppose it would be more accurate to say that time, plus working during that time, plus someone willing to pay you for the work that you do, results in money – if they actually do pay you. But when sentences get cluttered up with qualifications for the sake of accuracy, the proverb department tends to reject them.

The unconscious

Why do we do what we do? This is one of the big questions of psychology. Some of the things we do, we consciously decide to do. We think about what we want, we think of options, we consider the consequences of those options, we make a choice, and we carry out what we've chosen. If anyone asks us why we did what we did, we can explain our reasoning. This is conscious choice.

But a good fraction of what we do seems to bypass that conscious decision making process. When we sit, we tend to shift our weight around so that we don't cut off the blood supply to the skin that is bearing our weight for very long. But most of the time we're not really aware of doing this -- we're thinking about something else, and do this unconsciously. What if you had to make a conscious decision to breathe in and breathe out, each time you did it? Most of our breathing is completely unconscious.

Here's one of my favorite stories about the unconscious. There was a psychology lecturer who sometimes used the phrase "i.e." (which stands for the Latin words for "that is"). The students decided to see if reinforcement influenced the professor. So they counted the frequency with which he said, "i.e." Then they reinforced him for saying it, by nodding and looking interested and writing notes. The frequency with which he said it went way up. Then they went back to normal responding, and the frequencies of "i.e." fell. Then they reinforced him with attention and interest each time he said it, again, and the frequency went back up again. They had demonstrated that they could use reinforcement to change his behavior.

But here's the part that has to do with the unconscious. When they shared these results with him, he was totally unaware of the changing rates of his behavior, or that it was connected with his students' apparent interest. He had somehow calculated so as to bring out attentive behavior from his students, without even realizing he was doing so. This is another piece of evidence that we can make unconscious decisions.

Of course, we can get on shaky ground when we make a theory that someone did something because of a certain unconscious wish, when the person can't confirm or deny that theory. For example, suppose I think that

250

someone is acting angry at me because I remind him of his father, and he is unconsciously wanting to express anger to his father. If the person can't confirm this, it can be hard to get evidence that proves my theory.

But in understanding people, it's good to keep in mind that lots of times, we ourselves don't know exactly why we did something -- our unconscious mind has been doing some calculation that we are not aware of.

Defenses against mental pain

Psychologists who are interested in the unconscious have listed several maneuvers that we tend to do in our minds to make life less painful -- to protect or "defend" ourselves against bad feelings. Most of these come with a price, namely that of distorting reality or ignoring part of it, or somehow losing part of the truth. These defenses are sometimes used automatically or unconsciously, but sometimes people are aware of what they're doing. Let's go through some of the most important defenses.

Projection. In protecting ourselves against acknowledging something about ourselves that might make us ashamed, we convince ourselves that the shameful thing is done by someone else instead. For example, a political candidate who very frequently lies, is running against a candidate named Smedley, and he starts calling him "Lying Smedley."

Denial. There's something that would be painful to acknowledge, so we simply don't let ourselves believe it. For example, someone notices a lump growing in their body. Rather than think, "This is not normal. I need to get this checked out by a doctor," the person denies to herself that the lump is any big deal.

Repression. Something creates an unpleasant memory, so we just forget about it. For example, someone goes through a very traumatic experience of being abused. The person finds that they are unable to remember much about this experience.

Regression. To escape some painful situation, someone acts like they were in an earlier stage of development. For example, when a child's parents try to get him to sleep in his own room like a big boy, he starts using baby talk and sucking his thumb as if to prove that he's still just a little boy.

Rationalization. Someone does something for a reason that might cause shame to admit; they make up a more rational explanation for their behavior. For example, a high school kid hates a classmate because he is trying to take away his girlfriend. But when someone asks why he didn't vote for that classmate in an election, he mentions various ways in which he agrees more with the classmate's opponent.

Displacement: Someone has feelings that would logically be directed toward one person, but those feelings get directed toward someone else. For example, someone has been mistreated by someone at work, and feels like yelling at the boss. But instead, he comes home and yells at his dog. He has "displaced" his angry feelings from boss to dog.

Reaction Formation. The person has some urges that the person would be ashamed of. So instead, the person does things that work in the opposite direction from those urges. For example, the person has negative feelings about a certain racial group; as a defense, the person speaks and makes argument for racial justice and equality.

Sublimation. The person has some urges that are unacceptable. The person channels those urges into more acceptable directions. For example, the person thinks it would be fun to cut people; the person becomes a surgeon and gets money and respect for cutting people proficiently (and not forgetting to sew them back up).

Intellectualization. The person deals with situations that might be horrifying or depressing. But the person defends against those bad feelings by studying the situations in a scholarly way. For example, a psychotherapist hears from clients lots of stories of horrible traumatic experiences in which people were treated cruelly. The person studies the effects of trauma and ways of helping people reduce the ill effects of it, and is able to use problem-solving thinking rather than feeling demoralized or giving up on humanity.

Compartmentalization. The person is able to restrict thinking about certain upsetting situations to a certain time or place, and put it out of the mind otherwise. For example, someone has a job where they have to deal with important high-stakes decisions. But when the person comes home, they put the work decisions out of their mind and concentrate on being with family members.

Suppression. The person has a certain feeling that give them an urge toward unacceptable behavior. But they just don't let themselves do what they have the urge to do. For example, someone sees a stranger that he feels very attracted to. The person has an urge to go up and propose romantic activity with this stranger. But he correctly predicts that the stranger would be "creeped out" by this behavior, so he just suppresses the urge and doesn't let himself act on it.

Avoidance. The person consciously or unconsciously calculates that a certain situation would bring on bad feelings, so the person figures out a way to avoid the situation. For example, someone knows that if they go to a certain dance, they will feel extremely jealous of seeing a person they are very attracted to, at the dance with someone else. So the person manages to have too much work to do at the time of the dance, and stays away from it.

Fantasy. Someone hates a certain bully, and would like to "beat up" the bully. But they realize that they would probably get hurt badly if they attempted this. So in fantasy, they repeatedly conquer and dominate the bully.

Humor. Someone takes a situation that could cause great fear or sadness, and turns it into something funny. For example, someone is worried about the destruction of civilization through nuclear war. But the person manages to make up and sing a very funny song about the mushroom cloud of nuclear explosions that may happen "some fine day."

Passive aggression. Someone has feelings of anger and urges toward aggression. But they manage to get back at the other person in a way that they can't be blamed for. For example, someone is angry at a coworker. The person sees a mistake that the coworker made, that they could tell the person about and let the coworker correct it. But instead, the person does nothing, knowing that soon the mistake will come out in a much more embarrassing way for the coworker.

Sometimes it's not easy figuring out why we ourselves are doing what we are doing. Being familiar with these defense mechanisms can help us answer that

question. We can realize, "I'm using the defense of _____,"
and then decide, "Is this what I really want to be doing, or
not?" In other words, familiarity with defenses sometimes
helps us to follow the ancient advice that goes, "Know
thyself."

Definition of good economy, unemployment, and inflation

What is the meaning of a "good economy" for a
country or a region? In any economy, you have goods and
services being produced, and you have people buying those
goods and services. ("Goods" are things like cars, ears of
corn, pocket knives, shirts, or cell phones; "services" are
things people do for us, like clean our teeth, diagnose our
sicknesses, teach us, keep our money in a bank, provide us
a phone connection, and so forth.) People earn money by
producing the goods and services, and they use their
money to buy the goods and services that other people
produce.

In a "good economy," people get access to the goods
and services they need and that make them happy. For this
to happen, they need to be able to: 1) find a job with which
to earn money, 2) find the goods and services available at a
price they can afford. If no one will hire them, or if the
price of the things they need is too high, they can't get what
they want and need.

The two problems that are the opposite of these are
unemployment and inflation. In unemployment, jobs are
scarce; in inflation, prices are rising fast.

When people have lots of money, they want to buy
goods and services with their money, so companies tend to
spring up and add workers so as to meet the demand and

make money by selling the goods and services people want. So when people have lots of money, unemployment tends to fall. But if people have lots of money relative to the amount of goods and services available, sellers raise their prices, because there are so many people wanting to buy. So inflation tends to be a problem.

On the other hand, when people don't have as much money, there isn't as much demand to buy things, so businesses don't hire new workers or lay off the workers they have. So unemployment gets to be a problem. On the other hand, people don't have as much money to spend on goods and services, so if sellers want to sell, they have avoid raising prices, or even lower them. So people in government who can influence how much total money people have, need to strike a balance so as to avoid unemployment on the one hand and inflation on the other hand.

Demand for the goods and services that really increase long term happiness

Earlier I said that in a good economy, people get access to the goods and services that make them happy. In order for this to take place, they need to make good choices about what to spend their money on, and create demand for the goods and services that tend to make people happier.

The "gross domestic product" for a country is an estimate of how much money people spent, total, on goods and services in a certain time period, for example a year. Spending money on very good teachers adds to the gross domestic product; spending money on healthy food, or on remodeling houses to make safe and healthy places to live, or on providing health care, or creating books to teach nonviolence and conflict resolution, all add to the gross domestic product. On the other hand, the money spent on cigarettes, whiskey, guns, divorces, people suing each other, prisons, bombs, junk food, and weight loss programs to counteract the effects of junk food, also all add to the gross domestic product.

The big idea of this section is that a good economy is not just the total amount of goods and services delivered to people; it includes people's choosing to create demand for, and cause the production of, those goods and services that really make society better off. In some circumstances people are better off with lower sales of goods and services. For example, when people go out and take a walk together and have a good conversation, there's no contribution to the gross domestic product. When people buy video game hardware and software that enables them to go into their rooms and fantasy rehearse violent acts in large numbers, there's a larger contribution to the gross domestic product.

Increasing or decreasing the money supply is a lot easier for someone in government to do than it is to reshape people's wishes, so that people spend their money on the things that really make them, and the rest of society, better off!

Biofeedback

There is a part of us that is called our "sympathetic nervous system." Someone named it in an unfortunate way, because it doesn't have to do with sympathy and compassion. When it gets turned up, it helps with the "flight or fight" response -- the physical changes that help us run away from predators, or fight them. There are nerve pathways that run from our brains to many different organs of the body, that tell the body to get excited, to get ready to move. Many people have troubles resulting from too much of the flight or fight response -- so much anger or so much fear that the response disrupts their ability to make good decisions and carry them out. For example, they may scream at people and hit them, though they later regret the consequences of this; they may run away from the situation they are in or just be as if paralyzed by fear. There are probably very few of us who couldn't benefit from the ability to turn down the level of anger or fear every once in a while.

So someone could say, "Just turn down the activity level of your sympathetic nervous system." But most people would reply, "How in the world do I do that?" The sympathetic nervous system is part of the "autonomic" nervous system, and the word "autonomic" sounds a lot like "automatic." A lot of its activity starts and stops without our consciously trying to change it. At one point it was called the "involuntary" nervous system.

But people can learn to get conscious control over parts of the nervous system that were thought to be involuntary! One of the things that helps with this is biofeedback. Biofeedback means that you measure something that the body is doing, and experiment around with seeing what makes that something change; gradually you learn to change that something on purpose. Sympathetic nervous system activation tends to 1) increase heart rate (to get more blood to your muscles) 2) decrease fingertip temperature (as blood supply goes away from the skin and toward the muscles) and 3) increase sweating (to help you cool off from the exertion of fighting or fleeing). Turning down the flight or fight response does the opposite of these three things. You can measure your heart rate with a pulse oximeter, and fingertip temperature with certain types of thermometers, each of which can be bought for less than the cost of a restaurant meal. You can measure the sweating of your fingertips by instruments that see how well the surface of the skin conducts a very tiny, unnoticeable electric current; the more sweat there is, the better the electricity gets conducted.

There are various relaxation methods. If someone experiments with them, and finds ways of doing them that decrease heart rate, increase skin temperature, and/or increase the conductance of the skin, then the person is learning to turn down the activity of the sympathetic nervous system. And this can be a very useful skill!

There are other types of biofeedback, used for a variety of different purposes. But they all involve measuring something that the body is doing and using the feedback of those measurements to learn to control something that the body is doing or can do.

Communal rhythmic activities: dance, singing, and others

Here's an interesting thing about human beings: they tend to like to make and hear sounds that go in a steady rhythm, and they tend to like to move in time with those steady rhythms. It's easy to imagine some people from a different planet who would be very perplexed to notice this. They might see someone beating on drums, and think, "Why is that person spending their energy on that activity?" But for the humans on this planet, steady rhythms are central to singing, drumming, dancing, chanting, and waving your hands in time with a performer's song. For some reason, people like to get together in groups and do those things.

Why did we get so interested in steady rhythms? Probably because of the following important steady rhythms of life, some of which are walking, running, breathing, and heart beating.

Whatever the reason, if there is some module in the brain that makes us enjoy listening to rhythmic music and moving in time to it, we should enjoy it – it's a form of exercise that doesn't have bad side effects, unless people play the music so loud as to make us deaf!

The kindness -> mental health connection

What's a great way to improve the mental health of a large group of people? If there were some way to teach all, or most, of the people in the group to be very kind to one another, I am sure that this would have huge positive effects on the mental health of the population. There are hundreds of scientific papers that could be cited in support of this idea. But let's just think about a few of the reasons why this might be true.

Many mental health problems are due to traumas, or really bad experiences, that people have had, and the most damaging traumas seem to be the ones inflicted by other unkind people. If abuse of children or spouses were eliminated, that in itself would prevent a huge number of mental disorders.

Anxiety disorders come from being afraid. One of the most reliable reducers of fear is "social support" – having friends or family members whom you can count on, who are kind to you. On the other hand, when people bully you and are mean to you, you tend to be more afraid of what will happen next.

Depressive disorders are marked by feeling sad, feeling that there's nothing to look forward to, feeling as if nothing you do makes a difference. But if there are people who like to do fun things with you, who express a lot of enthusiastic reinforcement for the good things you do, and whom you very much wish to make happy, lots of the key ingredients of depression are greatly reduced, although not eliminated altogether.

Some mental disorders consist in people's being unkind and uncooperative and angry – they have names like oppositional defiant disorder, conduct disorder, antisocial personality disorder, and intermittent explosive disorder. Having learned to be very kind to other people almost all the time pretty much rules out these disorders.

Some mental disorders, such as schizophrenia and bipolar disorder, are well known to have a pretty strong genetic component and to have symptoms that respond to drugs, and are thus thought of as being "biological" disorders. But lots of research has shown that even for these, people do much better when they are living in a positive "family emotional climate" than when they aren't. And the key to a positive family emotional climate is for people to speak and act kindly to one another.
How would you go about teaching large groups of people to be kind to one another? Please see the big idea on "Methods of Influence" for some different sets of ways, each of which could include hundreds of different projects, programs, and practices. I'm guessing that major organized efforts would pay off greatly.

261

Desensitization

How do you get over fears that you wish you didn't have? This is the question for which "desensitization" is a very prominent answer.

Let's first think about how you learn to play the piano well. You start off with very easy things to do, and you practice doing those things well, and you gradually work your way up to harder songs and exercises, doing a lot of practice with them and trying to do them in a high-quality way. People have found that you can practice in your imagination, and that this helps you with your real-life playing.

The same general strategy works with getting over fears. Let's say you're scared of dogs. There are lots of possible situations with dogs; you list a bunch of them, and you rate how scary each of them is, on a scale of 0 to 10. The rating is called a SUD level; that stands for "subjective units of distress." Maybe it causes a SUD level of 1 on a scale of 10 to imagine looking at a picture of a sleeping puppy on the Internet, and maybe a SUD of 2 comes from actually looking at such a picture. Maybe a SUD level of 4 comes from seeing a portion of a movie where a boy has a really nice dog. Maybe it's a SUD of 6 to be on one side of a big room while someone holds and pets their little dog on the other side of the room, and 8 to come close to the person holding the dog. Maybe it's 9 or so to actually pet the dog or hold a leash while taking the dog for a walk. Figuring out things like these is called constructing a "hierarchy" of feared situations. This is an important part of desensitization.

After you have a hierarchy, you start with the situations near the bottom, and start practicing with them.

You can practice in imagination. You can write out "fantasy rehearsals" that describe the situation, the thoughts you want to have about the situation, the emotions you want to have, the behaviors you want to do, and the celebratory thoughts you want to have when you have handled the situation well. As you go over these fantasy rehearsals more and more times, the fear that they bring out tends to get less and less. You also can practice handling situations in real life. You gradually work your way up the hierarchy until you can handle all the situations you want to, the way you want. Practicing with the situations in real life as well as in fantasy is usually an important part of the procedure.

People have found it useful to practice relaxation, and to use relaxation methods as one of the possible behaviors in response to the situations. Measuring heart rate, skin temperature, or skin conductance (see our discussion of biofeedback) can give some information about how your body is responding, over and above that of the SUD level, and can make the whole process more interesting and fun.

People speak of desensitization as "exposure based" therapy, because a central activity is exposing yourself to the situations you are scared of. I prefer to think of the major healing element as "practice" rather than "exposure." If you are practicing handling the situation like you want to, desensitization works lots better than if you are practicing feeling terrified and counting down the seconds until you can get out of the situation. This is just as in learning the piano: you have to "expose" yourself to the challenge of playing the next song well, but it's the positive practice that makes you better, not the exposure itself.

Place value

What is MCMLX multiplied by XCVII? That's pretty hard to compute if you're using Roman numerals! But 5th graders shouldn't have too difficult a time in multiplying 1960 x 97, without a calculator.

With Roman numerals and other numbering systems of that sort, as numbers get bigger, you have to keep adding new symbols to stand for them. But with the system we use, the same 10 symbols, 0 through 9, allow us to write any number that we want, because the place that the number occupies determines how big it is. The 3 in 30 represents 3 10's, 10 times more than the 3 in the number 3; 3 in 300 represents 3 hundreds, 100 times more than the 3 in the number 3, and so forth.

The invention of a decimal point made it possible to express fractions in the same way -- 0.3 is three tenths, 0.03 is 3 hundredths, and so forth.

It was a smart person (or set of people) who introduced the use of 0 into the number system (it's not present in Roman numerals). The 0 in 30 allows us to say, very economically, "We're dealing with 3 tens and no additional ones." The 0 symbol was crucial for a number system that uses place value.

Literal numbers

A literal number, or variable, is a symbol for a number. The number could possibly take on a variety of different values -- that's why we call it a variable.

Suppose we have 2 liters of a solution of water and alcohol, and someone adds 2 liters of a solution that is 95%

water and 5% alcohol. We find out that the resulting solution is 80% water and 20% alcohol. Suppose we want to figure out what fraction alcohol was in the original two liters. This is a typical algebra problem. It is much easier to solve this kind of problem if we let a letter stand for the unknown quantity that we want to know. If we let x equal the fraction alcohol in the original 2 liters, then the original solution had 2x liters of alcohol. The solution we added had 2*0.05 or 0.1 liters of alcohol. The final solution had 0.20 * 4 or 0.8 liters of alcohol. Since the amount of alcohol we had plus the amount that we added equals the amount we ended up with, we can say that

$2x + 2*.05 = .20 * 4$

or
$2x + .1 = .8$
$2x = .7$
$x = .35$

So the original solution was 35% alcohol.

Letting x or some other letter stand for an unknown quantity makes problems like this much easier to solve. We could write, "The original fraction of alcohol" over and over, but even that is letting something other than a number, namely a bunch of letters, stand for a number -- that phrase is still a variable.

Another advantage of literal numbers, or variables, is that they let us write formulas. We might notice that for a certain rectangle, the area is 20 square centimeters, the length is 5 centimeters, and the width is 4 centimeters. For another rectangle, the length is 6 centimeters, the width is 3 centimeters, and the area is 18 square centimeters. But using literal numbers, we can summarize an unlimited number of rectangles by just saying that

$A = l \times w$

or Area = length times width. Area, length, and width can vary from one rectangle to another, but they always have the same relationship. Using variables lets us make statements about lots of different situations rather than thinking about only one concrete one.

Alphabets where letters stand for sounds

When the first people wanted to represent words by some sort of written markings, the logical idea is to draw pictures of what you're trying to say. If people develop a system of pictures where each symbol, or combination of them, stands for a word or idea, that is called a "logographic" system. This is the system used in Chinese languages. Many, many centuries ago, some people in what is now called the Middle East got the idea of making up an "alphabetic" system where letters stand, not for whole words, but for the sounds that make up those words. In languages like Spanish and Finnish, the correspondence between letters and sounds is pretty close. In English, what sound a given letter makes is less predictable. For example, the letter a makes one sound in apple, another in mama, another in cake, and no sound in breakfast. At any rate, the big idea is that there are lots fewer sounds in a language than there are words, so memorizing one written symbol for each sound takes a lot less time than memorizing a

266

symbol for each word. That having been said, it appears that logographic systems such as in Chinese languages seem to have done the job for them pretty well!

Parsimony in evaluating hypotheses

People sometimes make up test questions like this: Which number should come next?   3, 6, 9, 12, then what? Or if they want to make it a little harder, something like this:
Which number should come next: 3, 2, 5, 4, 7, 6, 9, 8, then what?

Perhaps the reason that people make up question like this is that the process of looking at numbers and figuring out some sort of rule that they go by is a lot like what happens in science, and other aspects of life. You get a bunch of data, often thousands of numbers, and then you try to boil it down into some much more simple summary that explains what's going on. Just as in the problems above, you use simple rules like "add three each time" or "alternate between adding 3 and subtracting 1."

But suppose someone gave a different answer to the first problem. The person says, "The answer is 332 million." Someone says, "How did you get that?" The person says, "The rule is, you skip count by 3s for 4 numbers, then you tell the approximate population of the country you live in. Then skip count by 3s for 4 more numbers, then tell the population of the country just south of you. Then skip count by 3s for 4 more, and tell the population of the country just south of that. It's a very orderly rule."

Can you say that the person is wrong? They have made up a rule that is totally consistent with the data. What the test makers want you to assume, but what they don't say, is: "Use the *simplest possible* rule to predict what number comes next."

It turns out that in science, some amazing things are predicted and explained by very simple rules. The motion of planets and satellites in orbits are predicted and explained by a handful of formulas that can be memorized by high school physics students. Albert Einstein's perhaps most famous discovery is that matter can be converted into energy. How much energy do you get when a certain amount of matter gets converted? The universe could have been set up so that the answer would have taken pages and pages of complex instructions to communicate. But instead, the answer is so simple that many people can rattle it off: $E=mc^2$. You just take the mass of the stuff you're converting, and multiply it by the the speed of light, times the speed of light again, and that gives you how much energy you get.

The idea of looking for the simplest explanation for things rather than cooking up an extremely complicated one is something we use in life all the time without even being aware of it. For example, suppose I look for my glasses, but they aren't where I expected them to be. It is possible that someone could have obtained a copy of a key to my apartment, crept in when I wasn't looking, and stolen my glasses, because that person knew something I didn't: top secret information was encoded in the frames. On the other hand, a simpler explanation is just that I took them off and put them down while thinking about something else. When I look at the table in the other room, I confirm the simpler explanation. (This illustrates that if we're writing a movie script, we should think up the most interesting or fun explanation, not the simplest one!)

Looking for the simplest explanation has been called the principle of parsimony. The principle has been associated with a philosopher who lived in the 1300s called William of Ockham, and has been called Ockham's razor -- as if we are shaving off the unnecessary assumptions. But Aristotle, who lived around 300 something BCE, mentioned the same idea.

Insurance

Imagine that you have a family with a young child, and your work provides all of the money to buy that child what they need. You think, "If I die, what will happen to my child? If someone sues me and wins all the money I'll ever make, what will happen to my child? If the house we're living in burns down some time when we are out, how will I ever make enough money to pay for another place to live, and still take care of my child?" Someone is smart to be thinking in these ways, even though the questions raise a good amount of anxiety.

The insurance industry is meant to reduce people's anxiety over things like this, for a price that is paid to the insurance company. The person pays a certain amount of money, called a "premium," to the insurance company, and then if they die, the insurance company pays their family a certain amount of money -- this is called life insurance. In exchange for a premium, the insurance company guarantees that if the house burns down, they will pay to build it back or get a new one -- this is homeowner's insurance. And in exchange for a premium, the insurance company guarantees that if the person gets sued in the course of their work, the company will pay the amount that the court forces them to pay -- this is called professional liability insurance.

Which would you rather do: have a 100% chance of paying a certain amount a year in an insurance premium, or keep the premium, and have a smaller chance of losing everything you own? The insurance industry exists because people would rather pay a premium than take the risk of losing a much larger amount of money. There are people called actuaries who work for insurance companies. These people figure out how likely it is that the insurance company will have to pay in response to some bad thing that has happened to one of its customers. They figure out how much the company can guarantee paying, and how much the premiums have to be, in order for the insurance company to make a profit.

If the insurance companies do what they promise to do, they can increase the happiness of their customers. However, if they make it very difficult for their customers to get paid when they should be, so that their customers have to take the insurance company to court to get money out of them, the insurance company loses the trust of the customers and ceases to make them feel more secure.

Atoms, molecules, and compounds

Suppose you take some iron, or gold, or carbon, and divide it into the smallest little bit of it that you possibly can. Iron, gold, and carbon are examples of elements, and the smallest unit of an element is an atom. If you could take the atom apart, it wouldn't be the same element any more. An element acts a certain way in reacting with other elements. Elements are made up of atoms that are all alike.

For each element, each atom has a certain number of protons in the center of it. Two or more elements can have their atoms bind together in some regular way, to make what's called a compound. For example, two atoms of hydrogen and one atom of oxygen can bind together to make water. The smallest unit of water, where if you take it apart further it isn't water any more, is a molecule. A water molecule has two hydrogen atoms and one oxygen atom, bound together to make the molecule. When there is a lot of water, each oxygen atom is attached to two hydrogen atoms. (Well, that's not exactly right – about one in every 10 million oxygen atoms has 3 hydrogens attached, and one in every 10 million has only one attached. But let's not worry about those.)

Each element has a symbol that is a letter. For example, hydrogen is H, Oxygen is O, carbon is C, nitrogen is N, chlorine is Cl. Sometimes the symbol is gotten from the Latin name of the element rather than the English name. This is why sodium is Na, gold is Au, lead is Pb, and potassium is K.

The chemical symbol for a compound shows how many atoms of each element are in the compound. For example, NaCl (which is table salt) has one atom of sodium for each atom of chlorine. CO_2, which is carbon dioxide, has one carbon atom and two oxygen atoms per molecule. $C_6H_{12}O_6$, which is glucose, a type of sugar, has 6 carbon atoms, 12 hydrogen atoms, and 6 oxygen atoms for each molecule of glucose.

Mind-body dualism vs. mind as a function of the body

The phrase "mind-body dualism" means that our minds and our bodies are two different things -- the belief that we have bodies, with souls, or ghost-like beings, residing within them, and those souls don't need the body to keep existing. The opposing idea is that thinking, feeling, being aware of one's existence, seeing, hearing, and moving are all functions that the body carries out, directed by activity of the cells in the brain.

As science has progressed, all the evidence points to the second view rather than the first. Long ago we realized that when certain brain functions are shut down by anesthetic drugs, thinking and feeling and behaving cease. We learned that injury to certain brain regions shut down the brain functions that are carried out by those brain regions. As brain imaging technology has developed, we have documented that certain types of actions cause the brain regions involved in those activities to "light up." Stimulation of certain brain regions with magnetic fields brings about effects that are consistent with our knowledge of the function of those brain regions. Drugs that have effects on brain chemicals affect the ways we think, feel, and behave in ways consistent with our knowledge of what those chemicals do. Severe brain illnesses such as Alzheimer's disease devastate the ability to think, feel, and behave. And so forth.

As of the 2020s some polls found that about 40% of people in the USA believe that ghosts exist. This gives evidence that if over 130 million people believe something, it still doesn't have to be true! (If you're one of the people who is sure that ghosts really do exist, you might take my last sentence as evidence that if someone writes about big ideas, not everything he says has to be true! And that definitely is true!) Part of the "big idea" of this section is that if a ghost were to decide to haunt someone, send a message to someone, make noises in an attic, or whatever else ghosts are supposed to do, they would need to have the brain regions that are in charge of decision making ... which they don't!

Laws don't include proper names

Suppose that famous actor Lala Pajama decides to smoke while riding on an airplane. The flight attendant says to them, "I'm sorry, there's a law against smoking on airplanes." Lala says, "Don't you know who I am?" The flight attendant might well instruct Lala that "Laws don't include proper names." For example, the law about smoking on planes didn't read, "You're not allowed to smoke on a plane, unless you are the famous actor Lala Pajama."

Rich, powerful, and famous people sometimes think that laws were meant for ordinary people, not extraordinary people like themselves. A well-functioning legal system applies the law impartially, regardless of how rich, powerful, or famous the person is. For this reason, you sometimes see a picture of a person symbolizing "justice" holding a scale in their hand, blindfolded. The scale symbolizes making a decision by weighing the arguments pro and con; the blindfold symbolizes that justice doesn't look at who the person is, but makes the decision on the weight of the evidence.

Does this mean that a rich, powerful, and very popular person is always just as likely to get penalized for a crime as a poor, powerless, and unknown person who commits the same crime? Unfortunately, our justice system does not always meet the standards of fairness it aspires to. In other words, no.

Flexibility, strength, endurance, speed, coordination, balance

This big idea tells us the types of goals to shoot for when we're trying to make ourselves healthy by staying in good physical condition. Flexibility means that we can move our joints as much as they were meant to move. Someone who can touch their toes without bending the knees is more flexible, at least in a certain movement, than someone who can't do this. Someone who can do the "splits" is more flexible than someone who can't. It's not necessary to be extremely flexible in order to be healthy, and it's important not to hurt yourself by overdoing the stretching that helps you get and stay flexible.

Strength is measurable by how much weight you can lift or how much you can use in resistance exercises. Strength is somewhat proportional to the size of your muscles.

Endurance, also called stamina, refers to how much physical work you can do over a sustained time. Marathon runners or triathlon athletes are examples of high achievers in endurance.

Speed refers to how much physical work you can do in a short time -- people who win 100 meter sprint races are high achievers at this.

Coordination has to do with the ability to teach your body to do complex moves successfully -- such as playing basketball, doing gymnastics moves, diving, juggling, dancing, playing the piano.

Balance is that part of coordination that lets you keep things from falling over, and the most important of those things is yourself! This is especially important when you get to be an old person and break more easily.

The many benefits of exercise

As a general rule, if you see some advertisement for something claiming to cure and prevent all sorts of different health problems, it's good to be suspicious. The word *panacea* means a "cure-all," and people who claim to have found panaceas are mainly interested in curing their own financial troubles.

However! There is something (the title of this section gives it away) that can: reduce the risk of diabetes, reduce the risk of heart disease and strokes, reduce or prevent anxiety and depression, preserve intellectual skills, prevent falls, make bones stronger, prevent certain cancers, give you more energy, increase your strength and endurance, help you fight off infectious diseases, help prevent or slow the progression of brain diseases like Alzheimer's or Parkinson's, improve sleep better than any sleeping pill, let you live longer and healthier, and provide other health benefits as well! And, what may be for lots of us more motivating than the health benefits: it helps you look better. One lecturer said that if it were marketed for sale, it might be called "Does-it-all." And that something is physical exercise: walking, running, jumping, stair-climbing, doing pushups, pullups, planks, and squats, helping people move stuff, dancing, biking, gardening, working out with weights, doing dance steps while you wash dishes, chopping wood, playing vigorous sports, doing physical labor, or doing anything else that makes you pant or makes your muscles tired.

Here's a theory about why "Does-it-all" does so much: In the many centuries in which our bodies evolved, our ancestors probably were moving around almost all their waking hours, looking for something to eat. Our bodies evolved to do best when we moved a lot. In today's age, where many people have to sit most of the day and interact with computer screens, our bodies get way less exercise than they are meant to get. Exercise helps our bodies do the amount of moving that they have been designed for.

Multiplication and exponents

What is multiplication? It's repeated addition (of the same number each time). For example, 3 x 4 means 4 + 4 + 4. We add together three fours. (We could also add together four threes, and get the same thing.)

What are exponents? They represent repeated multiplication (of the same number each time). For example, 5^3, or five to the third power, is the same as 5 x 5 x 5.

Powers of 10 are particularly familiar numbers. 10^2 is 100, 10^3 is 1000, 10^4 is 10,000, and so on. 10^{-1} is one tenth, 10^{-2} is one hundredth, 10^{-3} is a thousandth, and so forth. (The rule is, something to a negative exponent is one divided by, or one over, that thing to a positive exponent. So 2^{-3} is the same as $1/2^3$.)

Scientific notation

One great use for exponents is to express numbers that are lots bigger or smaller than the numbers we usually count up to. We can express any number as some number between 1 and 10, multiplied by a power of 10. And that's what scientific notation is!

So for some examples: 7,600,000 (or seven million, six hundred thousand) is 7.6×10^6.

0.00034 is 3.4×10^{-4}.

Want to know how many centimeters light travels in a second? It's about 3×10^{10}.

Want to know how many atoms there are in the number of grams of any element equal to the atomic weight of the element? (The atomic weight is about equal to the number of protons plus the number of neutrons.) It's about 6.02×10^{23}, otherwise known as Avogadro's number. Scientific notation keeps us from having to write out and count up a whole bunch of zeroes.

The big bang

How did the universe start? Physicists have gotten together a lot of evidence that about 13.8 billion years ago (1.38×10^{10} years ago), a huge amount of matter and energy started hurtling out from a very small spot where it all began. This event has been named The Big Bang. The idea that everything started in one spot, that things have been moving away from ever since, is consistent with scientists' findings that all the stuff we can see up in the sky, with or without telescopes, seems to be getting farther and farther apart as time goes by. The theory somehow predicted that a certain type of radiation, called cosmic background radiation, would be found, and years after that prediction was made, the radiation was indeed detected.

What existed before the Big Bang? Why did the Big Bang happen to bang? Did just one universe get started in this way, or are there a bunch of them somewhere or other?

If you enjoy wondering about questions like this (for which I don't know the answers) you will enjoy the subject of cosmology, which is a branch of physics.

What good nutrition is

Everyone knows that having a healthy, nourishing diet is good. But what is good nutrition? People's ideas change on this subject as more research comes in.

The first requirement for the food we eat is that there should be neither too much, nor too little of it! We'll talk more about this in the section on caloric balance.

There are several things we need to get enough of in our diets. Protein is a name for several different molecules we use in lots of different ways, including to make our bodies. It's found in particularly high concentrations in meat, milk, and eggs; peas and beans and nuts are also good sources of protein. Fats and carbohydrates are used by our bodies as a source of energy. Butter and vegetable oil and fat meat are examples of fats; sugar and starch are examples of carbohydrates. People who are overweight worry about getting too much fat or carbohydrate, but we all need to have enough fuel for energy. Fiber is the part of what we eat (especially from plants) that doesn't get digested as it goes through our stomachs and intestines. Having enough fiber helps our system of eliminating wastes work well. Vitamins are chemicals found in foods, that our bodies need for various chemical reactions. These have been named things like Vitamin A, Vitamin C, Vitamin B12, and so forth. Minerals, some of which are called electrolytes, are things like sodium, potassium, calcium, chloride ions, and so forth. And since our bodies are composed of somewhere around 50% water, getting enough water is also important for nutrition. Scientists discover other substances that may not be absolutely necessary for life, but help prevent illnesses, including cancer, and probably help our brains to function better as we grow old. An example of these is a group of plant components called phytochemicals.

Many students of nutrition have concluded that a "plant based" diet, where the major components are fruits, vegetables, nuts, and grains, give us the best chance of being healthy. A variety of evidence suggests that eating lots of red meat, for example beef, is not a good idea.

The biggest nutrition problem for most residents of developed countries is probably the tendency to eat too much "junk food." This category includes candy, cakes, ice cream, soda pop, potato chips, pie, doughnuts, butter, whipped cream, sugar, and others that have an abundance of sugar and fat, as well as all alcoholic beverages. (I'm sorry to say that fruit juices like orange, apple, grape, and pineapple juice, while containing some healthy substances that are lacking in soda pop, have so much sugar that people are more often counting them as junk food rather than healthy food.) Junk foods supply what has been called "empty calories" – they contribute little to nutrition other than calories for energy; our bodies often use them to put on weight. If, on the other hand, one is starving or greatly underweight, junk food is way better than no food, and it could possibly be life-saving.

We notice that many of the foods that people celebrate with the most, and like the most, fall into the junk food category. This is why people have "birthday cake" instead of "birthday bean and kale stew"! This is why people collect candy on Halloween rather than avocados and eggplants. Junk food tends to taste really good! There's a reason for this: during most of the many centuries of human evolution, the big challenge to survival was getting enough food. Getting too much was hardly a worry at all. The foods that delivered big supplies of energy to our ancestors helped them stay alive, so they evolved to like taking in concentrated calories. The result is that most of us like candy bars more than raw kale! But when food is plentiful, more people have health problems from too much rather than too little food. Food with concentrated calories gets the rather pejorative label of "junk food."

Caloric balance

A Calorie is a unit of energy. It's defined as the energy it takes to heat a certain amount of water by a certain amount. (The Calories people speak of regarding food are actually "kilocalories" to a physicist. There is a unit called a calorie, (lower case c) that is one-thousandth as much as the amount of energy in the Calories they talk about with food, in a very confusing choice of words.) The Calories that are in food refer to how much energy can be generated when our bodies use that food to make energy for ourselves, for example to keep ourselves warm or to move our muscles. If the number of Calories we take in, through our food, is greater than the number that we use to make energy, our bodies tend to store the energy in the form of fat (which is a very efficient way to store up potential energy for when we need it). If the number of Calories we use up for energy is greater than the number we take in, we tend to lose fat tissue as our bodies dip into the fat reserves to make energy. If we take in exactly the same number of Calories that we use for energy on any certain day, we are in "caloric balance" for that day.

How many Calories does someone use for energy? For the "average" adult, the number is about 2000 Calories per day. But if someone runs a marathon (which is a little over 26 miles) the number of Calories used that day is more than double that number. If someone is small, so that it doesn't take as much energy to keep the body going and move it around, and if the person isn't exercising much, the number can be fewer than 2000 Calories.

Here's an interesting thing about caloric balance. For each accumulation of about 3500 Calories over what we've used up, we gain about a pound of fat. For each expenditure of 3500 Calories more than we've taken in, we lose a pound. 100 Calories can be consumed in way less than a minute. About a cup of orange juice, or a cup of 1% milk, or a couple of bites of a doughnut, or about 1/5 of a McDonald's Big Mac hamburger, has 100 Calories. Suppose you take in just 100 Calories more than you expend, each day. That means that in 35 days, you've gained a pound. In a year, you've gained about 10 pounds. In 10 years, you've put on 100 pounds! By the same arithmetic, if you take in just 100 Calories less than you expend each day, in a year you lose 10 pounds and in 10 years you lose 100 pounds. (This assumes you had 100 pounds to lose!) But if you tried, each day, to calculate exactly how many Calories you expended and how many you took in by eating, you couldn't do it nearly accurately enough to detect a caloric excess or deficit as little as 100 Calories. This is why it's amazing that some people seem to stay the same weight, without making calculations. They must have a thermostat-like mechanism that is working well. This also helps us understand why more people find themselves gradually gaining weight and needing to try to be in caloric deficit rather than excess to reverse this process.

Why is caloric balance a big idea? I'm trying to select the ideas that are helpful in life, and most of us eat just about every single day of our lives. Eating, and weight, are "Goldilocks variables" (see the big idea on this) and every day we have the opportunity to eat too much, too little, or about in the right range.

People should never insult or shame other people for being heavy. The principle of kindness is paramount in dealing with other people, including "plus sized" people. At the same time, however, kindness to self and others involves not ignoring the health problems that can come from having lots of fat on the body. These include type 2 diabetes, heart disease, strokes, high blood pressure, osteoarthritis, gallbladder disease, some cancers, worsened migraine headaches, disorders connected with chronic inflammation, and others, including premature death.

People should also not insult or shame others for being too skinny. But some people have such a fear of fatness that they develop a condition called anorexia nervosa, where they keep losing weight to the point where they endanger themselves. Self-starvation can cause loss of brain tissue, difficulties with memory and problem-solving, hair loss, heart rhythm problems, weakened bones, and other health problems, including, with disturbing frequency, premature death.

So what is a "just right" weight for any given person? There are tables and calculators that the Center for Disease Control make available where one can enter one's height and weight and age; the calculator will tell you the "body mass index" (BMI) and whether it's in the "healthy range" or too much or too little. A problem with this is that the tables don't know the difference between weight contributed by fat and that contributed by muscle. Very muscular people can come out in the "too heavy" range for body mass index, even though they may have lots less fat tissue than average. For most of us, however, the BMI (body mass index) tables provide at least some degree of reasonable guidance.

If someone has a problem with caloric balance in the direction of "caloric excess," i.e. too many Calories being taken in, one way to shift the balance is by cutting out, or greatly reducing, junk food. In another section I speculated that it may be possible to get about as much pleasure from eating, if one eats "healthy foods" seasoned by the "best sauce," i.e. some hunger.

Systems of the human body

Skeletal system: This is our bones. These form the structure of our bodies, the hard solids that make us able not to be squishy. Our bones have joints, where two or more bones come together. They are like hinges, where one bone can move while pushing against or being supported by another.

Muscular system: These are our muscles. They are what allow us to move. Our brain sends messages to our muscles that tell them to shorten themselves, or contract. The contraction of some muscles lets us move in a certain way; then when others contract, we can move back the other way.

Cardiovascular system: This includes the blood and the blood vessels, which are the tubes that carry blood, and also the heart, which pumps blood around us from its position in our chests. The heart is a strong muscle itself, that never gets too tired to keep beating. Each beat squeezes blood out into our arteries. If you feel your pulse, you are feeling an artery get bigger and smaller, once for each heartbeat, as the heart pumps blood through it. The arteries branch into smaller and smaller tubes, and the very smallest ones take oxygen and nutrients to the other parts of our bodies. The blood also picks up the carbon dioxide that gets generated when the body uses energy. Then the blood keeps going and the vessels start coming together to make bigger ones called veins, that go back to the heart. The heart pumps the blood to the lungs, where again the vessels branch into very small ones and then come together to make big ones again. The small vessels in the lungs transfer carbon dioxide to the air in the lungs and absorb oxygen from it. Then, after the blood comes back from the lungs to the heart again, it's ready to start all over again and make its next trip through the body! The blood transports to our tissues not only oxygen, but also the breakdown products of the food we eat, to nourish the cells of our bodies. And it transports from our tissues the waste products that our cells generate.

Respiratory system: This includes all the parts of our bodies which are involved in getting oxygen into our blood and carbon dioxide out of it. The respiratory system includes the nose and mouth, where air enters and exits our body. From the nose and mouth the air goes through the back of the throat, the windpipe or trachea, on the way to the lungs. The trachea branches into smaller tubes, the bronchi. Finally there are tiny sacs, that make up our lungs, where the oxygen in the air goes into the blood and the carbon dioxide in the blood goes out into the air.

Nervous system: The brain is the headquarters of the nervous system -- it's where we think, feel, make decisions, initiate movements, and organize and appreciate all the information that comes in from our senses (such as seeing, hearing, touch, pain, position sense, smell, taste). Outside the brain there are nerves that carry information to and from the brain. Sensory nerves pick up information on what's happening and send it to the brain. Motor nerves take our wishes to move in a certain way, and send the signals from our brains to our muscles, so we can move as we decide to move. Nerves coming from the brain also go to organs other than the muscles, for example our hearts, blood vessels, intestines, sweat glands, adrenal glands, and others, and turn up or down the activity of these organs. Our nervous systems are made up of cells called neurons. These cells are specialized for storing and transmitting information and signals, in a way that can be compared to parts of a computer. Neurons use the movement of electrical charges to transmit information, not in the same way that wires conduct electricity, but in a way that depends on the movement of electrically charges across the membrane of the neuron. The membrane is the part of the cell that separates the neuron from the fluid around it. Our brains and nervous systems have evolved over millions of years. It is amazing that they can do what they do. One of the big goals of humanity is to help every person learn to use their brain capacity in the best way they can.

Digestive system: We need food to live, and the digestive system is in charge of processing the food we eat.

There is one long tube that is central to this. The tube starts with the mouth and throat, takes food through the chest in a part called the esophagus, to a place in our belly known as the stomach. In the stomach, chemical reactions go on that break food down into parts that we can absorb and use. From the stomach, the tube turns into the small intestine, where most of the absorption of nutrients goes on, and then the tube turns into the large intestine or colon, where water is absorbed. The end of the colon is called the rectum, and the place where the rectum ends is called the anus. This is where feces, or poop, comes out of the body. There are organs that help with digestion, including the pancreas, that contributes some of the chemicals that break food down, and the liver and gall bladder. The gall bladder empties into the small intestine. A very interesting part of our digestive system is the "good bacteria" that live in the tube we just described. This set of bacteria, called the microbiome, has various good effects on our bodies, if the bacteria are the right ones.

Urinary system: Every day we drink water (or liquids containing lots of water) and we urinate, or pee, out the liquid called urine. It's very important that we have dissolved in the water that makes up much of our bodies, just the right amounts of certain chemicals, for example sodium and potassium. There are other chemicals, including urea, that are waste products that the body needs to get rid of. Our kidneys are where blood enters and exits, leaving behind a certain amount of urine extracted from the blood, with just the right amounts of sodium and potassium and other chemicals present in the urine to keep things in a good balance. From the kidneys, the urine goes down tubes called the ureters to a sack called the urinary bladder.

When the bladder gets full, we get the urge to urinate. In males, the urine goes through a little tube called the urethra that goes through the penis and from there out into the toilet. In females, the tube from the urinary bladder goes to the urethra, which opens to the outside right between the clitoris and the vagina.

Endocrine system: The nervous system sends its messages along nerves via reactions involving electrical charges. The endocrine system also helps the body communicate with itself, but it does so by various organs (called glands) putting chemicals into the bloodstream. Those chemicals have effects on other parts of the body, and they are called hormones. The pituitary gland is very much connected to the brain, especially the hypothalamus. The pituitary puts hormones into the blood that regulate how much water is filtered out of the urine, and other hormones that regulate the action of other glands, including the thyroid and the adrenal. The thyroid hormones regulate how fast the body generates energy; the adrenal cortical hormones regulate a variety of functions including certain parts of the immune system and the absorption of sodium and potassium from the urine. The parathyroid glands have to do with the regulation of calcium in our bloodstreams and in our bones.

Lymphatic system: Most people are familiar with the blood vessels and the circulation of blood through the body. The lymphatic system is another system where fluid circulates. Some of the fluid from blood goes out into the tissues, and is called interstitial fluid. This fluid gets collected into little tubes called lymphatic vessels; these eventually empty back into the blood system. They have thinner walls than the blood vessels and for that reason are more difficult to see. On the way, the fluid of the lymphatic system goes through some other special organs of this system: the lymph nodes, the tonsils, the thymus gland, and the spleen. These have a special role in the immune system, which is the germ-fighting system of the body. White blood cells originally produced in the bone marrow are mobilized into action in these organs, so as to fight against infections. In addition, the lymphatic system helps the body to get rid of substances that are no longer needed – for example, the spleen takes old red blood cells and breaks them down into their parts, which can then be recycled! One other function of the lymphatic system is in absorbing fats from the digestive system. So there are several crucial functions of this fluid-circulating system.

Reproductive system: This is the system that is responsible for making new people, creating babies, letting the human species keep going on. The endocrine system is intertwined with it, because there are hormones that direct the activity of the reproductive system. This is a system that's quite a bit different for males and females. The reproductive system is designed to bring together a sperm, that a male produces, with an ovum, (a.k.a. egg), that a woman produces, to make an embryo, which is what you get when the sperm and egg join together. A sperm and an egg each have half the number of chromosomes necessary to make a person. The chromosomes are the strands of DNA that carry the genetic information; they determine what we inherit from each of our parents. The sperms are made by males in the testicles, or testes, that reside in a little sack called the scrotum that is right underneath the penis. Nearby the testicles and penis is the prostate gland, which makes the fluid that the sperms are suspended in.

The mixture of fluid from the prostate and sperms from the testicles is called semen. The ova (that's the plural of ovum) are made in two round organs, one in each side of the lower belly of a woman; these are called ovaries. The ova travel through tubes called the fallopian tubes that connect the ovaries with the uterus. The uterus is a very expandable sack where the embryo grows into what's called a fetus and becomes a baby. The sperms get into the woman through a tube called the vagina that leads from the outside world to the uterus. The male deposits the sperm into the vagina during sexual intercourse, and from the vagina they swim up; one of them might fertilize the ovum and contribute to the formation of a new person. If the sperm and egg get together at the right time, the embryo plants itself in the uterus. There grows an umbilical cord connecting the uterus with the embryo, so that the mother can nourish the embryo. Before a woman gets pregnant, each month or so, the uterus lines itself with a rich blood supply to prepare for nourishing a fetus; if an ovum doesn't get fertilized that month, the uterus sheds the blood it had stored up for the purpose, and the blood comes out the vagina in what is called menstruation or the monthly period. Evolution has made the survival of the species more likely by making sexual intercourse pleasurable (except when it's not, for example when one person is being mean to the other, or when pregnancy is very undesirable and people are scared that birth control won't work, or in a variety of other circumstances). The function of the clitoris in the female is to make sexuality more pleasurable. There are various ways that people have figured out to prevent pregnancy but still have the pleasure of sexual activity. One more part of the reproductive system is the breasts, which in the female produce milk for any baby that is born. The reproductive system is fairly complicated; my explanation of the physical aspects is incomplete. But the psychological aspects of human sexuality are even more complicated, and could fill several books. That's because the reproductive system is very much connected to the most complicated organ of all: the brain.

Integumentary system: Integument is a big word for skin. Our skin forms an absolutely crucial barrier that keeps germs out from our bodies, and keeps the fluids in our tissues in.

Immune system: You may have picked up that the author of this book is interested in peace and harmony and the absence of fighting and violence. However, I am in full support of an army that is in a constant fight to disable and kill hostile invaders – our immune systems. Our amazing bodies have evolved to protect us against viruses and bacteria and other tiny organisms, or bigger ones such as certain types of worms, that would like to take up residence in our bodies and produce huge numbers of offspring that eventually kill us. The immune system also works to reject nonliving foreign substances when they intrude, such as wood splinters, and if our bodies produce a few cancer cells (which is much more frequent than we might think) to recognize them as bad and kill them and get rid of them.

People speak of two divisions of the immune system: innate and adaptive. The adaptive immune system "learns" to recognize certain substances as bad, and to prepare the defenses against them. This is the point of vaccination: to mobilize and prepare the adaptive immune

290

system to kill a certain virus, for example. The innate immune system is built so as to recognize certain substances as bad without needing to be "taught" to do so. Lots of the white blood cells that circulate through our bodies are born knowing that certain tiny organisms are not to be trusted. Sometimes those white blood cells actually form something that looks like a mouth, and chomp on those germs, and use some chemicals call enzymes to destroy them.

The immune system has cells that are specialized to kill the bad guys in the body, and it also uses proteins that it puts into circulation, called antibodies. The antibodies recognize the bad guys and glom onto them so as to kill or inactivate them.

The business of deciding, for every possible thing that can be in our bodies, what's a good guy and what's a bad guy, is a huge task for the immune system. Unfortunately, it can't be right all the time. Sometimes it attacks important cells that we really need for good functioning. This produces an "autoimmune" disease. In one type of diabetes, the immune system attacks the cells in our bodies that make insulin, which is a hormone crucial in using sugars to make energy. Sometimes the immune system attacks the cells of the thyroid gland, and makes people need to take thyroid hormone by pills. In rheumatoid arthritis, the immune system goes after tissues in our joints. In multiple sclerosis, the immune system goes after parts of the brain.

A different type of mistake that the immune system makes is to overdo the reaction to certain foreign substances, in a way that is unpleasant, dangerous, or even fatal. People who sneeze and have their eyes water when they're around cats experience a typical allergy. Asthma is an overdoing of the immune response in the airways; this can be anywhere from mildly annoying to (in rare cases) fatal. An anaphylactic reaction is an overdoing of the immune response that also can be fatal.

So the immune system is not perfect. But given the millions of different things that can wind up in us, it does the best it can, and it's kind of amazing how well it usually succeeds!

The serenity prayer, or figuring out what you can control

"Grant us the courage to change the things we can change, the serenity to accept the things we can't change, and the wisdom to tell the difference."

This has been a very helpful piece of guidance for lots of people. It's not good to spend a lot of time and energy fretting about things that you can't control. And at the same time, it's not wise to passively do nothing when there are things you can do to make a situation lots better than it is. Figuring out what you have the power to change and what you cannot change is in many cases not an easy task. Seeking the wisdom to make that decision is a worthwhile activity.

I would add one more bit to the serenity prayer, and ask for "the joyousness to appreciate and celebrate the things that are good as they are and don't need changing."

Greenhouse gases, greenhouse effect, global warming, and climate change

Do you know how a greenhouse works? A greenhouse is a place to grow plants, where the air will be warmer than the air around it. There are glass or plastic panels that make up the roof and sides of the greenhouse. These let the sun's rays in -- especially the type of rays that get turned into heat when the rays strike something. (These are infrared rays.) But the walls and roof of the greenhouse slow down the rate at which heat escapes. So the sun's rays warm up the greenhouse, without as much need for heaters. This principle is the reason why the insides of cars can get so hot in the summer when the windows are rolled up.

The same sort of thing is going on with our whole planet earth. There are some types of gases in the atmosphere that let the sun's rays through, but interfere with the escape of heat from earth, so that heat doesn't go radiating back off into space as fast and as much. Two of these gases are carbon dioxide and methane. If the percent of the air that consists of either of these gases increases by a fairly small amount, the earth gains more heat than it loses, and it heats up. This has been happening, and the earth has been getting hotter.

Why has the percent of greenhouse gases gone up in recent years? The simplest to understand is carbon dioxide. Each time gasoline is burned to fuel a car, bus, or plane, one of the by-products is carbon dioxide. Each time natural gas or oil is burned to heat a house, carbon dioxide is given off. Each time coal is burned, more carbon dioxide goes into the air. Each time we breathe, we put carbon dioxide into the air, but fortunately this doesn't represent a very big fraction of the sources of carbon dioxide.

Meanwhile, what takes carbon dioxide out of the air? Plants use carbon dioxide to grow. Each time a forest is cut down to make a road or a city, the rate at which our planet removes carbon dioxide from the air is decreased.

Thus human beings, by burning lots of "fossil fuels" such as coal, oil or gasoline, and natural gas, that took carbon out of the air a very long time ago, and by cutting down the plants that would take carbon dioxide out of the air, have increased the fraction of the air that consists of carbon dioxide. That carbon dioxide traps heat, and thus we have "global warming."

But the warming of the earth has lots of effects other than just warmer temperatures. When the ocean is warmer, it's easier for hurricanes to get started. Warmer temperatures in some places can make it more likely for wildfires to get started. Melting of ice near the north and south poles will cause a rise in sea levels. Certain plants and animals will no longer be suited for the environments they once were adapted to.

Global warming has caused people to think about ways of producing energy without burning fossil fuels: for example, by wind, solar energy, hydroelectric plants (using the energy of water going over waterfalls), and nuclear energy. Nuclear energy seems like a good solution unless something goes wrong and lots of radiation escapes to where it should not be.

Global warming also gives us another reason to think about the question, how many people at any given time can this planet support? Is there some number for the earth's total population, that is the most sustainable number? Is that number smaller than the number currently living on earth, or the number that are projected to be on this planet in future years?

$E=mc^2$: The interchangeability of matter and energy

Have you ever seen the equation $E=mc^2$? This is a very famous formula discovered by Albert Einstein. Let's talk about what it means.

We can think of the universe as made up of two things: matter and energy. Matter is things, and energy is the ability to push or pull on those things. Bricks, people, cars, water, air, chairs, bacteria, and all other stuff are examples of matter. The atoms in hot air have more energy than those in cold air. A moving train has more energy than one that is sitting still. A bunch of water at the top of a waterfall has energy that can be used to turn something and change the energy into electricity; that energy can be used to light our lights or heat or cool our houses.

At one time, there was a law of conservation of matter, and a law of conservation of energy -- that both matter and energy could be neither created nor destroyed. But Einstein figured out that matter can be destroyed, leaving energy in its place. The disappearance of just a little bit of matter creates a huge amount of energy.

In Einstein's equation, E stands for the amount of energy produced. m stands for the mass of the matter that disappears. And c is a very big number, the speed of light. C^2 is the speed of light multiplied by itself.

The electrical energy used in all of New York City in a typical day is a lot of energy. If the amount of matter present in a pair of shoes -- about a kilogram, a little over 2 pounds -- were converted fully into energy, that pair of shoes could supply all of New York City's electricity, according to my calculations, for about 7 years! Of course, taking a pair of shoes and converting it completely into energy is not something we can do! But in nuclear reactions, it is actually possible to measure the tiny amounts of matter that get converted into large amounts of energy.

For this book, I've tried to pick the ideas that really help us to lead our lives better. How does $E=mc^2$ help you to lead a better life? I will have to confess that for most people, it doesn't, not unless you happen to get pleasure out of understanding how the universe works, and you're curious about things and enjoying finding things out, even if you'll never use them directly. For the curious bunch, this big idea's for you!

Reciprocal interaction, also known as ping-pong Interaction

If you're around an infant, one of the first really fun games that you can do requires nothing but a floor and a ball. You roll the ball to the child, and if the child goes after it, you make excited and approving noises. If the child pushes it back to you, you make excited and approving noises again. Now you push it back toward the child. Pretty fascinating game, huh? Well, if you're really interested in the development of that child, it is tremendously fascinating and gratifying, especially if the child smiles and otherwise seems to enjoy this.

Or: you hide your face, and the child watches. You reveal your face, saying "Peek-a-boo!" with a big smile, and the child laughs or smiles.

Maybe later on, the child takes on the hider-and-revealer role in the game, getting behind a pillow or something while the other person pretends to look around. Then the child shows their face, and the seeker makes a big excited and approving reaction to finding the lost child.

When the child starts learning to talk, having someone who listens and talks in response, in an understandable and fun way, is an enormous spur to the child's development of skill in using language.

Meanwhile, college kids out on a "quad" throw a football back and forth. Some senior citizens nearby hit tennis balls or pickle balls or ping-pong balls back and forth with each other.

Almost everywhere, people chat with each other, have social conversation, "hang out" together. People's conversation is the most important type of turn-taking game.

All of these are examples of "reciprocal interaction." People take turns. One does something. The second responds to what the first one does. The first one responds to the second one's response. Each of them, in their turn, responds to the other and gives the other something to respond to.

We probably have something built into our brains that makes us enjoy reciprocal interaction. When people cultivate the art of talking in an interesting and fun way with each other, they have a source of enjoyment that can last a lifetime.

We all are familiar with ways that reciprocal interaction can fail. Someone starts talking with us, and we think of what we'd like to say when it's our turn -- but our turn doesn't come! The person just keeps blabbing!

Sometimes the person keeps talking even if we yawn, look at our watch, or start fiddling with our phones! Another failure of reciprocal interaction comes when we say something to another person, but the other person doesn't respond -- instead, the person looks at their phone, looks at the TV, or otherwise ignores us. Maybe the person was in the middle of some important work and didn't want to be distracted, and we should have waited before trying to get reciprocal interaction going.

If you observe people, I think you'll notice that a large fraction of human happiness has to do with the extent to which people can have pleasant reciprocal interactions.

Types of reactions to bad experiences

Bad things happen to people. They get hit by other people. They get neglected by the people who are supposed to protect them. They get sexually abused. They have people speak to them in very mean and disrespectful ways. They get compelled or pressured to try to do things and then get humiliated when they fail. They get stolen from. They have their loved ones victimized by violence. They or their loved ones are victims of unsafe or unhealthy environments. They get threats that keep them scared. They lose people whom they are attached to. They make very regrettable mistakes.

The world is very unfair, and some people have way more bad experiences than others. Almost none of us makes it through life without at least some bad experience.

There are several ways that people can react to bad experiences. Some of those ways tend to make the person even less happy than they were, and some tend to make them more happy. The big idea of this section is that it's good just to be familiar with a few of the options that people pick.

1. **Identification with the aggressor**. This means that the person who has been bullied bullies other people. The person who gets humiliated and ridiculed by unkind words uses the same type of words with other people. This brings about very sad results.

2. **The repetition compulsion**. This means that the person who has had bad experiences for some reason keeps getting into situations where those experiences keep happening. For example, someone who has had an abusive parent keeps picking abusive persons as their romantic partners.

3. **Drug-seeking**. They seek to numb the pain that comes from remembering the bad experiences by using one or more drugs. If the drug is addictive, this creates a whole new set of problems.

4. **Acting out the need for help**. This means that the person does things that communicate to other people the idea, "I need help," sometimes without the person's actually realizing that this is what they are doing. They get crying spells, they lose their appetite, they get physical symptoms, they get into situations they need to be rescued from.

5. **Self-protection and self-healing**. They get away from mean people and bad environments. They learn about how to deal with trauma. They work on healing themselves from the bad effects of what happened to them, with the help of expert knowledge, gained in person or through reading. They try to become as expert as possible at making good decisions, perhaps telling themselves, "No matter what has happened to you, if you can keep making

good decisions at choice point after choice point, you're going to do OK!"

6. **Activism and altruism**. They take the emotions they feel about their suffering and harness them as motivation to improve the world. For example, someone whose spouse was a victim of gun violence starts an organization to try to reduce gun violence. Someone who was abused as a child becomes an expert at preventing parents from abusing their children.

Of course, I haven't listed all the possibilities. And lots of times people respond in a variety of different ways at different times. Many chance factors influence which of these directions someone will go in. It may be helpful for people to think about these options and try to choose, consciously, how they want to respond and how they don't. And on the chance that it is helpful, I list it as a big idea.

The distributive law

Let's make a row of five things, repeated 3 times. But let's think of the five things as separated into three and two more. Let's have the 5 things be the letter U (standing for unit).

UUU   UU
UUU   UU
UUU   UU

Having a total of 3 groups of 5 things represents multiplication: 3 x 5.
It's pretty clear from the picture above that 3 5's is the same as 3 3's and 3 more 2's, right?
Or in other words, (or symbols) 3 x 5 = 3 x 3 + 3 x 2.

Or otherwise, 3 x (3+2) = 3 x 3 + 3 x 2.

It is NOT true that 3 x (3 + 2) = 3 x 3 + 2. If we're going to make 3 repetitions of the 3 plus 2 things, we've got to repeat the 2's just like we repeated the 3's.
Let's give another example with other numbers.
4 x (1+2) = 4 x 1 + 4 x 2
Is that right? Yep, on the left side of the equation, we get 4 x 3 or 12. On the right side, we get 4 + 8, or 12.

We can use literal numbers, or letters that stand for numbers, to express this idea:
a x (b + c) = a x b + a x c

Or, since if we write two letters together it means to multiply them,
a(b+c) = ab + ac

This is called the distributive law.

People use the law all the time when solving algebra equations. You run into expressions like 3(x+2). You have to remember the distributive law telling us that this can be simplified to 3x+6 … and not 3x + 2!

Metric system versus the US system – units of measurement

The big idea of this section is that we measure things by deciding upon "units" of whatever we are measuring, and then figuring out how many of those units are in whatever we are trying to measure. We can use different units to express how much something is. And we can express things that we measure in terms of different units, and convert from one unit to another.

In the USA, we usually think of how tall you are as a certain number of feet and inches, and how much you weigh as a certain number of pounds (and a number of ounces, especially when you're a baby). We measure usually measure volumes of liquids in gallons, quarts, pints, cups, tablespoons, teaspoons, and fluid ounces. This system has been called the British Imperial System, but now people in Britain, as well as people in most other countries other than the USA, and scientists in the USA, use the metric system. In that system we talk of meters, grams, cubic centimeters, liters, and so forth as the familiar units. In the USA, if we're not a scientist, we usually measure temperature on the Farenheit scale, where water freezes at 32 degrees and boils at 212 degrees. Most of the rest of the world, and the scientific community in the USA, use the Celsius scale, where water freezes at 0 degrees and boils at 100 degrees.

In both systems, when we are measuring little things, we like to have smaller units, and for bigger things, bigger units. For example, the amount you take of most medicines, even in the USA, is usually measured in milligrams. I'm thinking of a certain pill that has 10 milligrams of medicine in it. It's a lot more convenient to say 10 milligrams than to say "1.1 hundred-millionths of a ton," even though both communicate about the same amount of medicine.

What's the big advantage of the metric system? It's mainly that the relation between big units and small units is so much simpler, because the ratios are powers of 10. For example, ten millimeters are in a centimeter; 100

centimeters equal 1 meter; 1000 meters equal a kilometer. How many meters are in 8 kilometers? That's easy, 8 with 1000 in each, that gives 8000. On the other hand: 12 inches are in one foot, three feet in a yard, 5,280 feet or 1,760 yards in a mile. How many inches in a mile? 5,280 x 12, which isn't very easy for most people to do in their heads.

The metric system uses prefixes that are the same for mass, length, or volume.

Milli = one thousandth
centi = one hundredth
kilo = one thousand

So a milliliter is a thousandth of a liter, a millimeter is a thousandth of a meter, and a milligram is a thousandth of a gram. A kiloliter is a thousand liters, a kilometer is a thousand meters, and a kilogram is a thousand grams.

There are other prefixes for bigger and smaller units. A nanometer, for example, is a billionth of a meter. A gigameter, on the other hand, is a billion meters.

One tradition that hasn't been changed and simplified much by the metric system is the measurement of time. There are still 60 seconds in a minute, 60 minutes in an hour, and 24 hours in a day, for 86,400 seconds in a day. We could have used powers of 10, and defined things that a second was a little shorter, so as to make 100,000 seconds in a day, 100 seconds in a minute, 100 minutes in an hour, and 10 hours in a day, but such a system never caught on. We do speak of thousandths of a second as milliseconds, and billionths of a second as nanoseconds. When it comes to the number of days in a year, we can't really make that a power of 10 if we want the years to start and end in the same season. We're stuck with 365.25 days in a year because that's how long it takes for the earth to make one complete trip around the sun.

Negative numbers

How can you have anything less than zero? In some situations where we use numbers, it doesn't make any sense. For example, Billy has 3 apples and you take 5 away from him. Wait – after you've taken 3 away you can't take 2 more away to give him -2 (negative 2) apples. However, we can define what we mean by numbers just a little differently, and have this same situation makes lots of sense. Billy has 3 apples, and he says to Joan, "In return for what you've given me, I'm giving you 5 apples. I have 3 now, and will owe you two more." Now the "owing 2 more" means that Billy has negative 2 apples. When he gets 2, and turns them over to Joan, his net apple ownership will be 0. When he had negative 2, he had a number such that when 2 was added to it, he had zero.

Suppose you have a bank account. When you deposit money into it, you increase the amount in it; when you take money out, you decrease it. What's the change in your total account value when you take $100 out? It's negative $100.

Suppose the temperature is 0 degrees Farenheit. That's really cold. Then the temperature goes down farther still, 10 degrees colder. Now the temperature is 10 degrees below zero, or -10 degrees, or negative 10 degrees.

Suppose there's a rating scale for how much someone likes sardines. 10 is that sardines just send someone into ecstacy. 0 is that eating sardines does not deliver any pleasure to the person. How do we rate it if the very smell of sardines makes someone want to vomit? It would make sense to call that -10 on our scale, and have our scale run from -10 to +10, with 0 meaning that eating sardines is a neutral experience, neither painful nor pleasant.

Suppose that we define sea level as the height of the sea, relative to the land. Suppose we call that zero. A mountain might be a good bit above sea level, and a very deep valley might be below sea level. The elevation of the valley would be expressed as a negative number.

Suppose that we define a coordinate system where there's a point we call 0,0, which is the origin. We decide to define the position of any point by measuring how far to the right of the origin it is, and how far up from the origin it is. So 10 units to the right and 10 units up is called (10,10). What do you think we should call the point 10 units to the left and 10 units down? We'd call it (-10, -10). This is another use of negative numbers. This, by the way, is a big idea inserted in this discussion of another big idea. The system we've just described is a big idea called the Cartesian Coordinate System, named after a man who introduced it; his last name was Descartes. (You may read elsewhere about epistemology, which is the field that asks, "How do we know what we know?" Descartes is famous for figuring out that at least he knew he existed. The famous quotation is, "I think, therefore I am.")

But getting back to the big idea of this section, in lots of situations negative numbers are very useful in expressing what is going on, and they aid us greatly in describing and figuring things out about this world.

Percents, fractions, ratios

A pretty high fraction of the math people need to use in everyday life, for example in managing their finances, involves percents, fractions, and ratios. (After composing that sentence, I realized that it referred to a fraction, and it could have as easily referred to a percent!)

The ratio of a first number to a second number is how many times more the first is than the second. The ratio of 6 to 2 is 3, because 6 is 3 times higher than 2. The ratio of 2 to 6 is 1/3, because 2 is 1/3 of 6. ("Of means times.")

One meaning of a fraction is, out of a certain number of things, how many of them have a certain characteristic? So: "In what fraction of the last 20 days have you laughed?" means how many out of 20 have you laughed. If the number was 8, the fraction was 8/20, which is the same as 2/5.

A way of thinking about percents is, "Out of 100 things, how many of them have a certain characteristic?" So, if 50% of the people I run across one day are really nice people, that means that 50/100, or ½ of them, are really nice. In dealing with money, percents are very often used. If someone lends $100 and gets 5% interest, that means the person gets $5 interest for the $100 that was lent.

We have to expand the meaning of fractions and percents beyond what I just said, to include fractions greater than 1 and percents greater than 100. If someone buys a house for $100,000 and the price goes up to $150,000, the new price is 3/2 of the old price. The new price is 150% of the new price. If the price goes up from $100,000 to $400,000, it went up by $300,000, or by 300% of the original price.

The concept of division is central to ratios, fractions, and percents. The ratio of a first number to a second is the first divided by the second. The fraction that a first number is of a second is the first divided by the second. And the percent that a first number is of a second is the first divided by the second, times 100.

Reflections and tracking and describing

Reflections are a type of utterance people make; tracking and describing is a similar type of utterance. Unlike most things that we say to other people, they are not meant to either tell the person something new, tell the other person to do something, or get the person to answer a question. They are meant to communicate to the other person that you are paying attention to them and understanding what they are doing or saying, and checking to make sure you are understanding right.

Here's an example of a reflection.

Person 1: I like seeing patients and being their doctor and helping them. But I hate all the time I need to be at the computer. I spend so much time in record keeping. And the computer programs for record keeping seem to make things worse rather than better.

Person 2: If I understand you right, you like your job of doctoring, but you find the computerized record keeping *very* frustrating.

What's the point of doing reflections? If there's any doubt in your mind about whether you understand what the other person said, you can let the person confirm or deny the way you paraphrased what they said. Even if there's no doubt that you understood correctly, the reflection lets the other person clear up any doubt in their mind that you understood correctly. And even if there was no doubt on their part, for most people it feels good to hear very accurate reflections. It feels good to know that the other person is performing the kind act of really tuning in and concentrating on what you're trying to communicate. And a final advantage of reflections is what they do not do: they don't give the person unwanted advice or bossiness, ask the person a question about something that's distracting from the direction they wanted to go, and they don't criticize the other person. They are purely listening, and checking out how accurately the listening is going.

Some reflections are "better" than others. The best reflections get to the essence of what the person is communicating, what it is that they really care about. Here's an example:

Person 1: I was eating supper with them, and they were so proud to serve me this dish that they make with lima beans. But I was thinking, "What am I going to do?" For some reason lima beans make me feel like throwing up!

Person 2: So you're saying you don't like lima beans.

That's correct, but it's not a very good reflection. Compare that with this one:

Person 2: So you're saying you were caught in a dilemma – you didn't want to disappoint your hosts who had made supper, but you also didn't want to gag on the lima beans.

Tracking and describing is like a reflection, only what you're putting into words is not a paraphrase of the other person's words, but a description of their actions.

Here are some examples of tracking and describing.

Someone watches a 3 year old play with toys: "Hey, there goes Mr. Farmer into the truck…. Putting all those cabbages into the truck…. He's taking them back to the farmhouse!"

A parent observes their adolescent child play with the guitar. "Sounds like a new song is getting figured out! … You're getting where all the notes are! … Now those notes are getting into a smooth rhythm!"

A spouse watches their partner start to exercise. "Exercise time, huh? … A bunch of squats. I bet those legs can really feel it now…. Getting the heart rate even higher!"

Both with reflections and with tracking and describing, the tone of voice that someone uses is really important. If the tones are of approval and enthusiasm, these provide a way of one person communicating good will, kindness, and love to another.

Pi, and other ratios in figures with similar shapes

We talked earlier about ratios. If you have something circular – a plate, a tree trunk, a hula hoop, a jar top, a tire – what's the ratio of the circumference of that circular thing (the distance around it) to the diameter (the distance from one side to the other, going straight through the center)? For example, if there's a perfectly circular lake, how much farther is it to walk around it than to paddle a boat from one side to the other, through the center? Someone might be tempted to say, "It probably depends on how big the circle is." But it doesn't! The ratio is the same for every circle, no matter how big or small.

And that ratio is called pi. It's a number not far away from 3 1/7. It's an interesting number because you can't express it exactly, as a decimal with any number of decimal places – there are always more, and they never repeat. Pi starts out like this: 3.14159265358. That's more decimal places than you'll need. Usually 3.14 is close enough. It's fun to think of pi sentences, where the number of letters in each word corresponds to a digit in pi. "How I like a sweet milkshake on summer morns and moonlit evenings," is one of them.

If someone tells you the diameter of a circle and asks for the circumference, you just multiply by pi. If someone gives you the circumference and asks you for the diameter, you just divide the circumference by pi.

Pi shows up in various mathematical ideas that don't obviously have to do with the ratio of a circumference to a diameter. What do you think the following number is equal to?

310

4 * (1 - 1/3 + 1/5 - 1/7 + 1/9 - 1/11… and so on forever…)

The answer is … pi!

By the way, the fact that the ratio of lengths stays the same no matter how big or small the figure is is not confined to circles. The ratio of a side of a square to the diagonal, the ratio of the length of one side of a triangle to another, the ratio of the length of someone's nose to the length of their ear when you enlarge a picture – the ratios stay the same in all cases. In fact, that is sort of what it means to say that two figures of different sizes are "the same shape."

The golden rule of equation solving

Suppose you have a mathematical problem that gives rise to an equation that you need to solve. Here's a simple example. Three times a certain number, plus 9, is 60. What's the number? You can translate the problem into symbols like this:

Let X equal the unknown number.

$3X + 9 = 60$

To solve this, we can use the "golden rule of equations," which is that when you do the same thing to both sides of the equation, the equation remains true. Just to illustrate this, suppose we start with

$13 = 13.$

We add 7 to each side of the equation, and we get
20=20.

We subtract 4 from each side, and we get
16=16.

We take the positive square root of each side, and we get
4=4.

If it works with numbers, it also works when the two things on either side of the equals sign don't look exactly alike.

To return to our problem,
$3X + 9 = 60$,
we can subtract 9 from both sides of the equation, and get
$3X = 51$.

Then we can divide both sides by 3, and get
$X=17$.
    We check our answer by seeing if three times this number plus 9 equals 60, and it does. Using the golden rule of equations gave us the right answer, and it can do so with much more complicated equations.

Things you can tell a computer program to do

    Computers, and the programs or "apps" that run them, have a huge influence on our lives. Everything that we do with computers involves code that programmers write that tells the computer what to do. There are many different languages that programmers can use to give instructions to a computer. The "syntax" of a computer language is the particular way you tell the computer to do something. The things that you tell the computer to do are similar from one language to another. The very complicated things that you can get computers to do are often constructed from fairly simple building blocks. Below are some of them.

1. Display something to the screen. Often the first program that people are asked to write is one that displays the phrase, "Hello, world!" on the screen. The syntax is usually pretty simple, something like
Print ("Hello, world!")

2. Assign a number or a string of characters or a list of such to a variable name. For example, you tell the computer to let the variable called A be assigned the value of 20. Or you tell it to assign the phrase "Please type in your answer and press the enter key." to the variable called B.

3. Get input from the user.
For example, you ask the user to type in their name, and you assign the result to a variable called username.

4. Do calculations with numbers.
For example, we make a variable called C and assign to it 5% of variable A.

5. Do manipulations of strings of letters or numbers or other symbols. For example, we tell it to look for "jamie" in a string of text and replace it with "Jamie."

6. Generate random numbers. For example, we generate two whole numbers between 0 and 10 for the user to practice with addition facts.

7. Make decisions depending on "If" some condition is true. For example, if the student gives the right answer, we tell the program to display the words "good

job" and add one to the variable keeping track of right answers; if the student gives the wrong answer, the program is to say, "I thought the right answer was …." and display the right answer, and add one to the variable keeping track of wrong answers.

8. Loop through a certain set of commands more than once. For example, in a program for practicing addition facts, the program loops back and generates more problems and responds to the user's answer until it's told to stop.

9. Create files, get information from or save it to information to the files, open or close files to use for these purposes. For example, a program for practicing math facts opens a file and appends to the end of the file the results of the student's next session of practice.

10. Create lines of code called functions, where you can tell the program to input something into the function; the function produces output of a certain type.

You may be surprised at how many thousands of computer programs or applications can be written just by using these basic commands! The art of computer programming involves figuring out how to break down a complicated task into simpler tasks such as those listed above.

Trial by jury, representation by lawyer

People who get into power tend to want to get still more power. Suppose someone gets into some powerful government position and wants to suppress the voices of any people who disagree with him. (I'm imagining the person as male.) The person appoints judges, and influences prosecutors to bring criminal charges against

314

those who don't like him. The leader lets the judges know that there are ways of removing judges from their jobs, that the leader has control over. Do you think there could be a very dangerous situation where the judges tend to do what the leader wants, and throw the leader's opponents in jail, or worse? Things like this have been known to happen, and examples in history are not scarce!

For this reason, criminal trials are supposed to be decided by juries of the accused person's "peers" – that is, people who aren't controlled or influenced by whoever is in charge, just ordinary citizens. This is a "check," or a barrier, against a leader taking too much control over the criminal justice system.

There are disadvantages of the jury system. Sometimes there are trials where a lot of complex knowledge is necessary to make a good decision, and most jurors don't have the knowledge to understand. In some places public opinion is so far one way or the other that most jurors will have their minds made up before the trial. And the amounts that jurors get paid for their service are so small that being called for jury duty for many people represents a big financial loss. Another issue is that most of the time "plea bargaining" is used to settle the criminal case rather than a trial. By plea bargaining is meant something a prosecutor might say like, "I'll charge you with a crime that gets a sentence of 20 years, but I won't if you plead guilty to a lesser crime that gets a sentence of 2 years."

Despite these disadvantages, it still is an important idea to try to get unbiased people, called jurors, to make court decisions, rather than rely totally on judges.

The importance of measurement in science

Suppose we want to know whether meditation makes people mentally healthier. If we want to approach this question scientifically, we need to do something other than just to think about the question -- we need to collect observations. Maybe we observe a bunch of people who meditate in various amounts, and see how mentally healthy they are, and see if the mental health is correlated with the amount of meditation. Or maybe we even randomly assign people to meditation or something else, and see after some time how the two groups compare on mental health.

But all this supposes that we have some way of measuring the variables we're interested in. How do we measure how mentally healthy someone is? How do we measure how much meditation they've done, or how well or how thoroughly they've done it? There are various ways. We can just give people a questionnaire to fill out, asking them about their mood, their relationships, their energy level, and so forth, and total up the ratings for the answers, and boom, that's how mentally healthy they are. Or we can do extensive interviews with everyone in their family, their work supervisor, their coworkers, and take the notes from these to get a rating of how mentally healthy they are. Or we can give them a bunch of situations and ask them what they would do in those situations, and have a panel of people rate from these how mentally healthy their responses are. There are all sorts of ways of measuring mental health.

And what do we mean by meditation? One person means, "I take my smartphone, and rather than listening to music, I listen to someone doing guided meditations." Another person means, "I listen to music that relaxes me --

for me, that's heavy metal music." Another person means, "I sit in a relaxed but alert way, with my eyes closed, and imagine one person after another, and wish for that person to give and receive kindness and live in compassion and peace."

The moral of this example is that the results that we get from our scientific study depend very greatly upon how we measure whatever we're trying to study! And lots of the very important things of life are very difficult to measure. Happiness, the family emotional climate, stress, the quality of life, the quality of education -- yes, people measure all these things, but they do it in many different ways that may not agree with one another!

Reliability and validity

The previous idea spoke about how science depends on being able to measure things accurately. Reliability and validity are ideas that have to do with the accuracy of measurements.

The reliability of a way of measuring something means: if we measure the same thing twice (or more), how well do our measurements agree with one another? For example, we measure the reading skill of a bunch of folks, and then a few days later we measure again. Or if we're measuring skill in option-generating, we get two raters to rate the options people think of for some situations, and we see if the scores agree with each other. Or if we're measuring depression, we give a questionnaire measuring how depressed someone is, and we see if the score from the odd numbered items agree with those from the even numbered items. All of these are ways of approaching the question, "Is our measurement reliable?"

The validity of a measurement is the answer to the question, "Are we really measuring what we want to measure, or what we think we're measuring?" For example, suppose someone is trying to help kids be careful not to set fires. They have a program to teach them about fire safety. The way they measure their results is to have the kids look at pictures that have to do with fires, and make up stories about the pictures; raters are trained to rate how careful about fires the people in the stories are. Maybe the raters agree with each other well, and the measure is reliable. But someone may ask, are you really measuring how careful about fires the kids are in their real life behavior? The scientist would need to prove that the stories children told had some power to predict what they would do in real life, before people would say that the measure of fire safety was valid.

Genetics and epigenetics.

Each of our cells (with some exceptions) has strands of DNA. The purpose of DNA is to tell the cell how to act -- what sorts of chemical reactions to do and what not to do. There are four different building blocks for DNA -- they are abbreviated A, T, G, and C. These can occur in all different orders, just as the letters in words or the digits in numbers, and like those, they work like a code. A sequence of DNA that tells a certain chemical reaction to go is called a gene. The orders of the parts of the DNA strands in our cells influence all sorts of things about us: how tall we are, what color our eyes are, what we look like, how fast we can run, how much we enjoy doing math, how easily we get angry, how likely we are to get certain diseases, and almost everything about us. I was careful to use the word

318

"influence" instead of the word "determine." For most of the things I listed, there are all sorts of things that happen to us and that we do that also influence those things. For example, if we spend a lot of time playing tag or racing people or playing full court basketball, that also can influence how fast we can run. If we grow up in a place where people often fight with one another, that also can influence how easily we get angry. Thus we speak of heredity (which is what we get genetically) and environment (which is what happens to us) as two big influences. In the things I listed, eye color has a big contribution from heredity and not much from environment. In the things I listed, enjoyment of math probably depends a lot on how well you are taught math, and is less dependent on genetics than eye color is.

The field of "epigenetics" has to do with how things that happen to us, our environments, can actually change the structure of our genes. Certain parts of the DNA strand can be activated or inactivated. For example, being treated very kindly or in a very mean way may turn on or off different parts of our genes.

There have in recent years been big advances in helping people with diseases that are influenced by genes, and advances in all sorts of other things having to do with genetics. But for most of us, at this point in history at least, directly manipulating our genes is not something we can do; trying to make the best choices and get into the situations where better things happen to us are the main ways to make life better.

Putting things into words as a way of resolving trauma

When bad things happen to people, particularly the sorts of bad things where people are treated very cruelly by other people, it's often hard to get over those experiences. Sometimes the image of them keeps flashing back into memory in a very unpleasant way. Sometimes people have nightmares much more frequently than they would otherwise. Sometimes people feel angry or sad without a reason that they can connect to whatever is going on in the present for them. We call the bad things that happen trauma, and when people have lots of unhappy lingering effects from the trauma, we might say they are suffering from post-traumatic stress.

There are many ways that people can help themselves to get over trauma. Long books have been written about this subject. But the one big idea for this section is that putting things into words often (but not always) helps. Telling the story of what happened, writing down or letting someone else write down what happened, seems to help, with some big "ifs." It's more likely to help if it's done with someone who is kind and caring. It's more likely to help if one can prepare for doing it and do it when one is ready, rather than being pushed into doing it when they don't want to. It's better to do it step by step, starting with the easier parts and working the way up to the harder parts. And when it's done, that is, how long after the traumatic event, seems to make a difference. There have been studies where it appeared better to "leave well enough alone" than to get people to "put the story into words."

Why does this help? We don't know for sure, but one possibility is that the parts of the brain that process language and that represent things in words are less likely to cause us pain than the parts that store bad memories that aren't coded into words.

Just as books have illustrations, sometimes people find it useful to have pictures going along with the story.

Putting the story of the trauma into words is not the only thing that helps us get over bad experiences. Learning how to make the best decisions we can, in each choice point going forward, is another very important thing to do. It's comforting sometimes to think: "No matter what happened to me in the past, if I can make good choices every day going forward, life has a great chance of working out well."

The worst forms of trauma appear to be cruel mistreatment by another human being, or group of them. Of course, the best answer to "post-traumatic stress disorder" is to reduce or eliminate horrible experiences that people have, especially those that come from the cruelty of others. We should all work toward a world where this is the case, even though no one is counting on success any time soon.

All or none with neurons firing

The cells in our brains, spinal cords, and nerves are called neurons. All the activity that we do -- all our thoughts, feelings, movements, sensations -- correspond to what happens in our neurons. Scientists have discovered that as a rule, neurons do what they do by either "firing" or not. By "firing," we mean that the electrical state of the neuron changes, by the movement of tiny atoms carrying an electrical charge, called ions, into or out of the neuron. And what does the firing of a neuron accomplish? Often, the result is to make one or more other neurons fire. It's not one neuron that makes us happy or sad, but the pattern of neurons firing in different places. For those neurons called motor neurons, the accomplishment of firing is to make a muscle cell, or several of them, contract. So if I decide to wiggle my right finger, some neurons up on the left side of my brain fire, and they excite other neurons that go down to the muscles in my hand and forearm, and the firing of the neurons makes the muscle cells move my finger. The process is complex, even for one simple movement. It's hard to even imagine what amazing things the neurons are doing, for example, when a concert pianist plays. Or when someone makes up the song that the pianist plays, or when someone makes an important decision.

After people discovered that the things we do, think, and feel are determined by whether neurons fire or don't fire, they invented computers. Inside computer chips are tiny little things called transistors that are either turned on or off. The amazing things that computers do are all determined by whether the tiny units are on or off, and the patterns of their firing relative to one another. In lots of ways computers are built to behave as nervous tissue or brains do. The transistors are to computers as neurons are to us!

Synapses and neurochemicals at synapses

In the idea just before this one, we talked about neurons firing or not firing. We talked about how very often, the consequence of a neuron firing is that it signals another neuron, or several of them, to fire next. How does one neuron tell another neuron to fire? First, it's good to know that neurons are not shaped like little round balls -- they often are balls with long branches coming off them. Some of those branches get messages from other neurons (those branches are called dendrites) and some of the branches carry messages to other neurons (those branches are called axons). The little gap between where one neuron stops and another one starts is called a synapse.

Since the firing of neurons has to do with electrical charges, one might think that the signal goes from one neuron to another by something like an electrical spark -- but that's not what happens. What does happen is that the end of one neuron releases a chemical, and that chemical is recognized by the dendrite of the other neuron in places called receptors, and the reaction between the chemical and the receptors causes the second neuron to fire. The chemicals that the body uses to transmit messages from one neuron to another are called neurotransmitters. Different synapses use different neurotransmitters.

One of the ways in which this idea is important is that certain drugs can increase or decrease the availability of neurotransmitters at the synapses, or can increase or decrease how easily the receptors respond to the neurotransmitters. Almost all drugs that affect the brain or nervous system do so in these ways.

It seems like the process of secreting a chemical into the synapse, having that chemical make its way over to the other neuron, and causing the second neuron to fire would be take a long time to happen. But all you have to do is to watch a concert pianist or a gymnast or a basketball player or almost anyone doing the complex things we do, to realize that the transmission across synapses happens super-fast!

The periodic table of the elements

All the stuff we can see and touch and smell, and we ourselves, are made of elements. Each element is made up of atoms. Atoms have protons (with a positive charge) and neutrons (with a neutral charge) in their nucleus, which is at the center of the atom. Revolving around the nucleus are electrons, which have a negative charge. What distinguishes one element from another is how many protons it has. An atom with one proton is hydrogen, with two protons is helium, with three protons is lithium, with 12 is carbon, with 16 is oxygen, and so forth. The atoms in pure elements have the same number of electrons as protons, so the positive and negative charges equal and make the atom uncharged. If we list the elements in order of how many protons they have, we go a long way toward organizing our thinking about elements. But it turns out that we can list them in order in rows and columns, so that the elements in the same column tend to behave like each other in certain ways. For example, in one column there are a bunch of gases that don't tend to react with and join up with other types of atoms. In another column there are metals that are very reactive, and in another there are gases that are very reactive.

Do you want to read an explanation of why the elements in a certain column of the periodic table act alike in some ways? Here goes. The electrons don't just go around the atoms randomly -- it's as if they fill up little sacks called "shells." The next heavier atom starts another sack, and as we look to the atoms that are heavier and heavier, the next sack gradually gets filled up. Atoms seem to "like" to be in the state where the sacks are filled up with electrons. So the atoms that have only one electron in a new sack tend to get rid of that electron by giving it to another atom. Likewise, the atoms that need only one electron to get a full sack seem to be "eager" to get electrons from other atoms. Sodium is an example of an element where the atoms are starting a new sack with only one electron in it. Chlorine is an example of an element where the atoms need only one electron to have a full sack. For this reason, sodium and chlorine like to partner up: sodium gives one of its electrons to chlorine, so they both have full sacks. The sodium atom is left with a positive charge from getting rid of its electron, and the chlorine atom is left with a negative charge from gaining an electron. Since opposite charges attract each other, the sodium and chlorine atoms tend to stick together in a crystal. We call resulting stuff a compound, called sodium chloride, more commonly called salt. So the next time you see salt sprinkled on food, you can imagine those atoms partnering up so that each of them is happier by having a full sack of electrons!

Lithium, potassium, and sodium all have one electron starting a new sack; they are arranged into the same column of the periodic table. Bromine, chlorine, and fluorine all need one more electron to fill the sack; they are in the same column. Helium, neon, and radon all have full sacks; they're in a column with each other that contains "inert gases." If you have ever tasted potassium chloride (it's sold as a salt substitute) you know that it tastes a lot like salt, but not quite. The elements in the same column behave a lot like each other, but not exactly like each other.

Being a good neighbor

Many of the places where people live -- apartments, condominiums, townhouses, and even houses -- have people living pretty close to each other. The quality of life depends a lot on whether your neighbors are "good neighbors." One part of being a good neighbor is being friendly, kind, and helpful when you encounter the people who live near you. Another part is having a good sense of when your neighbors would like to get together and socialize, and when they would like for you to leave them alone. But the big idea of this unit is that the important aspects of being a good neighbor are just NOT doing some bothersome things. Those are: 1) making too much noise -- especially when the neighbors may be sleeping. 2) Putting things into the air, such as smoke, that the neighbors shouldn't have to breathe. 3) Being careless about hazards, the most important of which is fire -- one of the most un-neighborly things to do is to catch the whole dwelling place on fire. 4) Leaving trash or other unwanted stuff, or bring lots of your friends and acquaintances, into the "common areas" of the place -- the lobby, the hallways, the yard, the sidewalk in front -- the places you don't own or rent. 5) This goes without saying, but I'll say it anyway: avoiding violence. Even more un-neighborly than accidentally setting the place on fire is deliberately hurting or killing your neighbor! Sometimes violence between neighbors results from conflict over the more minor things like too much noise or the presence of smoke.

If everyone did the things that this section listed, the happiness of the world could be increased by a large amount!

Perfectionism

Suppose someone has an essay to write. The person gets into mind the first sentence, but then the person thinks, "That's not a good way to start. That doesn't sound right. That's not good enough." Every time the person gets in mind a way to start out, the critical voice in the person's head says that it isn't good enough. So the person just can't get started at all, and the essay doesn't get written. We might say that this person's problem is "perfectionism." The person seems to believe that nothing short of perfect is OK, and therefore nothing gets done.

What's the antidote to perfectionism? Part of it is the idea of a "draft" that isn't the final draft. I'll get something down in the essay, and it's OK if it's not high quality -- I can always improve the quality in further steps. The idea is to start somewhere, and then progressively make it better and better, until it is "good enough" -- not necessarily until it is perfect. Sometimes the start we make helps us figure out how to start all over again with a different approach! But doing something is almost always better than doing nothing.

Perfectionism can interfere with all sorts of pursuits other than writing. For example, someone in social interaction wants to say and act in the perfect way that will make the other people think they are the greatest. The prospect of saying the wrong thing makes the person just avoid socializing, and miss out on lots of happy times. Someone wants to play a musical instrument, but the person finds that their very first efforts don't produce music that is very great to listen to; the person finds this so unpleasant that they give up playing the instrument. Again, in these circumstance, it's good to have the idea in mind:

My first efforts will be very imperfect; over time I can get them better and better.

It's good to figure out how to make the imperfection of the first efforts not be harmful. For example, beginning surgeons can practice doing operations on the bodies of people who have donated their bodies after their death, to medical schools, and do a lot of practice through fantasy rehearsal. Beginning pilots can use computer simulations of flights. Beginning drivers can start out on driveways or deserted parking lots.

GIOW in writing

In the previous section I gave an example of perfectionism in writing. Lots of people get "writer's block." They can't seem to make the writing come out well enough, and they can't turn off the critic in their minds, so their rate of progress goes to zero.

GIOW is a way not to try to do everything at once while writing. It's a way of separating the writing task into 4 parts, 4 tasks. While doing any one of the tasks, it's good not to worry about the others. That way you don't overload your brain from trying to do too many things at once. G is for generating ideas. You just write down ideas as they come to you, things you may or may not want to say in whatever you're writing. I is for inclusion: which of what you've jotted down do you think should be included in what you're writing, and what should be discarded or saved for something else? You cut and paste some of the jottings to a separate place, maybe at the end of the file, and get them out of the way. O is for ordering: in what order do you want to say the things you have left that you want to say? You move them around to get them in the right order.

And W is for wording: how do you want to improve your sentence structure, punctuation, grammar, and so forth. How can you reword things to make your point more clearly?

The more you do these things one at a time, the easier it becomes, eventually, to blend some of them together. Writing, like all other skills, is something that gets easier and easier with practice.

Adequate sample size

Suppose that you are the mayor of a city, and you think that things would be lots safer in your town if the speed limits for cars were much lower, and if there were electronic devices all over the town that used cameras and computers to send bills for fines to people who are breaking the speed limits. But you don't want to get behind this change if it's just going to make people angry and get them to kick you out of office. So you ask someone to take a poll, and see what the people in your town think of this, so you can predict how they would react.

Suppose the imaginary person comes back and says, "The people are going to approve of this, by about a 3 to 1! I asked 4 people, and 3 liked the idea, and only 1 of them hated it!" If I were the mayor, I think I would listen politely, thank the person, and then hire someone else who really knew how to take a poll. Why? Because 4 people aren't nearly enough to let you draw conclusions. The statistical experts would say that you don't have "adequate sample size" -- you don't have enough individuals in the set of folks you are sampling.

On the other hand, if your city has a couple of hundred thousand people, you don't need to ask all of them! For polls like this, you can get a pretty good prediction from maybe a thousand people, as long as they are a "representative sample" of the people you want to know about. By "representative sample," we mean you don't want to just include only people who are over 70 years old -- they may feel differently about it than the 20-somethings. You don't want to sample only people who don't have cars, and you don't want to sample only the people who never cross streets on foot. The best way to sample would be pick randomly from all the people you want to make a conclusion about, although this is seldom possible to do.

The concept of adequate sample size applies whenever we are trying to draw conclusions from observations, not just when we are conducting polls. Suppose there is a drug that is suppose to help someone make better decisions and behave better. The very first day that the person tries the drug, the person behaves worse than usual. Should they give up right there? Probably not, because one day is not enough of a sample size to make conclusions. The person could have just had a bad day for random reasons not having to do with the drug.

Suppose someone has known someone for a month, and they've had a great time with the person. One of the persons says, "Let's get married." The idea of sample size applies here, too. For something so important as marriage, it's good to collect a whole bunch of observations about how the person acts (and let them collect observations about you!) You want each person to have "adequate sample size" to know what they're getting into before taking the plunge!

What does it mean to throw things away?

If you live in a "developed country," just about every day you put things into the trash. You are constantly getting things or getting food, and they come in different containers, and you are "throwing away" the containers. Or there is stuff that you bought, that you don't want anymore, and nobody else will take it either, so you "throw it away."

But where is "away"? Someone comes and takes it "away" in a truck, but where do they take it? Some of it gets recycled; some of it gets burned up and turned into gases that go into the air; some of it goes to a "land fill" where it's dumped and covered up with a layer of dirt or gravel. And a lot of it winds up somehow in the ocean or in rivers or in the air or where it causes trouble. Some of the lead and mercury that get thrown away end up harming people when they work their way into people's bodies. And little bits of plastic are working their way into bodies of water, including the ocean, and into bodies of fish and of people.

The idea of this unit is that there is really no "away" -- the stuff we get rid of goes somewhere, and it goes somewhere that isn't very far away from at least some people or animals!

Back a long time ago when the earth had a lot of space where no human beings lived, and there weren't so many human beings, the problem wasn't so bad. But now, figuring out what to do with all the stuff that we want to be "away" from us is a big problem for human beings to solve.

A universal language

Isn't it amazing that people can pick up their phones or activate their computers, and start talking with people anywhere on this planet? Wouldn't it be a great thing to help people understand each other better, if people in the USA would just spend time chatting with people in China, Russia, India, Kenya, Argentina, or anywhere else, all over the world? And if two countries are having conflicts with one another, wouldn't it be a good idea for the leaders of both countries to spend a lot of time conferring and negotiating with each other, but also just talking and getting to know and understand each other better?

There's a problem that gets in the way of this vision: people speak different languages. It takes a long time to learn even one other language from the first one you learned, and then there are many others -- the idea of being able to speak with all the people on this planet seems impossible.

People have long thought, here's an easy solution to this: Let's make up a language that is regular and easy to remember. Let's have the letters in its alphabet make the same sounds every time they appear. Let's not have people waste their time with tons of exceptions to grammar rules. Let's not make people memorize which objects like books or tables we're going to think of as masculine and feminine. Then let's let everybody learn this language as their second language, in addition to whichever one they were raised with. That way everybody can speak with everybody else!

In fact, this has been tried. A man named Ludwig Zamenhof, in 1873, made up a language that came to be called Esperanto. Lots of people have learned it and have spoken it with each other. But the idea has not caught on nearly strongly enough to let everyone speak to everyone else. There have been other languages that people have made up for the same purpose since then. But getting everyone to agree on one of them and to get busy learning it proves to be an extremely difficult task.

As computer technology advances, the problem may get solved in a different way. At the time of this writing, it is already possible for computers to translate from one written language to another, in a "fairly good" way. And it is possible for computers to analyze spoken words, translate those, and produce translated spoken words, in a "halfway decent" way. But doing the job in an "excellent" way, so that people can communicate as well as they could if they both spoke the same language well, is a very difficult one. It's lots easier to get computers to play chess than to do this!

Why is it so necessary to be able to speak with people all over everywhere, when there are already more than we can get to know, who speak our own language? The answer is that we are all in the same boat on this planet, we all affect each other, and it's good if we can stop seeing some of us as "us" and others as "them" -- we are all "us." Or at least that's what people like Ludwig Zamenhof thought.

Women's liberation

For most of the history of this planet, and in most cultures, men have been more powerful than women. The "founding fathers" of the USA didn't give women the right to vote. The 19th amendment to the USA constitution finally extended this right to women across the country in

1920, although localities had begun giving them the right in more limited ways earlier. For centuries men could beat their wives and get away with it. In some cultures women were not permitted to drive cars until very recently. Women were kept out of the most powerful professions. There are still differences in how much women and men get paid. Jobs like early childhood education, which are mainly staffed by women, get paid far less than jobs staffed mainly by men, for example running "hedge funds" that buy and sell stocks for people. Some religious organizations push the idea that women should be obedient to their husbands, but not the idea that men should obey their wives. In families, men have controlled the money more than women, and women have done more of the household chores like cleaning up. And so forth.

But yet, women are as smart as men. In one very important way, they appear to be superior: in every culture I' ve seen data on, men are much more violent than women are. The murder and assault rates for men are much higher than those for women. But men tend to be bigger and stronger than women, and perhaps this is the reason why there got to be differences in power -- the unfortunate fact that "might makes right" that the world has not completely gotten away from. An author, Stephen Pinker, has documented that the more influence women have in societies, the less violent those societies tend to be.

In the second half of the twentieth century, change began to speed up in major ways as women reclaimed some of the power they had been missing out on for so long. The changes in customs and ideas and ways of doing things was called the "women's liberation movement." According to the most recent figures available at the time of this writing, medical school classes are made up of just a little over 50% women. Before the 20th century, such classes were approximately 100% men. Yale Medical School started admitting women in 1916 and Harvard Medical School in 1945. There are more women now in powerful positions in government and business and all sorts of professions. In families, women are less likely to be bossed around by their husbands.

In my opinion, society still has a big task on its to do list: the valuing of the jobs that women historically specialized in, such as rearing and teaching children, and the translation of that valuing into rates of pay. In a society where people who try to figure out which stocks to buy and sell can become billionaires, and people who help the next generation of human beings develop their minds and their personalities can live at the poverty level, something is wrong!

Civil rights versus racism and other "isms"

For much of human history it was considered OK and normal for people to believe that people of certain races were inferior or superior to others, and for people of certain races not to have the same rights as others. This has applied to many different groups of people throughout history. There has been horrible violent discrimination against Jewish people. When groups of Italian and Irish and Asian people came into the USA, there has been discrimination against them, as there has been against Hispanic immigrants. For the history of the USA, the most obvious discrimination has been against black or African-American people, who during the first years of this country were bought and sold as slaves. After the USA's Civil War (but not immediately after), slavery ceased, but discrimination against African-American people did not -- they were often not allowed to go to the same schools, eat at the same restaurants, sit where they wanted on buses, get jobs for which they were qualified, live where they wanted to live, and importantly, to have the same voting rights as other Americans. The 1960's in the USA saw very important laws come into effect that banned such discrimination; what has taken much longer has been changes in people's attitudes. At the time of this writing, much progress remains to take place with respect to people's judging one another on the basis of their character and not on the color of their skin.

With consciousness of the evils of racism, there has been growing consciousness of how ethical principles should extend non-discrimination to other groups, with non-discrimination on the basis of gender, sexual orientation, status of various handicaps, age, economic background, religion, and others. The big idea is: when we make decisions about people, we're obligated to get information about individuals, not just what group they can be classified into.

Organic farming

One of the big tasks of humanity is producing enough food for itself. When we try to grow food, two problems occur very frequently: bugs eat up our crops, and other plants (that we call "weeds") start growing and competing for the plants that produce our food. Scientists worked hard to discover and make chemicals that would kill the bugs and weeds without killing the food plants, and they succeeded. These chemicals are called pesticides (for the bugs) and herbicides (for the weeds). The result was that more food could be produced, more cheaply. However, the more they have studied the effects of these chemicals, the more chemicals have been discovered to be bad for people. Even the fertilizers that are used in farming can have bad effects: they can dissolve in rain water and be carried to rivers and lakes and disrupt the balance of plant and animal life. For example, they can feed the growth of toxic types of algae.

For this reason, there is a movement to discover and refine ways of producing food without using chemicals that can cause harm. This has been called the organic farming movement.

Descriptive statistics

The major purpose of the field of statistics is to make sense of a bunch of numbers. It's to boil down information that is too detailed to make sense of, into summaries that we can make sense of. For example: suppose someone wants to know how well the kids in a certain school are reading. There's a certain test that they think measures reading skill, and they give it to every student in the school. So to answer the question about how well the kids in the school read, the person could start rattling off the scores for every single student. If it's a very big school, they might have to keep going for several hours! And by the time they finished, most of the people listening to them would have walked out from sheer boredom, and any that stuck around would not be able to make any sense out of all the numbers they heard!

So someone had the Big Idea of calculating things that would summarize the numbers without having to list every one of them. If we add up all the numbers, and then divide by how many numbers we added up, we get a statistic called the mean, or average. This is one way of deciding what a "typical" score is. It answers the question, "If we had a group of people with the same total score, only with each of them having the same score, what would that score be?" A different way of deciding what a typical score is, is called the median. If we arrange all the numbers in order, from lowest to highest, the number in the middle is the median. This answers the question, "What's a number with half of our observations greater and half lower?"

When we have a bunch of numbers, we often want to know not just what a typical score is, but also how spread out the scores are. Let's say there are two countries, and for each of them, the average yearly income for families is $60,000. But one of them has lots of people who get many millions of dollars each year, and many people who have to get by on almost nothing. The second country has almost all the people with incomes between $40,000 and $80,000 dollars. There's quite a bit of difference between the two places, that isn't communicated just by the average income, right? One way of expressing the spread of a bunch of numbers is by getting a sort of average of how far each of the numbers is from the mean of the group. The way of averaging that's called the "standard deviation" gets a "sort of" average deviation from the mean. ("Sort of" because rather than just averaging the distances from the mean, it squares them, averages them, and then takes the square root of that.) Another way of communicating how spread out the numbers are is by saying what the numbers are such that

25% and 75% of the observations are below those numbers. These are called the 25th and 75th percentiles.

There are also ways of graphing the big bunch of numbers, in ways that give pictures of what typical values are and how spread out they are. Histograms, stem-and-leaf plots, and box plots are ways of boiling a bunch of numbers down into pictures that allow us to make sense of them.

All of these methods are called "descriptive statistics." They just show what the batch of numbers is like, in ways that summarize the important aspects of the whole group of them.

Inferential statistics

The word "inferential" comes from the word "infer," which means "to draw a conclusion." The conclusions we draw using statistics may result in a statement like this: "When people get a certain treatment for an illness, their chances of surviving are between 2 and 3 times greater than if they had no treatment, and we're about 95% confident in that." Or our conclusion can be communicated with fewer numbers, but it may sound something like this: "We're pretty sure that treatment A is really better than treatment B, and that it didn't just happen to do better than treatment B by chance." Or it can sound like this: "We have some good evidence that eating this type of diet causes people to be healthier in these sorts of ways."

The ways that studies are set up so as to make inferences possible, and the types of calculations that people make from the numbers they get, are part of the subject of inferential statistics.

339

Public health

When most people think of medicine and doctors, they think of the people you go to when you are sick or injured. And if people figure out ways of curing illnesses or injuries, that's great.

But there's another way of improving the health of a group of people: to prevent the illnesses or the injuries before they even happen. For some examples: rather than just trying to figure out ways of curing people from polio, we use a vaccine that keeps them from getting it. Rather than just trying to cure people from the diseases they catch from sewage that gets into the water supply, they figure out sanitary ways of getting rid of sewage and making water supplies free of bad germs. Rather than just trying to use surgery to fix the injuries from car accidents, we build seat belts and air bags into cars so people will get hurt less severely from such accidents. Rather than just trying to help people who have been poisoned by lead or mercury, we try to get lead or mercury out of the environment so they won't get get poisoned in the first place. Rather than just trying to figure out how to help people who have been badly burned, we teach people ways of preventing fires from getting started. Rather than just making medicines for heart disease, we teach people how diet and exercise and not smoking and other things can prevent heart disease in the first place. Rather than just having treatment programs for people who are addicted to drugs, we try to teach people about the dangers of certain drugs and to make addictive drugs less available, so fewer people will need such treatment. Rather than just trying to treat the psychological problems that result from bullying, we try to teach people not to bully each other so as to prevent those problems.

The various ways of doing these things are the subject of public health.

Tones of approval and enthusiasm

We have talked about the role of "positive reinforcement" in the lives of all people -- we tend to do things in order to make desirable results happen. And since we are social animals, one of the most universal reinforcers is the approval of other people -- getting the message that people like us, that they like or admire something we did. Closely related is that we tend to do things in order to know that we have "made a difference" to other people -- we've had an effect, we aren't just nobodies.

One of the ways that we get the message from others that they like what we've done is by the meanings of their words. "Thank you for doing that. I very much appreciate that. You have helped me greatly. You are very good at that." We enjoy hearing sentences like this from other people.

But the meanings of the words are only part of what make us feel good. Perhaps a more important part is the tones of voice with which the words are delivered. The word "monotone" means that the words are all said in about the same pitch. Such speech seems to have little emotion connected with it. On the other hand, speech that goes up and down a lot in pitch can communicate lots of emotion.

Do an experiment in your mind, please: imagine someone saying to you, in a monotone, "Thank you for doing that. You really helped me." Now imagine someone saying, in a very excited tone, "THANK you for DOING that!!! You REALLY helped me!!!" For most of us, the second makes a much bigger impact. The moral of this big idea is that if we want to communicate to other people how we feel, we should think of the tones of voice we use as well as our words. A related idea is that if we want people to do more of the things we admire, it helps to communicate our approval in enthusiastic tones of voice!

An optimum population for the planet

Lots of the bad problems of our planet seem to be related to how many people are living on our planet. For example, the more people use energy that burns up fossil fuels, the more carbon dioxide gets into the air, and the more global warming beomes a problem. The more people buy things that produce trash, the more waste products pollute the planet. The more people need to be fed, the more fertilizers and chemicals get into the environment and disrupt things. The more people need houses to live in, the less wild space there is for animals to live in, and the more animal species become extinct. The more crowded we get, it's perhaps more likely that people fight wars in order to get control of more territory (although this last point is disputed by the fact that people seem to have been fighting wars since the beginning of recorded history, even before the planet was nearly as crowded as it is today).

The word "optimum" means "best." What's the best number of people for the planet Earth to host at any given time? This section doesn't take on the task of giving a number that's the answer to that question. But the big idea of this section is that there probably is an answer. My guess is that the answer is a lot fewer people than we currently have.

Advantages of biodiversity

Among the various "isms" we spoke of earlier is "species-ism." Human beings have tended to consider themselves as really the only important species on this planet -- all the others are often judged as being important or unimportant only insofar as they affect our species. There is growing acceptance, however, of the big idea that other species have a right to thrive, and not to become extinct, for their own sakes.

But even if we think only about the self-centered needs of our own species, there are reasons for preserving the existence of other species. An amazing diversity of plant and animal life evolved over millions of years on this planet, and the various species grew to become interdependent in different ways. The waste products of some became the usable supplies of another. For example, the carbon dioxide breathed out by all animals and produced when they burned things, was of great use to huge numbers of plant species in the tropical rain forests. When those tropical rain forests and the many species within them are destroyed in order to grow single crops, the balance between carbon dioxide put into the air and that taken out gets disrupted a little bit more.

Another way of thinking is that the various ways that plants and animals depend upon each other are so complicated and varied that there is a very great deal that we still don't know. Just in case a species happens to be useful to ours, it's lots easier to keep it from going extinct than to try to bring it back once extinction occurs.

The type of environment in which there are lots of species of plants and animals living together interdependently is called biodiversity. All other things equal, biodiversity is a good thing.

Animal liberation

On the subject of animal liberation, there are many more gory details than I want to go into, but the ways people have treated the animals that we use to make food for ourselves have often -- perhaps usually -- been extremely cruel and inhumane. When you see eggs for sale at the grocery store, some are labeled "cage free" -- this is because thousands of chickens have been forced to live their whole lives in cages where they hardly have had room to move. They have been used as egg-producing machines, and then slaughtered for meat. Even some of the chickens called "cage free" are still kept in overly crowded and inhumane conditions. Cows produce dairy products for people after they have had calves; the milk they give was meant for their calves, and they appear to care very much when their calves are taken away from them. Some calves that become "veal" are fed unbalanced diets and restricted from running around, to make their meat more tender, and then killed for their meat.

Caring about whether animals suffered from such treatment hardly ever occurred to many people, until "animal liberation" joined the liberation movements of the 20th century. Somehow people started to think: cows, geese, ducks, chickens, turkeys, sheep and others have feelings. They can suffer. It's hard to see ourselves as kind people without wanting to keep the suffering of animals as low as possible.

Some people respond to this idea by not eating any animal products. Others respond by trying to get rules made and enforced that ensure that when we do use animals for our own purposes, we try to let them lead happy lives, and if we kill them, we at least do it in a way that is as painless and free of suffering as possible.

The idea of animal liberation extends to pets, also. We are getting away from the idea that people "own" their pets, in the sense of being able to do with them whatever they please. People who take on pets have an obligation to take care of them well -- to let them get adequate exercise, have an adequate effort-payoff connection, have enough of what the most enlightened research tells us makes for a happy animal versus a miserable one.

It is probably true that many of the people who have pets should not have them. It still remains true that millions of animals are mistreated for the sake of producing food for us as cheaply as possible. But the big idea of animal liberation at least is much stronger than it used to be.

Optimizing versus satisficing

The two terms, optimizing and satisficing, refer to two ways of making a decision. With optimizing, you are trying to generate all the reasonable options you can, consider the pros and cons of many of them, and pick the option that will work out best of all. This can take a lot of work. With satisficing, you stop generating options when there is one that is "good enough," and you go for it. Optimizing is best for important, high stakes decisions: what career should I try to go into? Where should I live? Satisficing is best for low stakes decisions where it won't make much difference in your life which one you pick.

Which parking space (in a lot where they are all legal) should I park my car in? Which socks should I put on this morning? Which brand of oatmeal do I want to pick from the grocery store shelf? When I pass someone, what greeting do I want to say?

So: when you make a decision, first it's good to make a decision about the decision (consciously or unconsciously): is this a decision where I want to optimize, or satisfice? (Or somewhere in the middle – that's also possible.)

The daily to do list

There's a field of study called time management – how to get the most out of the time you are allotted in life. By "getting the most," we don't mean the most money, or the most fame, or the most achievement, or advancement, necessarily – we mean the most of what you really want, what your goals are. One of the major techniques of time management we have already spoken of: thinking, and rethinking, what your goals are, and writing them down.

The daily to do list is another major time management technique. To use it, you simply write down what you want to accomplish, or to do, during the day. You refer to this list during the day to remind yourself. You think about your long term goals when you make your list. Many people have long term goals that they strongly wish for, but they devote approximately zero minutes a day to accomplishing. They can avoid this by putting on the daily to do list activities that make progress toward the long term goals. An important part of the to do list is to order the activities in priority. Especially if the list is long, you decide on what the most important one is, and put the

346

number 1 by it; you put the number 2 by the second most important, for perhaps the top 5 priorities. Then, when you get time that isn't already scheduled for something else, you concentrate on the number 1 priority. After that, you concentrate on the number 2 priority, and so forth. And when you make progress on any task or activity or finish it, you celebrate and feel good. You might write "Done!" next to the item.

Using a daily to do list doesn't mean you have to be "working" all the time. Maybe one of your goals is having a good relationship with family members, and perhaps an item for the to do list is just to goof off with a family member. Or maybe a goal is to enjoy relaxing, and an item for the to do list is to spend some unstructured time in a pleasant way.

So the big idea of the to do list has several parts:

deciding on goals,
activities that make progress toward goals,
order in priority,
concentration on one at a time,
celebration of accomplishment.

Ways of being frugal

The proverb, "A penny saved is a penny earned," means that you add to your wealth just as much by not wasting a certain amount of money, as you do by earning it. Actually, if about a third of your income goes to taxes, "A penny saved is 1.5 pennies earned." (Because you only get to keep 2/3 of those 3/2 of a penny, or one penny.)

The word *frugal* means not wasting money. Why should we be frugal? One of the reasons is that doing so gives us more time to do what we think is most important in life, rather than doing only what people are willing to pay money for. For example, suppose someone spends a certain amount a month on junk food. They get paid a certain amount per hour. If you divide the amount spent on junk food by the amount the person makes per hour, you get the number of hours the person wouldn't have to spend working, if they didn't waste money on junk food. If the happiness they would get by spending some work time in some other way exceeds the happiness they get from eating junk food, then they should save the money. Of course, if the person's work gives meaning and fulfillment and helps humanity, and the person knows that they would waste a few extra hours on video games, then the reasoning changes! Another benefit of being frugal is that it allows something to contribute more to charities that make the world better.

In being frugal, it's good not to be "penny wise and pound foolish." For example, you don't want to waste time clipping a coupon worth 35 cents off something at the grocery store that you don't particularly like, while wasting thousands of dollars in other ways. Two big expenditures for most people are housing and transportation. Not having dogs and cats enables people to save big on housing – finding places that allow animals takes money. Not having lots of possessions taking up space lets you save big on housing, by letting you live in a smaller space. Buying only used cars, and cars that cost as little as possible for fuel, or if one is a city dweller, not having a car at all, saves lots of money. Buying computers, clothes, or anything else used rather than new is a great way to save money.

Comparing the prices of things is an activity that frugal people do. For example, coffee at Starbucks at the time of this writing costs between 2 and 6 dollars, not counting a tip; a cup of instant coffee made at home from a jar of it bought at a grocery story cost a little under 5 cents! And drinking water instead of coffee would be almost 0 cents. Getting almost anything at a restaurant usually costs many times more than preparing an equally nutritious meal at home.

For a person who enjoys being frugal, wasting money on cigarettes, alcoholic drinks, marijuana, or any other drugs meant to give pleasure is out of the question – they directly cost money, and the money that is lost if one becomes addicted is far greater. Hoping to make money at a gambling casino is also completely out of the question.

Using things till they wear out, rather than getting something new as soon as something gives signs of being old is another way to be frugal.

Is going to an elite private college worth the money, as contrasted to going to a state-supported college that can cost a couple of hundred thousand dollars less? If someone is frugal, and they have this choice, they at least think carefully about this question.

Frugal people think about the "opportunity cost" of "non-performing assets." For example, they don't leave much money in accounts that pay them no interest, if there are other places where their money would earn interest for them. If they buy some expensive equipment that they no longer need, they sell it and put the money they make into something that earns interest for them, rather than letting the equipment pay them nothing.

Newton's 3 laws of motion

Isaac Newton lived in the 1600s and early 1700s. He came up with many big ideas; one set of them is his three laws of motion.

The first is that an object at rest (that is not moving) will stay at rest unless something pushes or pulls on it (in other words, unless there's a force applied to it). That's not surprising, is it? But the first law also states that an object in motion will keep moving in a straight line, at the same velocity, unless there's a force to change its motion. When I first learned this, I was surprised. If I threw a ball, it kept going for a while and stopped. If I got up some speed on roller skates or on a bike, and just coasted, I coasted to a stop. If what Newton said was true, why didn't these things keep moving forever? The answer is that there is a force that slows down the motion – it's friction. When a ball is rolling along, it bumps into the air molecules, and into the little bumps on the ground or floor, and each of these little bumps gives a push that opposes the ball's motion and slows it down. When my bicycle coasts, there is friction in the motion of the wheel around its axle, and with the tire on the ground, and with the air. That force is what makes the motion stop. By the way, friction force is also what makes a car stop when you put on the brakes. When someone is skiing down a hill and wants to stop, they turn the skis sideways and let the edges cut into the snow, so that there's a lot more friction than there is when the skis are pointed straight down the hill.

The second law has to do with acceleration, which is a change in the amount or direction of the velocity with which an object is moving. How do you get something to move faster? You push or pull it in the direction you want it to move. How do you get it to move slower? You push or pull it in the other direction. The more massive the object is, the harder you have to push or pull to change its motion. For example, if there's a baseball coming at you, you don't have to push very hard to stop its motion. If there's a car coming at you, it would take much more force to stop its motion (so, if you wisely don't try to stopy it with your baseball glove, but run out of the way, you're using Newton's second law!) Newton's second law says that how hard you have to push or pull to accelerate something increases the more massive the object is, and how much acceleration you want to get. In other words, F=ma, or force equals mass times acceleration.

The third law says that when you apply a force to something, it applies a force to you that is exactly as strong, but in the opposite direction. Sometimes when people get mad, they hit their fists against a wall, which is a decision I officially do not recommend. One of the main reasons for not recommending this is Newton's third law: when your fist hits the wall and pushes against it, at the moment of impact, the wall pushes back against your fist just as hard. The harder you hit the wall, the harder the wall hits your fist. Hitting the wall has turned a perfectly peace-loving wall into something that has broken bones in people's fists! The way Newton's third law is often stated is, "For every action, there is an equal and opposite reaction." It applies not only to fists and walls, but to every force that anything exerts on anything else!

If I hold a book that weighs 2 pounds, the earth is pulling on the book with 2 pounds of force, the book is also pulling back on the earth with 2 pounds of force. If I drop the book, the force the earth exerts on the book accelerates it, making it fall toward the earth. Why doesn't the equal and opposite force the book exerts on the earth accelerate the whole earth toward the book? Because of Newton's second law! The earth is more massive than the book, and it would take hugely more force to accelerate it! But if the book were as massive as the whole earth, and somehow they found themselves close to each other, they would both be accelerated toward each other. (Don't worry – I'm going to stop writing soon!)

Symptoms and diagnoses

Sometimes, in medicine, a very important idea is: "Don't just treat the symptom; figure out what the diagnosis is. That will lead you to the best treatment." For example, if someone has a cough, that's a symptom. The cough could be a symptom of several different illnesses – tuberculosis, asthma, pneumonia due to Covid, pneumonia due to a certain bacterium, or others. You don't just give cough medicine to each of these people – you try to figure out what the diagnosis is and treat the underlying illness.

However, sometimes it's best not to worry very much about the diagnosis, but to treat the symptom. For example, a child acts very aggressive and angry at home. The parent worries about whether the child's diagnosis is oppositional defiant disorder, or disruptive mood dysregulation disorder, or any of several others. But someone helps the parent realize that the child is getting much attention, and getting his way, by being angry and aggressive, and the child finds it hard to get his parents' attention in other ways. When the parent learns to pay attention to the child when the child is acting OK and to ignore the child as much as possible when he is angry and aggressive, the aggression goes away.

So it's good not only to know about diagnoses, but to figure out when diagnoses are useful and when they aren't!

What to do versus who's at fault

Suppose Person 1 tells a family member, Person 2: "The car is stuck in a ditch." Suppose Person 2 responds, "Who was driving, you? How did you get it stuck? Don't you know not to park on the side of the road when there's a steep slope into a ditch? Why didn't you just keep going, until you found a level place?"

Now let's replay the conversation. Person 1 says, "The car is stuck in a ditch." Person 2 responds: "Are you hurt? No one else hurt? Good, we don't have to deal with that. Is the car damaged, or just stuck? How about I take a look at it with you. We can decide whether we want to try to get it out ourselves, or whether we want to call for a tow truck. Is there anything blocking the way?"

In the first conversation, Person 2 was using the strategy of finding out who's to blame, and punishing that person (with reprimands). In the second conversation, Person 2 went straight to trying to figure out what strategy to use to make things better.

Which version of Person 2 would you rather have as a family member? Which version would you feel most comfortable talking about problems with? For most people, it would be the second version: the problem-solver rather than the judger and punisher.

Figuring out who is at fault and punishing that person, like many of the patterns of interaction that are overdone in the world, does have its place. If someone is stealing from your family, over and over, figuring out who's doing it and bringing that person to justice sounds like a good plan. If someone in a work situation is being mean to all the customers and making them want to go elsewhere, the boss's best strategy is probably to find out who is doing this and either get them to change their ways or fire them. There is a whole court system that largely revolves around figuring how who is to blame for things and how people should be punished, and very few people feel that this system should be abolished.

But in many, many situations, the first question should be "What should we do?" and not "Who's to blame?" Let's finish this with one more example: an airplane is headed straight down, in a nose-dive. In version 1 of the story, the pilot in charge thinks, "Who is responsible for this? Somebody must have done something bad. Was it my copilot? Was it me? Was it the person who inspected the plane? I need to get to the bottom of who's fault this is." In version 2 of the story, the pilot in charge thinks, "I'll try this to pull the plane out of this nose-dive. If this doesn't work, I'll consider this other technique instead." Version 2 of the story is more likely to have a happy ending, right? And that's the point of this idea!

We are all "influencers"

Why do we do what we do? One of the big reasons is to get results that we want. We pick our behaviors based in large part on our past history of those behaviors' paying off for us. In other words, we tend to do what has resulted in reinforcement, and to avoid what has resulted in punishment, and also not to do those behaviors that don't pay off, those that result in "non-reinforcement."

The idea of this section is that any time we interact with another person, any time we make any little utterance or gesture, the other person responds – or doesn't respond – in some way. The person's response either is pleasant, unpleasant, or neutral. Or maybe it's a mixture of pleasant and unpleasant. The person's response either reinforces what we just did, or punishes it, or non-reinforces it. In any case, the chance is high that we are influenced at least a little bit. The upshot is that in every interaction, people are constantly influencing one another.

Suppose I say to someone else, "I just had an idea about how to reduce violence in the world." The other person looks off into space, and says, in a dismissive tone, "Oh." OR the person looks at me and responds with a curious, "Oh?" OR the person raises the eyes wide, smiles, looks very excited, says, "Oh!" and then looks at me expectantly. Even though I picked the same word for these imaginary responses, the degree of reinforcement in them varied tremendously, didn't it?

This idea is particularly important for parents who want their children to be happy and healthy. Every time a parent speaks to a child or interacts with the child in any way, some influence is being delivered. If the summation of the thousands and thousands of little influences is positive, the child's chances for success and happiness are increased. The idea is also important for people in a romantic relationship or friendship. When the person you are in a relationship with gives lots of positive reinforcement, and gives it for your wise and good and happiness-producing behaviors, that is one of the hallmarks of a "good relationship!"

Utopias and dystopias

The word *utopia* comes from a work of fiction published by Thomas More in 1516; the word was constructed from Greek words so as to mean "no place" – that is, existing only in imagination. The place called Utopia in More's book was imagined as a good society – a good way for human beings to organize themselves. For example, in Utopia, the citizens never fight in wars (although they aren't above paying others to fight for them); the leaders focus on governing their existing country well and not on taking over other countries; there are free hospitals; the essential work of the society is done in a six-hour workday; people don't waste their efforts obtaining jewels and fancy clothes; there's no need for locks on the doors of houses.

Many other authors have shared their imaginings of what a good society should look like, in other utopian stories. A famous one, written by Plato around 375 BCE, is called *The Republic*. Plato took on the question of how a society should come up with good and wise people to be its rulers. The imagined answer was to prepare the future rulers from a very early age, teaching them to be wise, courageous, temperate, and just.

Another utopian novel called Walden II, by B.F. Skinner, imagined a society in which the principles of behaviorist psychology were used to produce a harmonious and happy community. Children in Walden II were taught the skill of self-discipline by taking on tasks such as carrying candy around while resisting the urge to eat it.

Other novels are called *dystopian* because they imagine a society that has gone wrong. In the novel *1984*, there is widespread surveillance, constant propaganda meant to increase loyalty to powerful leaders, a state of constant warfare, and language conventions meant to interfere with people's ability to think clearly. In *The Handmaid's Tale*, there's a dictatorship that oppresses women (and uses some of them purely to bear children for other people); in *The Hunger Games Trilogy*, bad rulers force youth to fight with each other to the death as a form of entertainment for the masses and to punish rebellious ideas.

The idea I'm talking about here is that it is possible for people to imagine good and bad ways that people have a society, live together, govern, and have social customs, and this is probably a very useful thing for people to do. Most of these novels, both utopias and dystopias, deal with very important aspects of society, such as these:

1. Who is in charge, how much control do they have, what do they make people do, how much are people free versus controlled?

2. How are children brought up – how are they indoctrinated, how are their personalities shaped?

3. What sources of information do people have – are they allowed to seek and find truth and facts, or does someone or some group systematically bias and deceive people?

4. What are the basic social units, how do people group themselves? For example, do "nuclear families" live together, apart from others, or are there communes, where people are expected to help with other people's children as well as any they have?

5. How does the work of society get divided up? Are there alternatives to having a bunch of highly paid executives benefiting from the labor of low-paid workers? Are there alternatives to some people working oppressively long hours, and others unable to find work at all? Is there some way of focusing on the work that really helps people and omitting the work that doesn't?

6. What is done with people who break the rules? Are they killed? Are they "brainwashed," or somehow indoctrinated to follow the rules from now on? Do the people somehow know to follow good rules and disobey bad ones, without the author telling how they achieved this skill?

7. How much tolerance for diversity of behavior is there in the society? Does everyone have to act the same and believe the same, or can people have very different customs and habits?

8. What are the customs regarding love, marriage, and romance? Do governments intervene, or do they stay out of this and let people make their own choices?

9. What do people in the society do for fun and entertainment?

Why is it useful to grapple with these questions, and other questions that such novels bring up? Because if people have clear and well-thought-out images of what they want and what they don't want from the societies in which they live, they have a better chance of improving the human condition.

Stimulus control: the special case of guns

One of the most important psychological skills that was listed in another section is nonviolence. When people are afraid that other people will hurt or kill them, this fear greatly reduces the quality of life, even if no one ever actually does anything violent to them.

One of the important methods of influence that was listed in another section is stimulus control. This means that if you want more of a certain behavior, have the things that tend to bring out that behavior close at hand and convenient; if you want less of a certain behavior, have the stimuli that bring out that behavior absent or difficult to get at. For example, if someone wants not to drink alcohol, it's wise not to have alcoholic drinks in the house. If someone wants to exercise more, it's probably wise to have a pair of dumbbells lying around in plain sight, reminding the person to exercise with them. If someone wants to study more, it probably is a good idea for that person to have a good study place where there are not lots of other distractions.

The principle of stimulus control would suggest that if we want people to kill and injure each other less, it's wise to arrange less access to guns, since the major purpose of a gun is to kill or injure someone (or some animal) or to make them scared you're going to do so.

Do people kill each other less often in places where guns are less accessible? You can look up lots and lots of statistics on this question. Here's one interesting comparison. In the USA there are more guns than people. With respect to privately owned small firearms, in the USA the rate is around 90 guns per hundred people, whereas in Japan the rate is about 0.6 per hundred people. Thus the rate of gun ownership is over 100 times as much in the USA as in Japan. Do people in the USA kill other people more often in Japan? If so, how many times more often -- as many as two or three times as often? According to some measures, in the USA people kill each other about 30 times as often as people do in Japan!

If you look at lots more statistics, it appears that the principle of stimulus control seems to apply to guns and violence, just as it applies to bowls of potato chips and potato chip consumption!

The idea of making weapons less convenient and accessible as a way of reducing violence also applies to nations and their bombs. For decades, peace activists have been trying to persuade governments to get rid of the nuclear bombs that can destroy huge amounts of property and millions of people in one blast. So far, these efforts have been as unsuccessful as the efforts to reduce the guns in the USA have been.

Peaceful transition of leadership

How does a country decide who's going to lead it? The best way that people have come up with is to hold elections. But what if the person who is in power doesn't want to give up that power? That person might order the military to arrest the person who got elected and order the courts to convict that person and sentence them to prison. Sometimes someone whom the people have elected have been overthrown with the help of foreign governments and replaced with someone else whom the foreign country's leaders like better. Sometimes someone in power uses their power to rig the election process in their favor, so they get to stay in power.

The more a country can count on its customs and expectations and norms to insure that the person who is legitimately elected gets to be in office, and that people who are not elected give up their claims to office peacefully and voluntarily, the better off that country is!

Cognitive testing

There are tests that are designed to measure how well a person can figure things out, solve problems, think clearly, use words well, remember things, and do other things that people call "cognitive tasks." People have noticed that various types of tests seem to be correlated, or to predict one another -- how someone does on a vocabulary test lets us predict to a certain extent how they do on a test of figuring out what geometric figure should go in a certain box to make the pattern consistent. Some people speak of the results of such tests as indicating "how smart" or "how intelligent" the person is. It is a very interesting finding that how people do on such tests tends to be fairly stable over time -- people who do great on them at age 10 tend also to do very well on them at age 20 or 30. And another interesting finding is that in today's world, where many jobs, and particularly the high-paying ones, involve a lot of thinking and information-processing, how people do on those tests tends to predict success in life.

But there are lots of reasons why such tests can be invalid. If the person isn't even trying to get the answers right, or is giving a very half-hearted attempt, the results won't be meaningful. If the person is sick or sleep-deprived or receiving a medicine that affects thinking, this will bring down the score. If the person has had some really stressful bad thing happen, it's probably less easy for the person to concentrate on the test. And if the test asks for knowledge, such as what certain words mean, the person can be very intelligent but not know the answers if they have never seen or heard the word in use. It's very difficult to make up a test that isn't influenced by one's past education and experience.

One of the best uses of tests is to figure out where to start in teaching someone in a specific subject matter, such as reading or math. If someone scores at 9th grade level on a good test of overall math skills, and someone else scores at the 3rd grade level, it usually doesn't make sense to teach both of those people the same math lessons. Testing can be a useful aid to hierarchy-ology: to figuring out how to educate people in a way that their challenges are not too hard, not too easy, but just right.

Replicability

Suppose someone makes a very important scientific finding, and reports the results. For example, the person discovers that children seem to learn a lot better when teachers treat them a certain way. Or the person discovers that a safe food supplement helps people get over a bad mental problem. Or the person discovers that exercise helps people get over depression. Or that a certain protein in the brain may be responsible for a bad illness. Or that a drug that chemists have synthesized cures a certain illness. Or that you can see certain things through a telescope that lead to a conclusion about how the universe works.

What next? Do we assume those results are true, and act as though they are true forever afterwards? Sometimes researchers do a study with one particular group of people who respond differently from a different group. Sometimes certain results just happen by random chance. Sometimes researchers have biases that affect the results of the study, that the researchers aren't even aware of. And, with people being imperfect, sometimes scientists lie about their results. For all these reasons, and others, people who repeat, or replicate, the study may not get the same results. For that reason, if a finding is really important, the study that showed it should be replicated, ideally by different researchers. (This is one reason why scientists should describe their methods very clearly: so that other researchers will know how to replicate.) If different groups of researchers carry out the study repeatedly and keep coming to the same conclusions, we are lots more confident that the finding is believable. The finding has passed the test of replicability.

Not all yes or no questions can be answered yes or no

Sometimes people ask yes or no questions, and seem to feel entitled to get a yes or no answer. In courtroom dramas, or real-life congressional hearings, questioners may insist, "Please answer the question, yes or no."

There's an assumption behind the idea that questions should be answerable yes or no. That assumption is that every statement is either true or false. If it's not true, it's false. If it's not false, it's true.

This assumption works well for lots of statements. "Two plus two equals five": false. "Lead is denser than water": true. "The earth revolves around the sun": true. These are either true or false. And if they are false, the "negation" of them is true, and vice versa: "Two plus two does not equal five": true. "Lead is not denser than water": false. "The earth does not revolve around the sun": false.

But there are several reasons why some statements are neither true or false.

How about this statement: "Very hot pepper makes chili taste lots better." For some people that is true, and for others it is false. The truth of the statement depends on whom we're referring to. It's the same way with this statement: "It's a good idea to walk at least 3 miles each day." What if you're only one year old?

Similarly, some statements are opinions that vary from person to person. Different things bring on different degrees of pleasure and pain for different people. "Taylor Swift's songs are more pleasing than Guiseppe Verdi's." "Salvador Dali was a better artist than Pablo Picasso." These statements justify the idea, "It's no use arguing over matters of taste."

Another case is that the yes or no question carries with it an assumption that may be false. For example, suppose someone asks me, "Have you stopped snorting cocaine?" If I answer, "No," that sounds like I'm still snorting cocaine. If I answer "Yes," that sounds like I used to snort cocaine and stopped. So the answer to the question is: "That question appears to imply that I once snorted cocaine, but that assumption is not true." Here's another yes or no question of that sort: "When you cheated on your tax payments, did you feel guilty? Answer yes or no!"

A third reason is that the statement or question refers to itself in a way that makes both "yes" and "no" answers lead to a contradiction. Consider the statement: "This statement is false." If it's true, then according to itself, it's false. But suppose it's false. If it's false that it's false, then it should be true. So we can't answer yes or no to whether the statement is true or false – either way, we appear to contradict ourselves.

Serious philosophers and students of logic have exercised their thinking muscles with paradoxes that are very much like this. Here's a paradox raised by the philosopher Bertrand Russell. Let's think of the set of all sets that don't contain themselves as members. So if we define set K as {a,b,c}, K is a set that doesn't contain itself. If we define set J as {a,b,c, set J} then set J does contain itself. Here comes the mind game, yes or no question: does the set of all sets that don't contain themselves contain itself? If you want to, you can figure out that either a "yes" or "no" answer leads to a contradiction of that answer. If it does, then it doesn't; if it doesn't, then it does.

So sometimes, the best answer to "Answer yes or no," is "Sorry, it doesn't communicate well to answer yes or no!"

Converses, inverses, and contrapositives

The words converse, inverse, and contrapositive are terms used in the study of logic. They have to do with "if-then" propositions.

Let's say we start with the proposition

If A, then B.

A and B can be any sort of statement: for example, If you take a certain medicine, you will get well. Or if you are a baby, you weigh less than 100 pounds. Or if I lift weights every day for a month, I will be stronger at the end of the month.

Here's the converse:

If B, then A.

The converse does not follow, logically, from the original proposition. For example: If someone is president of the USA, that person is a USA citizen. The converse is not true: "If a person is a USA citizen, that person is president of the USA" is NOT true.

Here's the contrapositive:

If not B, then not A.

The contrapositive does follow from the original proposition. If someone is not a USA citizen, that person is not president of the USA. That's the contrapositive to the proposition above, and if the original statement is true, the contrapositive has to be also.

Here's the inverse:

If not A, then not B.

The inverse doesn't follow from the original proposition. If a person is not president of the USA, then the person isn't a USA citizen -- that doesn't follow from our original statement. The inverse is logically equivalent to the converse, and both of them can't be inferred from the original statement.

A very frequent error that people make is thinking that the original proposition implies the converse. Let's imagine that for someone it's true that, "If you're a person I'd be happily married to, I find you attractive." This does not imply: "If I find you attractive, you're a person I'd be happily married to!" Here's another example: "If I have a brain tumor, I will get a headache." This doesn't imply, "If I get a headache, I have a brain tumor."

The sort of thinking that goes on in these examples is different from that which we usually encounter in life, where instead of

If A, then B,

we're more often dealing with propositions like,

the truth of A increases the probability of the truth of B by a certain amount.

So, for example, if I have a brain tumor, the probability of headache is higher than if I don't, but still not 100%. If I have headaches, the probability that I have a brain tumor is a tiny bit higher than if I didn't, but not much higher and nowhere close to 100%.

Dealing with probabilistic statements makes things more complicated than simple "If A, then B" propositions.

Syllogisms and the transitivity of subsets

Logic is the field that studies how you come to conclusions about what's true and what isn't. Being given two statements that are true, and figuring out that a third must be true, is making a deduction or deducing something through logic.

367

One of the simplest forms of deduction is called a syllogism. Here's an example of a syllogism:

All Beagles are dogs.
Myrna is a Beagle.
Therefore, Myrna is a dog.

Here's another famous example of a syllogism:

All men are mortal.
Socrates is a man.
Therefore, Socrates is mortal.

Syllogisms can be understood as having to do with the concept, "is a subset of." Here's how we could rephrase the first syllogism:

The set of Beagles is a subset of the set of dogs.
Myrna is a subset of the set of Beagles.
Therefore, Myrna is a subset of the set of dogs.

We say that the relation, "is a subset of," is transitive. This means that if B is a subset of A, and C is a subset of B, then C is a subset of A. The relation "equals" is also transitive: if E=F and F=G, then E has to equal G. The relation "greater than" is also transitive: if John's height is greater than Mary's, and Mary's is greater than Tina's, then John's is greater than Tina's.

Syllogisms simply follow from the fact that "is a subset of" is transitive. To apply this to our second syllogism:

The set of men is a subset of the set of mortals.
Socrates is a subset of the set of men.
Therefore Socrates is a subset of the set of mortals.

Predicate logic

We talked about syllogisms and subsets as a way of figuring out that something is true when we know that some other things are true.

How about this inference:
All apples are fruits.
All bananas are fruits.
Therefore all apples are bananas.

That clearly isn't a sensible conclusion, is it? Apples are a subset of fruits, and bananas are a different subset of fruits, but the two subsets don't overlap. This sort of false inference has been called predicate logic, because the words "are fruits" are in the predicates of the sentences, and the false inference comes when someone thinks that because the predicates are the same, the subjects have to be the same.

With the example above, the inference is clearly false. However, sometimes people use predicate logic without it being so obvious to them that they are making a logical mistake. Suppose there's a trial for a crime. It's known that the criminal was a male with black hair, in dreadlocks, who was wearing a hoodie and who has type A positive blood type. An accused man, Rashad, has black hair, worn in dreadlocks, owns a hoodie, and has type A positive blood type. Therefore, a juror reasons, Rashad is the criminal. This is the same sort of predicate logic that we used to infer that apples are bananas, isn't it? There are

369

thousands of men, other than Rashad, that meet all the characteristics listed for the criminal, and it's a logical error to home in on Rashad without more evidence.

Here's another example of predicate logic:

Someone who is alive at age 95 eats bacon every morning.
I eat bacon every morning.
Therefore, I'll be alive at age 95.

The conclusion doesn't follow, does it? Here's another example of predicate logic:

A person who had a usually fatal illness and took a new medicine, got well.
I have that illness and I will take that medicine.
Therefore I will get well.

That's still predicate logic, isn't it? But here's another example:

5000 out of 5000 people who had a usually fatal illness and took a new medicine, got well.
I have that illness and I will take that medicine.
Therefore I will get well.

That conclusion seems more logical, doesn't it? But the reasoning really follows the format of predicate logic. Predicate logic sometimes gets more logical when the evidence mounts up and up and up.

Parts of speech

How does language work? It's amazing that the sounds we make that come out of our mouths, or the marks we make that people can see, can communicate so many things -- such as the ideas in this book! There are lots of different languages, but they seem to work in very similar ways. There are words that do different types of jobs. Those different types of jobs that words do in sentences are called the "parts of speech."

The simplest sentences have a word for someone or something that did something, and another word for what they did. Tyesha ran. Smedley spoke. Tyesha and Smedley are the names of persons, places, things, or ideas, and are nouns; ran and spoke tell about actions or states of being and are verbs. Tyesha and Smedley are the subjects of their sentences, and ran and spoke are the predicates or verbs of those simple sentences.

A little more complex sentence adds what received the action. The men built a train. Men is the subject, built is the verb, and train is a noun that is the direct object. Fred kicked the ball. Fred is the subject, kicked is the verb, and ball is the direct object.

We can use pronouns in place of nouns: After saying "Fred kicked the ball," we might say, "And then he ran to get it." The word *he* is a pronoun that we use instead of repeating the name Fred.

We add words called adjectives, that describe nouns or pronouns, and words called adverbs, that describe verbs, adjectives, or other adverbs. The big man quickly kicked the round ball. Big is an adjective telling about the man, round is an adjective telling about the ball, and quickly is an adverb telling about the verb.

371

Words called prepositions tell the relation of something to something else. The person goes over the water, into the water, under the water, between the trees, beside the river -- words like over, into, under, between, and beside are prepositions, and the water, the trees, the river in the phrases above are called the objects of the prepositions. A preposition with its object(s) makes a prepositional phrase. A prepositional phrase can act like an adjective, by telling about a noun: for example, the man from Kansas is here. From Kansas describes the man. Prepositional phrases can also act like adverbs: in the sentence, "He ran to the tree," to the tree is a prepositional phrase that tells where he ran.

Words called conjunctions join other words. In the sentence, "Jack and Rasheeda went to a party but left early," and is a conjunction joining two nouns, Jack and Rasheeda, and *but* is a conjunction joining two verbs, *went* and *left*.

Words called interjections express emotion without doing so via any of the other parts of speech. In the sentence, "Oh, hey, don't do that!", *oh* and *hey* are interjections. But in the sentence, "I'm feeling upset and surprised," *upset* and *surprised* are adjectives, not interjections.

A special part of speech is the word *to*, as in the sentences "I like to run," or "To err is human; to forgive, divine." The word *to* is one way of making verbs act like nouns or adjectives or adverbs; the phrases are called infinitive phrases. Another way of making verbs act like other parts of speech is by adding *ing* or *ed* to the verbs, as in "Walking is fun," or "I see the flying ducks," or "There's some baked bread." In those sentences walking is called a gerund, flying is called a participle, and baked is also a participle.

We've listed 9 parts of speech: nouns, pronouns, verbs, adjectives, adverbs, prepositions, conjunctions, interjections, and the infinitive. And we've listed infinitives, gerunds, and participles as ways of making verbs do some of the jobs of the other parts of speech. And those are all we need to make whole books, whole libraries full of books, in all sorts of different languages!

Thinking about how language works is especially useful if you're a writer. And most people need to be writers, at least part time, to communicate with others! Another reason to think about language and the parts of speech is to get more insight into how we think. Very much of our thought is expressed or at least expressible in language.

Child-directed, adult-directed, and rule-governed activity

As if you didn't know: every human being starts out life as a young child. It's good for young children to learn to do three sorts of activities well, with whatever adults are looking after them.

Child-directed activity means that the child is able to take the lead, and the adult participates in the activities that the child selects and carries out. For example, the child has crayons and paper, and draws or makes marks however they want to, and the adult pays attention and comments in an encouraging way. Or, the child explores an object and sees what it can do and what can be done with it, and the adult "tracks and describes" the child's actions. Or the child plays with toy people and vehicles and houses, and the adult joins in and portrays one of the characters but does not direct the child. Or the child makes up a sequence involving chasing and being chased and hiding and being discovered, and the adult plays the part in carrying out this sequence in a way that's fun for the child.

Adult-directed activity means that the adult directs the child to do something, and the child complies; the adult ideally gives a reinforcing response to the child's compliance. For example, the adult asks the child to count some objects; the child does so; the adult excitedly says, "That's right, you got it!" Or the adult shows the child some pictures, and asks the child, "What's this"; the child answers and the adult reinforces. Or the adult reads the child a story and then asks the child a question or two. Or the adult shows the child how to do something on a piano and asks the child to do the same thing.

Rule-governed activity often means taking part in a game with rules: for example, the person who's "it" chases others, and when that person tags someone else, the person tagged becomes "it." Or I'm the leader and you imitate the actions that I carry out, and then you're the leader and I imitate your movements. Rule-governed activity can also include doing certain things in a certain sequence. For example, first I tell something I'm glad I did, and we name what skills I used; then it's your turn and we do the same (this is called the "celebrations exercise.")

Why is thinking about these categories a big idea? Because when we're nurturing the development of young children, we want to think about helping the child to be good at all three of them and helping the child to enjoy all three of them. A child who has lots of fun in child-directed activity with an adult develops a positive relationship that makes the other two activities lots easier to nurture. But a child who is accustomed only to child-directed activity can have a rude awakening -- or else give teachers and parents a rude experience -- when it's necessary for the child to comply more. A child who is trained to comply well but to suppress the sort of spontaneous activity that makes up child-directed activity may miss out on some joyousness skills, some social interaction skills, and the development of curiosity about the world; these are major contributors both to success and to happiness. Rule-governed sequences of behavior are good to learn to enjoy also -- they play a part in all sorts of routine activities, such as buying something from a store, getting from home to school, figuring out who gets to talk in a classroom, how you act at a party, and so forth.

Connotations and denotations of words

The denotation of a word is what it refers to, what its official meaning is. The connotation of the word is what it suggests about whether what is going on is good or bad, worthy of approval or disapproval.

If we say that someone is persistent, we mean that the person doesn't give up, keeps on trying. If we say that the person is stubborn, we mean about the same thing. But the word persistent connotes that we like the way they keep trying, and the word stubborn connotes that we wish they would stop!

If we say that someone is self-confident, we mean that the person obviously feels competent or otherwise capable of success. If we say that the person is conceited, we mean something similar, but the connotation of *conceited* is that the person's positive view of themselves is irritating to us, that we find it obnoxious.

If we say that someone has an alcohol use disorder, we're meaning that the person uses alcohol in a way that interferes with their life. When we say that the person is a drunkard, we are communicating the same thing only with a lot more disapproval of the person we're referring to.

If we say that someone is articulate, we mean that the person can use words well, and can express what they mean to say fluently, clearly, and elegantly. If we say that someone is glib, we also refer to a proficient use of words, but there's more of a connotation that the person is superficial or insincere or that we otherwise have some fairly mild disapproval of their use of words. If we call the person a blabbermouth, the connotation is that we very much dislike their enthusiastic use of words.

Being aware of the connotations of words helps us to communicate more effectively. Becoming aware of the connotations of the many words in one's language is a big job!

Leaders' involving stakeholders in proposals and decisions

When we speak of stakeholders in some decision, we're talking about the people who are affected by it – the people who may be made better or worse off. When we speak about leaders, we are talking about people who have some authority – mayors, governors, presidents, heads of businesses, heads of subcommittees, superintendents of school districts, principals in schools, department chairpersons in colleges, heads of families (parents), presidents of clubs that teenagers belong to, and so forth.

One way for leaders to behave is to come up with some plan or proposal, gather information about it, and tell everyone what should be done. The stakeholders in the decision have to just live with whatever the leader's choice is.

But often, there's a second way: the leader makes the decision and announces it, but if the stakeholders dislike it enough, they can veto it.

The big idea of this section is that there's a third way: the leader calls together representatives of the stakeholders at the beginning of the decision process, and gets their input as the plan or proposal is being made. The leaders ask stakeholders to give their opinions all during the process. Finally the plan is presented not as something that "I the leader" am imposing on everyone, but something that "We, the leader and the stakeholders" have figured out will be a good plan.

Suppose there is a big highway that goes through a neighborhood of low income people. There is very high crime in the neighborhood. For a long time people have thought about tearing down that section of highway and making some very attractive public land there in its place. Some of the low income housing might get torn down, and the residents may be offered other places to live.

Suppose the mayor and the city planners just meet and deliberate and weigh pros and cons. Then they announce the plan. There are beautiful drawings of what the neighborhood will look like. If you were living in the low income neighborhood, and you found out that someone had planned to tear down the place where you live and let you move somewhere you've never heard of?

How would you feel? Perhaps scared or angry? Inclined to protest so much that the plan gets abandoned?

Now suppose that the mayor and city planners meet, from the very beginning, with people who will be affected by the decision, including those that live in the neighborhood. The people in the neighborhood get to think carefully about what the new place to live will be like, and whether a move would make them better or worse off. They get to negotiate about what will happen. A plan is drawn up that they, as well as other stakeholders, approve of. The plan is announced without its being a surprise to any of the groups of people affected by it.

Let's imagine another story. A four year old child frequently has temper tantrums. The parents have been trying to give the child whatever the child wants, to end each tantrum. But they decide that in doing so, they are reinforcing the tantrums. They make a plan to withhold attention as much as possible while the child is raging, and to give as much positive attention as possible when the child is acting nice and happy. They don't ask the child whether this is OK or not. But even so, they discuss the new plan ahead of time with the child, and they explain why the child's life will be better off with the it. They explain to the child why they are doing the new plan. They answer any questions the child has. They are communicating with one of the stakeholders, even if that stakeholder isn't permitted a veto.

Dangers of moralistic thinking

On the one hand, the concepts of right and wrong, of moral and immoral behavior, the ideas that we should do some things and shouldn't do other things, are the basis for people's being able to live in happiness and peace with each other. A society in which the ideas of ethics and morality didn't exist would be a dangerous one to live in.

But on the other hand: people can often do very cruel things, and justify them by thinking that they are doing the right, good, and moral thing – that they are defending the most important principles of right and wrong. Many examples of this can be cited. At the time of this writing, in over 10 countries, being gay is a crime punishable by killing the person. The story of Joan of Arc involves people who felt justified in cruelly killing (by "burning at the stake") a 19 year old woman partly because she wore men's clothes and had religious ideas that conflicted with authorities. When wars are launched, or acts of terrorism committed, the justifications that are offered almost always have to do with defending some "good guys" against the actions of "bad guys." (They almost never say, "I'm just a bad guy myself.") People have been killed for what was thought to be an immoral act of getting into a romantic relationship with someone of a different race. People justify the inhumane treatment of prisoners by the need to uphold moral standards. If you want to read much more about how principles of morality can justify immoral acts, there's a book about this, called, *Virtuous Violence: Hurting and Killing to Create, Sustain, End, and Honor Social Relationships,* by A. P. Fiske and T. S. Rai.

The message of this idea is: if we think that our actions are good, right, moral, ethical, and just, we should think twice about whether we are using the concept of morality to justify actions that might be bad, wrong, immoral, unethical, and unjust! We should do this self-questioning particularly when the action we're considering is punishment or aggressive defense in response to what we think of as someone else's bad behavior.

Education and success

If by "success" we mean getting a job versus being unemployed, or earning more versus less money, many studies have found that more education leads to more success – on the average. If by "success" we mean staying alive versus dying, current statistics in the USA are that a 25 year old with a college degree is expected to live about 10 years longer than a 25 year old who didn't finish high school. If by "success" we mean giving a higher rating of your own happiness to the researcher who is doing the study, a number of studies have found that more education leads to more happiness. If by "success" we mean less chance of either getting killed by someone else or killing someone else, several studies suggest that these bad outcomes get less likely the more educated people get.

There are always exceptions. There are some people who don't finish high school, who go on to become rich and famous. There are many who have little education but seem very happy. But on the average, more education tends to lead to good things.

Why is this the case? I've spoken with lots of high school students who wonder, what's the point of this? Why should I be compelled to write an essay on the symbolism in some really boring novel? Why should I have to solve math problems that don't seem to have any connection with anything in life? Why should I spend time learning a language that I have no interest in ever speaking? Why

380

should anybody other than a chemist grapple with balancing chemical reaction equations?

Part of the answer is that when we meet challenges by reading, remembering, thinking, and expressing, we practice those mental skills, and the skills will apply to lots of challenges that really do make a lot of difference. Another part of the answer is that by meeting such challenges, we demonstrate to employers and others that we have the wits, and the fortitude, that are necessary to overcome difficult mental challenges that jobs or other situations might pose.

This is not to say that education is perfect the way it is. Would the world be better if students had more choice about whether they wanted their education to emphasize more "academic" skills such as analysis of literature and equations for ellipses, or more "practical" skills such as how to grow and harvest food crops, remodel buildings, fix broken pipes, and so forth? My guess about the answer to that question is "Yes!" There are all sorts of things in this world to learn, and I think that students should be given much more choice about where to devote their efforts.

But if someone can choose between "I'm not going to try in school, because it's pointless," and "It's something of a game, but I'm in it to win it," the latter attitude would be the one to pick. The game of "How skilled can you get at algebra," or "How well can you write," may seem pointless. But people have great fun in games that are much more pointless. The games of "How long can your character on a video screen survive" or "How many times can your team get a ball into a certain place" can muster great passion and millions of hours of intense effort from human beings. People who can get into the game of academic achievement and enjoy it have reason to celebrate.

Frontiers for humanity

The word "frontier" has meant the border between settled land and wilderness, as in "Settlers recently started going to the frontier town." It also has meant the border between what has been achieved and what people want to achieve, as in "Her work extends the frontiers of our understanding of the immune system." People have used the word in both senses to refer to humanity's ability to go to "space," that is, the moon, Mars, other places very far from earth, travel in space ships, and so forth. Space has been referred to as the "new frontier" and the "final frontier."

The big idea of this section, though, is that a very productive way of thinking about the frontiers for the human species is to think about the achievements that are much more strongly needed than the conquest of space. Whatever these goals are, thinking about them as the important frontiers may tend to focus our efforts on them.

What are some of the goals, some of these desired achievements? Here are some nominations: 1. The reduction and eventual elimination of warfare and other violence. 2. Ending poverty (which includes having food, water, housing, and medical care universally affordable and available). 3. Promoting positive connections between people, reducing loneliness and isolation, increasing kindness and joyousness in relationships. 4. Achieving sustainability for the planet – getting population, use of resources, disposal of wastes, reduction of unnecessary junk-production, and so forth into processes that don't burden future generations. 5. Reversing or stopping global climate change. 6. Finding cures, or better still preventions, for health problems. 7. Producing energy in ways that are safe and non-polluting.

One could go on, but these are enough to absorb the efforts of a good number of frontiers-persons. OK, that brings up one more: 8. Figuring out ways that society can create more jobs that harness people's efforts to extend humanity's frontiers in the best ways (and fewer jobs that harness efforts in wasteful or harmful ways.)

Meet the challenge versus frustrate the authority

Suppose a parent says to a young child, "Let's see how quickly you can get yourself dressed, all by yourself!" Child A thinks, "Sounds like a fun game, I'm in it to win it!" The child gets dressed quickly and presents to the parent; the parent says, "Wow, that was so fast! And everything is on just right!" On the other hand, Child B thinks, "They're on one side of this game; I'm on the other; I bet I can win it!" And the child not only doesn't put the clothes on, but throws them around the room. The parent gives signs of being very frustrated, and the child takes that frustration to mean, "I've won the game."

The two children are playing different games: the first is playing the "Meet the Challenge" game, and the second is playing the "Frustrate the Authority" game. The first is a cooperative game, where both participants can win; the second is a competitive game, where the authority and the other person play against each other.

People other than children can play both of these. When a president from one political party is in power, and sets out to solve some problem, lawmakers from the other party have been known to get so strongly into the competitive spirit and the Frustrate the Authority game that they oppose whatever the president wants – even things they themselves have said they wanted.

If a high school teacher makes a rule, how cleverly can someone break that rule? If people create unwritten rules about how I should dress, how thoroughly can I break those rules? Having a rebellious spirit is central to the Frustrate the Authority game.

Sometimes the Frustrate the Authority (or defeat, refuse, or depose the authority) game is a very wise one to play, when the authority is asking you to do bad things. For example, widespread civil disobedience of laws enforcing racial discrimination eventually led to the defeat of those laws. Sometimes it's wise to compete and not cooperate!

On the other hand, when parents, teachers, work supervisors, and others really do have people's best interests at heart, it's good to be able to play the meet the challenge game. It's important for children not to get stuck in the frustrate the authority game. As with so many other choices in life, the goal is to be able to assess situations and make wise choices about what to do in which situations!

Time on task, time in deliberate practice, work capacity

The big idea of this section is that the more you work at something, the more you tend to accomplish. For example, people who have practiced playing the violin or piano for seven or eight thousand hours tend to be lots better at their skill than those who have spent only 50 or 60 hours. People on swim teams who practice swimming for 3 or 4 hours a day, year round, for a few years, tend to defeat those who work out for half an hour three days a week for four months a year. That doesn't seem very surprising, does it? But there are some more ideas that go with it. There are certain skills that take the average person a certain length of time to acquire. For example, people have estimated that it takes about 600 hours for a person who has only spoken English to learn to speak Spanish, not like a native speaker, but well enough to get by. If someone hopes to learn Spanish in 15 minutes a day for 6 weeks, that person probably won't succeed. The state I live in recommends that people practice driving for 50 hours or so before taking a driving test. Someone who practices for an hour or two is unlikely to succeed.

An idea that goes along with this is that of work capacity, or attention span. If I can only tolerate a short amount of time working on something, there are limits to how much I can accomplish at that thing. But: the more skilled we get at something, the longer our work capacity gets at working at it. For example, when a child is a very poor reader, the child may only be able to tolerate practicing reading for a few minutes before starting to think, "When can I stop this?" But as children get better at reading, they can tap into the pleasure that reading can give, and some of them spend hours at a time immersed in their favorite books. Or for another example, the better someone gets at basketball, the more their shots tend to go through the hoop, and that makes practicing more fun; also, the person starts getting respect and approval from teammates and others, and the incentives that increase work capacity tend to pile up. So: work capacity increases skill, and skill increases work capacity.

In the field of mental health, researchers often try to find out how successfully a course of psychotherapy improves a certain problem. For example, someone who has had temper outbursts for years undertakes a training program to improve this problem. The amount of time on task in those studies tends to be in the range of 10 to 30 hours. Even with that amount of time, there are sometimes measurable effects. But what if the amount of time on task that it really would take to learn all the skills to solve this problem were ten or a hundred times as much? What are realistic amounts of time on task for various goals, given various starting points? Our finding out more about this will represent progress in our thinking.

Operational definitions

When we are trying to communicate, it's good if words mean the same thing to the persons giving and receiving the message. If I say that you are glib, and I think I'm paying you a compliment by saying that you can use words fluently and well, but you take what I say as an insult because to you the word glib means that those words are insincere or even lies, we haven't communicated well! So how we define words is important.

People speak of two ways of defining words. The first is called "constitutive" definitions. These define a word by giving other words that mean about the same thing. So for example, a constitutive definition of the weight of an object might be how heavy it is, or how hard it presses down on the ground or a floor if you place it there. An "operational" definition tells what procedures you go through to measure whatever you're talking about. So for an operational definition of weight, you specify that you get an object called a scale, and you put the object on it, and read or calculate the number that the scale gives you.

Suppose someone is doing a study about pain in children. A constitutive definition of pain might be something like, "suffering or discomfort, of the type often caused by illness or injury." An operational definition would specify how pain was measured in the study: "We gave children a line, with a smiley face at one end and a crying face at the other. We said, if this end of the line represents not hurting at all, and this end represents hurting as bad as you think someone can hurt, where is what you feel right now? Put a mark on the line to show how much pain you're in, how bad you hurt, right now."

A good thing about operational definitions is that they should be very specific. They should leave little doubt about what you're talking about. Another advantage is that they make it clear when one person defines something one way, and another person, another way. For example, two people might both have the same constitutive definition for physical fitness: "Being able to perform physical tasks effectively." But one measures physical fitness by how fast someone can run a mile and a half, whereas the other measures physical fitness by how many pushups the person can do. The conclusions the two people reach about physical fitness may be different, because their operational definitions are different.

Sometimes when we try to make operational definitions, the procedures we specify to measure the concept suffer from not being concretely defined themselves. For example, people have tried to make up operational definitions of autism. One of the operations involves deciding whether the person has "difficulties adjusting behavior to suit various social contexts." How many people have not had at least some difficulties figuring out how to respond to things other people do? What sort of difficulties are we talking about? How often? Are we talking about the "social context" of being locked up without cause, being called obscene names daily at school, or someone saying, "Hi, we haven't met, what's your name?" Another one of the criteria for autism is "excessively circumscribed or perseverative interests." So suppose someone concentrates night and day on making a big scientific breakthrough, persevering on it and excluding all else including playing golf and watching movies, and the person finally makes the big breakthrough. Sounds like pretty circumscribed and perseverative interests to me. Now we need a definition of the word "excessively." The point I'm making by this is that making up really good operational definitions of some concepts is more easily said than done. Of course, people can still describe the operations they use. For example, "We gave the Smedley autism scale to the parent to fill out, and if the score was over 14, the child was considered to have autism."

Despite the difficulties, the big idea of operational definitions has helped a great deal in letting people know better what others are talking about.

Breaking tasks into parts – avoiding cognitive overload

The concept of "cognitive overload," includes trying to do so much at the same time with your brain that you can't do any of it. The problem of cognitive overload can often be solved by separating a task into parts and focusing on one part at a time.

Many times people get "work block" when they are trying to write something. They try to get started on what they are writing, but they just can't get moving. Often, I find, they are trying to do everything at once. There's just too much for the brain to juggle. As I mentioned in an earlier idea, they can often overcome the work block if they break the writing task down into the following:

1. Generation of things to say. What do I want to get across?
2. Inclusion: Of those possibilities that I generated, which of them do I want to include?
3. Ordering: Let me cut and paste and arrange the order of what I want to say.
4. Wording: Now I focus on how to put the ideas into words, how to make clear and correct sentences.

With other tasks, the barrier to getting started may not be cognitive overload so much as tedium overload – the task involves so much boring or unpleasant work that it gets put off. For example, the task of "cleaning up and organizing the place where I live" may be like this. Making a list of the subtasks, for example wash the dishes, get things off the floor and put away, clean the floors, take the

389

trash out, do the laundry – no one of these is so
overwhelming as the whole job seems.

When we break down a big task into smaller parts,
it's good to celebrate the completion of each smaller part,
by saying to oneself something like, "Hooray for me! A
task is completed! That's real progress!"

What you feed your mind matters

By "what you feed your mind," I'm referring to
everything that you read or hear someone say, see on TV or
movies, observe on the Internet, hear someone say, watch
someone do, and so forth – the totality of the information
you take in. We are taking in information constantly.

Our information diet influences us greatly. Those
who frequently watch or read from news sources that pitch
certain political points of view tend to have those
viewpoints strengthened. Those who hear and read ethical
indoctrination, for example that it's good to be kind to
other people, or that the best thing is to be able to defeat
one's enemies, tend to endorse those ethical ideas.

Advertising is one of the prime examples of how
information that people take in influences them. Why are
companies willing to spend billions of dollars on
advertising? Because they have strong reason to believe
that the advertising will influence people to buy their
products, and their investment in advertising will pay off.

Getting control of the information that people
receive is a major way for people to achieve and retain
power. A dictator who controls what information the
people in his country can and can't get will often be
successful in persuading people that his leadership is
wonderful for them, and that they should keep him in

power for a long time. In a country like the USA, when people run for political office, they constantly ask for donations to their campaigns. They use a lot of that money to pay for advertising that is meant to persuade people to vote for them. Thus being wealthy or having very wealthy supporters is a major advantage.

People whose information diets consist very greatly of violent movies or violent videogames tend to be influenced by them. On the other hand, those who choose information diets where they read about the cause of nonviolence, peace, and harmony between people tend to be influenced in a different direction.

As one more of the countless examples that could be given for this big idea, people whose information diets consist mainly of news about horrible things going on in the world, horrible things that people have done to each other, and bad things that are forecasted to happen, probably tend to be less hopeful, more pessimistic. On the other hand, people who are actively involved in groups or causes that are trying to make the world a better place, and who read often about successes that people have had here and there, probably tend to be more hopeful and optimistic.

I hope that reading about the big ideas presented in this book will help you, and other people, take pleasure in knowing that the world is a very interesting place, and that cultivating ideas is a wonderful activity.

Index

www.ingramcontent.com/pod-product-compliance
Lightning Source LLC
Chambersburg PA
CBHW051812090426
42736CB00011B/1441